MINISTRY IN
THREE DIMENSIONS

MINISTRY IN THREE DIMENSIONS

ORDINATION AND LEADERSHIP
IN THE LOCAL CHURCH

Steven Croft

DARTON · LONGMAN + TODD

First published in 1999 by
Darton, Longman and Todd Ltd
1 Spencer Court
140–142 Wandsworth High Street
London SW18 4JJ

Reprinted 2000 and 2002

ISBN 0–232–52313–4

A catalogue record for this book is available from the British Library.

Designed by Sandie Boccacci
Phototypeset in 9½/12¾pt Palatino
by Intype London Ltd
Printed and bound in Great Britain by
The Bath Press, Bath

CONTENTS

v

CONTENTS

PREFACE

Ministry in Three Dimensions is about the development of ordained ministry in the present and in the coming decades.

The book is written with a variety of different readers in mind, among them:

- a Christian thinking through their vocation and what ordained ministry might mean
- an ordinand in training as a text book in courses on the nature of ordained ministry and on leadership
- serving clergy as they reflect on the shape of their own ministry, particularly in times of appraisal, review and transition between different posts
- the wider church as part of an ongoing debate about the nature of ordained ministry in the context of a church in mission

The book is primarily addressed to an Anglican and to a British context although I hope its message will be relevant to ordained ministers in other denominations and in other places. The book arises out of two contrasting experiences in my own life.

The first is the experience of thirteen years of parish ministry, first as a curate, in St. Andrew's Church, Enfield and then, most formatively, as vicar of St. George's Church, Ovenden from 1987 to 1996. Ovenden is an Urban Priority Area parish on the north side of Halifax in West Yorkshire. I was twenty-nine when I was instituted as vicar. The church already had a good-sized and committed congregation. Becoming an incumbent there felt at the time like putting on a jacket which was several sizes too big. I grew more, I think, in my first year as vicar there than in any other year of my life before or since (and rather faster than I ever want to grow again). Growing inevitably meant learning many lessons, most of them the hard way!

By the grace of God and through the gifts and support of many people, our years in Ovenden were very fruitful. The church there was enabled to grow both in numbers and in other ways. Many adults became Christians. I found myself continually learning new lessons and needing to find new paths of ministry in the midst of this growing congregation. Gradually I was drawn into sharing some of those lessons, engaging with other clergy and congregations and thinking more widely about the life of local churches and ordained ministry. For my final three years in Ovenden I worked also as Mission Consultant within the newly renamed Missionary Diocese of Wakefield, engaging with questions of church life over a wider area.

The second formative experience is that of being appointed to my present post in 1996 as Warden of Cranmer Hall, one of the Church of England's theological colleges (another jacket that felt several sizes too large at the time). The change meant that I had to begin to work through and think hard about my own understanding of ordained ministry as an important part of helping others prepare for their own ordination. In particular I began to develop a course for those in training in leadership and ordained ministry. The course was harder to write than I anticipated, largely thanks to the quality and the questions of those who took part. On many occasions, over several years, I have emerged from a lecture, mentally torn up the notes and the understanding of ministry I was trying to present and gone away for an afternoon's very hard thinking.

The results of these two kinds of experience are offered in *Ministry in Three Dimensions* in the hope that they will be useful and helpful to others at different stages in their thinking. The book covers a great deal of ground in terms of ministry: biblical, historical, theological and practical. Different readers will, no doubt, want to approach the text in different ways. You may want to read the text as an individual or use it as a basis for group study.

I have tried to acknowledge within the text where I am indebted to the writings of others and my hope is that this book will lead people on to read different authors on ministry, church life and leadership. However, I would like to acknowledge here all that I have learned from others about ministry informally along the way and through discussion; the congregation of St. George's, Ovenden deserves particular thanks for their patient endurance of many schemes and 'bright ideas'. I am grateful to my ordained and lay colleagues there for many discussions about ministry over the years which have helped my own understanding: among them to Tim Mayfield, Bill Goodman, Paul Hinckley, Jean Hoggard, Andii Bowsher, Catherine Townend, Barbara Brownridge and many others.

I have learned a great deal from the writings of and in discussion with my fellow Emmaus authors over six years of working together with Stephen Cottrell, John Finney, Felicity Lawson and Robert Warren. If this book is found to be useful, it will owe a great deal to those who have taken part in the leadership courses within Cranmer Hall from 1996 to 1999, especially those who have asked the most awkward questions and made me think more deeply (and they probably know who they are!). The material was also tested on a number of clergy groups at different stages of the writing. My thanks especially to the Ripon Deanery Chapter who asked me to speak at their annual residential in 1998.

More specifically, a group of people have taken the trouble to read all or parts of the manuscript of the book in draft form and commented upon it. Particular thanks to Rita Acarnley, Alan Bartlett, Mark Bonnington, David Day, Bob Fyall, Gordon Khurt, John Rice, Catherine Townend, Michael Turnbull, Tim Yates, Gavin Wakefield and Frank White. The views expressed here in no way represent those of other people: at several points those who have read the book have disagreed with me – but their comments have nevertheless been extremely helpful. Any mistakes remain, of course, my own responsibility. My colleague and secretary, Margaret Trivasse, has helped the book forward not least by helping to protect space for writing and revision. My editors at Darton, Longman and Todd have been supportive, creative and encouraging throughout the project. Ann, my wife, has shared the whole of the journey of ministry which is the background to the book. My thanks to her especially for continual patience, encouragement and love.

My hope and prayer is that those who engage with *Ministry in Three Dimensions* might be helped to think through the great challenges of ordained ministry in the coming years and be better equipped in some ways at least for the task before them.

STEVEN CROFT
January, 1999

A Note on the Pronunciation of Greek Terms

You will find three Greek words used quite often in the text. I trust they won't be too offputting to those who are not used to ancient languages. The first is *diakonia*, which is pronounced exactly as it is written: *dia* as in 'Diana'; *kon* as in 'gone'; *ia* to rhyme with 'spire' (sort of). This is the Greek work meaning 'service' from which we take the term 'deacon'.

The second Greek word is *presbyteros*: *pres* as in 'Elvis'; *byt* as in 'bit'; *eros* as in 'eros'. It is the Greek word meaning 'elder' from which we take the English words 'presbyter' and 'priest' (on which more below).

The third word is *episcope* which means 'watching over'. It is the hardest to pronounce until you get used to it. It is not meant to sound like 'periscope'. The *ep* is as in 'Pepsi'; *is* as in 'is'; *cop* as in policeman; and *pe* to rhyme with pay: ep-is-co-pe.

PART ONE

UNDERSTANDING THE PROBLEM

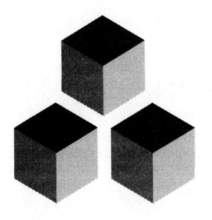

1

THE CHALLENGE
TO THE CHURCHES

The Mission of God and the Shape of the Church

All through history, the Church has reacted with the culture in which it has found itself. Sometimes the surrounding culture has been hostile, as in times of great persecution. This hostility has shaped the way the Church orders its life and its ministry. At other times and in other places the prevalent culture has been transformed by the Christian gospel and this in turn has shaped the Church's life and institutions. Each generation of Christian people has needed to understand the times and the culture in which it is set and respond accordingly, drawing from and seeking to be true to both the Scriptures and the tradition.

Different times and seasons in the Church call for different patterns of ministry and of mission, even though the gospel message itself may be unchanging. The call of the Church to engage in the mission of God has shaped its life profoundly and continues to do so. The New Testament documents were written because of the needs of young Christians and fledgling churches to receive, first, guidance from the apostles in the form of letters and, later, more detailed accounts of the ministry, death and resurrection of Christ. The familiar shape of the Christian year arose from the desire of the early Church to communicate the faith in deep and life-changing ways to those who came to be baptised. Communities of men and later of women came together to share a common life to enable them to pray for, witness to and live within a decaying society and the monastic movement was born. The system of geographical dioceses began and was expanded in the Church of England to enable the Church to be effective in its mission to the whole community. The large Sunday School buildings which stand beside many of our Victorian churches in the cities are a testimony to an earlier

3

generation of Christians' call the mission of God to his world by teaching the Christian faith to the children of their communities.

As the call to mission throughout the centuries has transformed the Church, so the need to fulfil that mission has continually formed and reshaped the Church's understanding of Christian ministry. In times of great theological controversy, the call has been for scholars and theologians who can set out the Christian world-view cogently against the philosophers of the day and be guardians of the truth: an Athanasius, Augustine or Aquinas. In times of great cultural darkness, the dominant model changes to that of pioneer missionaries and pastors: a Patrick or a Cuthbert. In a time of the flowering of culture and learning, as in the fifteenth and sixteenth centuries in Europe, there came a need for ministers who were educated and trained to the highest level and equipped to teach others: the skilled preachers and teachers of the Reformation. As the cities grew and the Industrial Revolution gathered pace, the learned country parson was no longer sufficient. The Church needed powerful preachers able to address working people in their own context and develop ways for them to help each other continue learning and growing: hence the rise of Wesley and the Free Church tradition of lay preachers.

In our generation, the Church faces a similar challenge. The models of mission and of ministry that have nourished the Church through previous centuries are no longer proving effective or sustainable for the majority of congregations and of clergy. This way of 'being church' and of 'doing ministry' has been described in a number of ways as Church in 'Christendom', 'pastoral', 'maintenance' or 'inherited' mode.[1] At its simplest level lies the assumption that within society most people are born and brought up as Christians. The primary way of learning faith is within family, church and school as children grow to adulthood. The main functions of the ordained ministry are to lead worship within and to pastor a largely stable congregation of adults, children and young people, paying particular attention to those within the community who are sick, bereaved or in other times of difficulty or transition. The normal assumption within this model is that the congregation have a single building in which to meet (a parish church) and that the minister will be full-time and paid; and possibly assisted in the leading of

4

worship and pastoral care in this stable community by a very small number of other people, ordained or lay.

The principal training for this kind of ministry is therefore seen to be training in the leading of worship well; of caring for individuals or families in times of difficulty or transition; and teaching the faith to children and young people. These tasks, it is assumed, will take up the majority of the minister's time, along with a small amount of administration.

There are still many churches in the United Kingdom which are operating on this model. Some still have comparatively large congregations in areas of the country where churchgoing has not declined as steeply as in others. Denominations that have been most effective in teaching the faith to children and young people, particularly the Roman Catholic and Baptist Churches, are the slowest to feel the effects of change. But the majority of congregations which are functioning in this way are, in actual fact, in decline, either rapid or steady depending on the age profile of the congregation.

The forces for change that have been affecting our culture and society have to affect the whole way we are church; the way we engage as churches in the mission of God in our generation; and therefore on the nature and task of those who are ordained ministers.

The End of Christendom

The largest change of all, from the Church's point of view, is the slow end of Christendom in the West. For hundreds of years it has been possible, at least from an Anglican perspective, to assume that the majority of people in these islands were Christian. The structures of the Church's ministry and mission have been, understandably, entirely geared to that assumption. Our main priority and aim in teaching Christian faith has been to teach the faith to children within Sunday Schools and day schools with continued Christian education of adults through Sunday preaching. In so far as evangelism has been directed towards adults, until comparatively recently, the assumption has been that most have a residual understanding of Christianity left over from their childhood. Hence the role of the evangelist has been to call people back to a faith and a community they have left behind rather than to teach Christianity from the very beginning. Structures of pastoral care and of worship have been geared to the maintenance of congregations who, it is assumed, have been Christians for the whole of their lives to date and are likely to remain so until their death.

But with the end of Christendom, all of those assumptions change. Only a very small minority of the population now grow up in a Christian context or in any meaningful contact with the churches. If the only way we pass on the gospel is through teaching the faith to children already within our churches, then we are restricting the Christian faith to a small proportion of the population, many of whom are not likely to remain active members of the churches in adult life.[2] This means that all of the mainstream churches have to make a profound shift from teaching the faith to children only to learning how to communicate and teach faith to adults as well – often adults who have little or no background knowledge of Christianity. One of the most encouraging features of the Decade of Evangelism has been the way in which this shift has been happening across the traditions and the denominations and is now becoming a mainstream feature of local church life.[3]

However, this in turn means that where church congregations are thriving and beginning to grow, they are also changing quite profoundly in their nature and composition. A growing congregation is no longer made up of people who have been Christians for the whole of their lives; who have lived largely in the same place; who are stable in faith and who are likely to remain regular attenders for the rest of their days. Because of the wider trends in society, even those who have been Christians and regular worshippers since childhood are likely to leave a church or congregation and to drift away.[4] Those who begin the Christian faith as adults have much greater expectations of Christian community and a much greater need of both continuous Christian nurture and teaching and ongoing pastoral care. They are also more likely to want to be more actively involved in some way in the life of the local congregation.

A local church therefore has very little choice as to whether it attempts to engage in mission to the adults within the local community and draw others in, as many are realising. Churches which do not attempt to engage in mission in this way will, in the course of time, simply have to close. The existing congregation grows older and declines as people become too infirm to attend church or as they die. The income of the church declines and so the congregation is unable to support a full-time vicar or minister. The pastoral oversight they receive from the denomination by way of part-time ministry has energy only for maintenance of the existing congregation. The decline continues until the circuit or diocese makes the decision to close the building and focus its energies elsewhere. Cities, towns and some villages are already full of redundant church buildings: painful reminders to Christian people that the Church needs to change and to be changed.

But this shift towards engaging in mission and teaching the faith to adults profoundly affects the work and shape of the ordained ministry. It becomes essential, of course, for clergy to become proficient in nurturing faith in adults and the very different kind of pastoral care which is needed by those who are coming new into the faith[5], but there are more subtle changes as well. Leading worship in such a way that it is both attractive and welcoming to those who are new to the faith and sustaining to those who have been Christians for many years is a continual challenge and increases the demands on the ordained minister. The new generation of Anglican liturgy is a much better resource for congregations but generally demands much more creativity on the part of those leading worship.

A Christian community that is continually welcoming others into its life and worship is continually being changed and reformed by those who are joining. In an urban or suburban area, the Christian community will no longer consist of people who have known each other all of their lives from schooldays onwards but will be an associational network of people who may have been strangers to one another before they came into the life of the church. The opportunity for friendship and a sense of belonging is one of the most attractive features of the Christian life in a society in which many people are isolated. The minister will therefore need the gifts and abilities to enable this community to be continually built up, nurtured and developed.

As Robert Warren and others have argued, the call is for the whole Church to be changed and to become a missionary congregation. If the journey to faith of an adult is one which commonly takes several years then many different aspects of the church's life will be important and will play a part in that journey.[6] The minister is therefore called to be an agent of education and change throughout the whole Church in order that the church may be effective. As many serving clergy will testify, bringing about change within a congregation can be an extremely difficult and painful process, even when handled with skill, wisdom and grace, partly because in most cases you are resident among and part of the group of people who are being challenged to move on.

But the most substantial change for the minister, and the one which is the most difficult to make, is the necessity to work collaboratively and involve others in the tasks of pastoral care, nurture and mission.

Where churches are growing in the United Kingdom, in the vast majority of cases, they are smaller congregations enabled to grow through the evangelistic and pastoral gifts of the clergy. People commonly join the congregation through a contact with the vicar, in an Anglican setting; and what cements them into the community is that relationship with the pastor.[7] Churches of this type are commonly called 'pastoral' churches for this reason.[8] But sooner or later, the church will reach the point where the pastor is unable to sustain a community which is any larger. From that point onwards, although new people may be joining the congregation, others will be leaving and drifting away at the same rate. The minister will probably be working slightly too hard in sustaining all the pastoral relationships which have been created and there will be a sense that things are not really under control. As in so many areas of life, so in the life of the church: where the numbers of people involved increase, the quality of the event or activity decreases.[9] The number of people able to be sustained in a church in that pastoral model, itself a relic of the Christendom era, seems to be around 100 to 120 adult church attenders. Church congregations used to be larger (and still are in some contexts). It is true that a large congregation consisting of people who have been part of the church all their lives and know each other well can be sustained and cared for by a single full-time pastor. But if that same congregation consists largely of those who have recently joined the church and are new Christians, the 'pastoral care ceiling' is much lower.[10]

For growth to continue beyond that ceiling, it is not enough to attempt to add more clergy or full-time lay ministers. There needs to be a sea-change in the life of the church, away from dependence upon care by the ordained, and towards the nurturing of the capacity for care and support for one another. This does not mean, as we shall see, that the clergy should stop caring, cease to be pastors and become managing directors (although some advocate this). But it does mean that this task, like the task of mission, needs to be owned by the whole body of Christ and not simply the ordained. Another 'essential' is added to the job description of the vicar: to enable the pastoral care of the congregation by the congregation, if the church is to continue to grow and to be effective.

Changes in Culture

There are other major changes in our culture which have a significant effect on the way the Church engages with mission and the task of the ordained ministry.[11] The pace of change in what has been called a white-water society has its own effect on the life of the Church. Congregations who are being disturbed by change in every other area of their lives are therefore sometimes much more resistant to necessary change within the Christian community: this dimension of life at least should stay the same. Geographical and social mobility have had a radical effect on almost all communities. Churches have traditionally related to geographical areas, particularly in the Church of England with its parish system. But very few sections of society network geographically: in most communities only the elderly, mothers at home with young children and, sometimes, the un-employed. It is no coincidence that these sections of society are the very ones the Church traditionally serves through its midweek activities. The largest proportion of our residential communities have different networks (which are not geographical) for work, leisure, shopping and other interests and most may not know many people even in the street where they live.[12]

This geographical and social mobility has an effect on the Church's composition as well as upon its mission. People who own a car, and some of those who don't, will have no hesitation whatsoever in travelling outside their own geographical community to church, just as they travel for almost everything else in their lives. The reason for attending a particular church then becomes, usually, one of personal taste and preference. The exercise of choice is one predominant feature of modern society. A consumer mentality then begins to affect both congregations and ministers. In some of its features this will need to be resisted; in others, worked with; but its reality as a dynamic in the minister/congregation relationship needs to be acknowledged. In many facets and areas of their lives people both observe and expect excellence. Rightly or wrongly, this expectation is often projected onto the churches people join as new Christians or, particularly, as transfers from other congregations.

Lastly, there has been and still is a breakdown in the hierarchical structure of society. People want and expect to relate to one another as individuals and as people, by Christian names rather than by titles. They also expect and value the opportunity to be involved and participate fully in the life of the church and congregation. In general, those joining the church are looking for far more than a service to come to on a Sunday morning. They are seeking community and the chance to give, to participate and to share in the life of a church, including in its direction and decision-making processes. Again, this impacts on the life of the clergy. 'Professional' distance which once was acceptable in the parson becomes something which alienates members of a congregation – particularly when it is re-introduced as a modern management technique. A congregation will, rightly, want to be consulted and be part of key decisions affecting the life of their community. If there is no opportunity for consultation and involvement then people will be estranged from what is happening, sometimes to the extent that they will find another church to attend. But again, this impacts on the skills required in the ordained minister. Collaborative leadership of a Christian community becomes an essential skill for ministers in the emerging Church of the present and certainly of the future.

The Emergence of Lay Ministry

If these changes were not enough in themselves, the Church has been engaging with its own agenda of renewal over the last thirty years, which has involved the recovery of many elements of the Christian tradition that had become neglected and the development of others. Many parts of the Church, including the Church of England, have begun to ordain women; charismatic experience and spirituality has played an increasingly important role in church life; there has been growth in a more creative use of liturgy. Alongside all of this has come a recovery of the theology of the whole Church as the people of God and of the ministry of the laity alongside that of the clergy.[13] Baptism and not ordination is seen as the foundation for the ministry of the whole people of God. The ministry of the ordained has come to be seen more and more as secondary to this calling of all the baptised.

This recovery of a vital element in theology has manifested itself, among other ways, in the development of new authorised ministries and training courses (for example, Bishop's Certificate in Pastoral Ministry; Deanery Lay Ministry initiatives) and a blossoming in at least some parishes of a whole variety of informal lay ministry within the Church. There has also been a steady, if slower, recognition of lay vocation and ministry as being much wider than the confines of the local congregation.

The recovery of lay ministry within the churches has, however, caused a rise in the level of frustration felt by many lay people who have invested a great deal of time and energy in long periods of preparation for ministry only to discover that their gifts and energies are not used to anything like their full potential. This may be because their present incumbent or congregation are not as open to lay ministry as the wider Church (which is true in many contexts still). It is more likely to be because their minister or incumbent is still operating in 'inherited mode' and has not wanted or been able to learn the different way of working collaboratively, using and supporting the gifts and ministries of others. Again this shift then highlights the need for a different set of skills among the clergy from those in which they have traditionally been trained and have operated.

The Change in the Deployment of the Clergy

The 'inherited' model of being church assumes a predominant pattern in the deployment of the ordained minister: a single full-time and stipendiary clergy person is entrusted with the cure of souls of one parish and, usually, a single congregation. The inherited wealth of the Church of England has meant that this pattern has been sustainable until comparatively recently in our towns and cities. However, multiple benefices and clergy looking after six or more parishes and congregations have been a necessary part of ministry in rural areas for much longer. In some of the Free

Churches, which do not have the Church of England's inherited resources, again the reality of ministers having the care of several congregations is normal rather than exceptional.[14] Financial realities and a limited number of stipendiary clergy in the Church of England are changing the inherited pattern even in towns and cities, and pastoral re-organisation is almost routine with every change of incumbent. Team Ministries, Group Ministries and informal clusters of churches are, for Anglicans, increasingly the order of the day in all but the largest parishes.

Alongside changes of deployment are developments in patterns of ordained ministry. Non-Stipendiary Ministry has been a feature of Anglican church life for a generation now and is well established in many parishes and diocese. Ordained Local Ministry (OLM) is being developed currently in about half the English dioceses as a different way of expressing and focusing the ministry of the whole people of God. OLM carries with it, in most of its expressions, a much stronger emphasis on collaborative ministry and leadership both within a parish and between different parishes in a wider area.

Again, these changes in deployment patterns call for a different set of skills and a different mindset among the clergy. We are moving further and further away from the concept of the ordained as the person whose primary responsibility is to lead the worship of the people, to do the primary work of pastoral care, and teach the faith to the children and young people. We are moving much more rapidly towards the primary skills of the ordained being focused around leading and building communities of faith who are able to engage in God's mission to the world.

New Ways of Being Church

The final area of change is the massive amount of flux, change and thinking which has been taking place within the last decade on the shape of the local church, responding to the changes which have taken place within Church and society over the last twenty-five years. No clear pattern is emerging yet for 'the church of the future' although there are some definite trends beginning to emerge.

Among the different developments through books and conferences have been:

- The development of Emmaus and Alpha groups and courses and the re-orientation of local church life around evangelism and nurture[15]
- The call to local churches to think creatively about becoming and building missionary congregations[16]
- The recovery of the catechumenate, of which Emmaus and Alpha form part, and the consequent revision of liturgy and the life of many Catholic parishes[17]
- The 'seeker service' movement initiated by Willow Creek Community Church near Chicago[18]
- The interest in cell-based churches in both denominational and non-denominational Churches[19]
- From a slightly different perspective, lessons learned by local parishes from the base ecclesial community movement worldwide[20]
- The steady growth and engagement with church planting in all sections and traditions within the Church[21]
- The rise and development of services geared to and engaging with emerging youth culture which often take on radically different forms of expression[22]
- New material on Natural Church Development, which again draws on the insights of the World Church, with its emphasis on building the quality of congregational life as a key to growth[23]

Digesting, assimilating and learning from these new movements in the Church takes time and energy and itself makes demands of the ordained. Without wise leadership, a Church can easily rush from one trend to another, pursuing the latest fashion and looking for that one solution which will lead to success. What each of these new ways of being church has in common is that they all have similar implications for leadership and the ministry of the ordained. *Empowering* is one of the twelve features of the life of missionary congregations. *Enabling leadership* is one of the eight key areas identified in Natural Church Development. Once again, whichever avenue is pursued, the same new set of skills is demanded of the clergy.

The Need for Enabling and Empowering Leadership

The call for enabling and empowering leadership to become a more recognised part of the vocation and training of ordained ministers has been widely recognised. In 1993 the Church of England published revised criteria for selection for ministry and for the first time included a section on leadership and collaboration in response to the perceived need in Church and Society. The summary paragraph reads:

> Candidates should show ability to offer leadership in the Church community and to some extent in the wider community. This ability includes the capacity to offer an example of faith and discipleship, to collaborate effectively with others, as well as to guide and shape the life of the Church community in its mission to the world.[24]

The commentary on the paragraph in the report stresses the differences between Christian and ministerial leadership on the one hand and secular and managerial styles on the other, a distinction we shall explore in the following chapter. The possibility of different ways of leading is acknowledged. The need for clergy to be self-aware, to manage themselves and to have the maturity to handle authority well is stressed. Discernment and the the leadership of a community is a vital skill:

> A basic ability required of leaders is to identify where the group or community stands and what it should aim to achieve. Leaders should then be able to set out the means to obtain the objectives, drawing the group or community towards the aim and motivating its members towards the goal. This is an essential cooperative task and depends on the ability not merely to stand over against the community but also to be responsive, understanding and sensitive to it and its corporate vision ... Of particular importance are the inner security and maturity to recognise, affirm and encourage the gifts of others and to respond to change and assist others to face it and use it creatively. There needs to be in leaders an observable readiness to develop the ministry of the whole people of God.[25]

Testing the conclusions of this chapter against the present perceived needs of the Church can be done in a very straightforward way by turning to the back pages of any recent edition of the *Church Times* or the *Church of England Newspaper*. See how many advertisements for incumbents or priests-in-charge contain language which asks in one way or another for these qualities and skills. Adverts requesting that a vicar come simply to lead worship and care for the people are few and far between.

- Chaplain required **to lead the growth** of this new congregation . . . must be able to **help the congregation** to grow in numbers and discipleship (post in Warsaw; Intercontinental Church Society)
- Senior Colleague required **to develop work** at a newly refurbished Church Centre . . . there is a **strong lay team** and many young families (Second Curacy in Bristol Diocese)
- A Priest-in-Charge is needed **to lead the mission** and varied worship (Diocese of Exeter)
- A person of **vision**, committed to **encouraging the continuing growth** of the church . . . a lively village church **needing a leader** . . . She/he will continue to **encourage the development of the ministerial team** in the parish (Diocese of Rochester)
- We are praying for **someone of vision** who will **build on the growth** of recent years . . . who **encourages lay ministries** and **can work collegially** with a small staff team (Diocese of Oxford)
- We are looking for **a gifted leader in mission** . . . Someone with **vision** . . . is wanted **to equip the congregation** to serve God in their neighbourhood (Diocese of London)[26]

Conclusion

The inherited mode of being church called for clergy who had the primary responsibility for leading worship, the pastoral care of stable congregations, and teaching the faith to children and young people. Any skills of enabling leadership which the clergy brought in addition to these tasks were welcome and appreciated but secondary to this primary call.

Changes in society and emerging ways of being church however call for new ways of being church and therefore make new demands on the ordained ministry. A cluster of skills which, for the moment, we will call enabling or collaborative leadership skills has now become one of the primary skills of those who exercise their ordained ministry within the local church.

However, challenging and changing the way in which the clergy see themselves is not an easy task, particularly in a time of uncertainty, multiple stresses and low morale. The next chapter moves on to look at the clergy's understanding of themselves and their response to ideas of 'leadership'.

FOLLOWING A FALSE TRAIL: SECULAR MANAGEMENT MODELS FOR ORDAINED MINISTRY

Understanding Clergy Stress

The 1990s have seen a growing realisation that many who share in ordained ministry of the Church are under increasing stress and pressure. The symptoms of this stress are easy to detect in lives which are overbusy or imbalanced; where there is too much work and too little leisure; too much activity and not enough stillness; too many superficial contacts and too few deep relationships and friendships.

Stress is not a simple phenomenon. However, all the indications are that the clergy are suffering in a more widespread and intense way than was the case even five or ten years ago. The dominant mood at the Deanery Chapter meetings I attend is one of tiredness and preoccupation often combined with a sense of frustration at intransigent congregations on the one hand and central structures on the other, which are sometimes seen as unappreciative, demanding and out of touch. The common threads in conversations with those who have recently been ordained centre around how much work there is to do and how little time to spare.

A survey conducted on behalf of the Evangelical Alliance in 1990 of 3000 evangelical clergy across different denominations makes sobering reading:[1]

> - 7 out of 10 clergy feel overworked
> - 3 in 10 feel their families suffer because of their work
> - Only 2 in 10 have received training in management or leading teams

> • Out of a typical 60-hour week, an average of 22 hours is spent in administration
> • In contrast to this just 38 minutes per week are spent in personal prayer

The consequences of so much stress in the lives of the clergy are not good. They are to be seen in the increase in marital breakdown among clergy; the breakdown in health or in relationships within churches; an increase in burnout and breakdown which is stress related; and, more commonly, the less spectacular running out of steam and loss of effectiveness which many of the ordained experience in mid-ministry.

Identifying the cause of this rise in stress levels is not straight-forward. Certainly we live in a much more needy society. A vicar in an average parish will be dealing with extremely demanding pastoral situations on an almost daily basis week in and week out, in continuous contact with people who are in emotional and spiritual need. As the tide of faith continues to recede across society, people outside the churches have fewer and fewer resources on which to draw when facing the difficulties which come in every life: particularly those of illness; conflict and bereavement. Many clergy are sharply aware of the need to exercise the kind of collaborative ministry and enabling leadership referred to in the previous chapter but lack the skills or the support to make the transition. Most clergy of every tradition acknowledge the need for local congregations to change, develop and grow but also recognise the pain and the difficulty in bringing about that change and the skills and support which will be needed by those in leadership.

In response to this trend there has been a significant growth in publications aimed at either analysing or helping clergy to combat the effects of stress. Some of these contain simple practical guidelines for good practice in the caring professions.[2] Others provide clergy and others with sensible patterns for the proper ordering of work, rest, worship and study that are sorely needed.[3] A third group focus on particular aspects of the task of ministry and ways in which it can be made more manageable.[4] Other studies have attempted to seek out the deeper root causes of stress and build strategies and remedies on the basis of that richer understanding.[5]

The most persuasive and thorough analysis in this final category is Andrew Irvine's book *Between Two Worlds: Understanding and Managing Clergy Stress*, which is based upon an extensive study of the working habits and values of clergy in Scotland and in Canada and the fruit of more than twenty years of thinking and reflection around these themes.[6] Irvine's thesis is that, although the symptoms of much clergy stress may be busyness, overactivity and burnout, the causes of that stress are to be found by looking deeper at the twin roots of identity and isolation. Of these two, questions of identity are of prior importance, for it is the clergy's understanding of who they are and who they are called to be that lead to patterns of work and behaviour which in turn lead to isolation.

Irvine argues that the clergy's understanding of their own identity has been eroded from both outside and within the churches during the past fifty years. As the Church has declined both numerically and in its place within society, so the wider society's view of the clergy has been eroded. Two generations ago the parson or minister was a respected figure within most communities. Clergy in the 1990s have to work against a perception in society that the vicar is, at best, a figure of harmless, eccentric irrelevance and, at worst, someone whose holy exterior masks a tendency towards immorality or abuse.[7] Almost all of the ordained are therefore seen to be marginal to the wider society and its concerns. The Church is commonly seen by the community in which we are set as having failed, and portrayed in that way by the media. By implication it is not difficult for the clergy to see themselves as having failed also, caught up within the wider trends of society's retreat from faith. In the context of that marginalisation and perceived failure, the question of how the clergy see themselves and their ordained role in relation to the wider community becomes central: what does it mean to be ordained in this generation and what am I meant to be doing?

The most obvious route for the ordained to take is to retreat within, become preoccupied with and find their role within the community of faith: the Church. Many congregations thus become captive to a 'Father knows best' theology and model in what have become stagnant backwaters of church life, unlikely ever to be renewed in mission.

However, within the broader and still moving stream, retreat is not possible. As noted above, there has been a rediscovery and reemphasis on the ministry of the whole people of God. This is an entirely right and healthy development. The Church has made significant progress from seeing itself as a hierarchy, modelled upon its picture of God the Trinity as a hierarchy, to seeing itself as a community proceeding from the Holy Trinity as an open community of love.[8]

Within the old model, it was at least possible to discern easily the specific identity and role of the ordained minister: he or she is acting primarily as a representative and intermediary, standing between God and the community. In this capacity, the priest preaches the word of God, administers the sacraments and extends care to the needy and vulnerable. He or she is dealing primarily with individuals already formed into a community by the other circumstances of their lives. The group which gathers in the parish church Sunday by Sunday is simply a sub-group or cross-section of the wider community of the geographical parish and the priest has a clearly defined and visible role within that perception of reality.

However, in the new ways of seeing church and being church, there is no pre-existing community within the geographical parish, whether that parish is full of tower blocks; suburban houses with large gardens where people never see their neighbours; or the village transformed by an exodus of its young people and an influx of the retired into new estates. One of the key tasks of the Church is the creation of primary communities in a desert of isolated lives. This is a task which involves the whole congregation, not simply the clergy. Others within that congregation, in the main stream of church life, are rightly encouraged to use their gifts and to undertake many of the tasks and functions once the preserve of the full-time stipendiary priest. This is the very way in which community is formed and relationships nurtured. What, then, is the role of the ordained? To allow our concept of priesthood and ordination to shrink into the only unique preserve of the ordained is a route which some have followed. The whole of ordained ministry becomes more and more focused around presiding at the Eucharist, with disastrous consequences for the mission of God to the world and for the enabling of community and ministry among the people of God. Others are drawn down the route of abandoning the distinctiveness of ordination altogether, or even the need for ordained ministers. Once again, our inherited concepts of what it means to be ordained cannot stretch to embrace the task and calling of the clergy in the Church of the future.

Irvine's appeal is for the development of a new understanding of the identity and role of the ordained which takes account of these changes in Church and society. He argues, persuasively, that such a new understanding needs to be grounded and tested in each of the four areas of a theological quadrilateral: Scripture, the tradition, reason and experience.[9] Because we are *Christian* ministers, our understanding of the people we are called to be and the task we are called to fulfil must be securely rooted in and consonant with the Scriptures and with the understanding of the Gospel, of Jesus Christ and the Church which we find there. It is not enough simply to be pragmatic, to argue from what we think we need to be to what we should therefore become.[10] Similarly, we stand as inheritors of almost 2000 years of Church history and tradition. The understanding of ministry which we develop at the beginning of the third millennium must draw on the evolving traditions of the Church and its ministry through the ages, and not simply on understandings of leadership drawn from society around us.

However, just as we are called to root our understanding of ministry in Scripture and in the tradition we have inherited, we must also be faithful to reason and contemporary experience. Our inherited understanding of ordained ministry in pastoral mode does not make sense and is not working. This is true from the perspective of our call to mission, from the perspective of the health of existing congregations, and from the perspective of the health and well-being of the clergy.[11] The Christendom model of one stipendiary priest caring for a stable congregation is breaking down. A new understanding of ordained ministry is called for which makes sense of our changing situation, yet remains faithful to our roots and our rich inheritance.

TABLE 2.1

Scripture	Tradition
Reason	Experience

The Flight into Management Models

- We have inherited a model of ministry which is no longer working.
- Clergy urgently need to develop a new self-understanding.
- There is a change demanded in the role of the clergy which we have already explored: new skills seem to be required in the areas of enabling and collaborative leadership.

It should not surprise us therefore that the place where large sections of the contemporary Church have looked for inspiration and for models for the role of the clergy have been in secular models of management and leadership, often dressed in a veneer of Christian language. Clergy and churches in the evangelical tradition have led the way in this development, although they have not been alone. Evangelicals have generally been quicker to perceive the need for enabling and collaborative leadership skills among the ordained from the perspective of mission and have been in the forefront of the development of lay ministry (and therefore of some kinds of collaborative ministry).[12] When talking to evangelical clergy and ordinands about 'leadership' I have found that there is no need to justify the use of the word or argue that it is part and parcel of the role of the vicar. Most evangelicals understand this intuitively, as it were, without the ideas being unpacked or argued out. In fact, for many younger evangelical clergy the primary focus of what it means to be ordained is focused in the very exercise of leadership skills.

Inherited Styles of Evangelical Leadership

Generally speaking, the evangelical tradition has not drawn its concepts of leadership directly from secular management sources, as have other traditions in the Church, but it is possible to discern two main influences at work. An older generation of evangelical clergy, now mainly approaching retirement, were prepared for the exercise of leadership in the Christian Church not through their theological colleges but through their public schools, universities and national service and a related network of Christian camps and organisations.[13] The leadership values which underpin their ministries have been those of unquestioning obedience within an organisation in

22

order to achieve a desired end; discipline, hard work and self sacrifice; not revealing weakness or pain; courage, endurance and the passing on of the highest example to others. Leadership within this tradition has largely been seen as exercised by men.

Much was achieved in post-war evangelicalism by leaders cast in this mould by their early years of formation. Other Anglican leaders came from similar stock.[14] However, this is not a tradition which finds the sharing of weakness, collaborative ministry or the sharing of authority easy.[15] Leaders who continue to operate in this way in the closing years of the century are too easily perceived as aloof and somewhat distant, perhaps more representative of a different social class in a society which no longer defers automatically to someone of a particular accent or background. The culture now favours a much more collaborative style. Leaders who have been fashioned in this mould are also often operating intuitively and uncritically in a certain leadership style, which may have its strengths but which has not engaged with the deeper insights of Scripture and tradition.

Leadership Styles and the Church Growth Movement

The second strand of evangelical thinking influenced indirectly by secular leadership styles is still very much with us in the methods of church development popularised by the Church Growth Movement. Leading proponents of this school have emanated from Fuller Theological Seminary in California and have included Peter Wagner, John Wimber, Eddie Gibbs and, latterly, Carl George. Eddie Gibbs's substantial book *I Believe in Church Growth* was first published in Britain in 1981 and was highly influential on a generation of Anglican clergy trained at or around that time, myself included. John Wimber's work has had a massive influence on the stream of Anglican Church life which was already caught up in charismatic renewal from 1983 until the present. The influence of Vineyard concepts has been mediated through four highly influential and large Anglican churches: St Michael-le-Belfrey in York, St Thomas', Crookes in Sheffield, St Andrew's, Chorleywood, and Holy Trinity, Brompton in London. In the 1980s regular meetings for leaders at Chorleywood and Sheffield propagated Vineyard-style concepts among influential Anglican church leaders in between the annual training conferences led by Wimber himself. John Wimber died in 1997 and direct Vineyard influence on the Church of England has decreased. The inspiration and lead given by Holy Trinity, Brompton has continued, largely through the development and growth of the Alpha course. The Vineyard became known in Britain largely through its emphasis on and recovery of signs and wonders and healing, particularly in evangelism. However, much of the teaching in conferences and seminars was in management and leadership concepts mediated through the Church Growth Movement, of which Wimber himself was a pioneer.

As with the earlier model discussed, the Church Growth Movement has been responsible for a great deal that is good in the life of the Church. Along with many others I have been inspired by its vision, the models of leadership it has produced and the insights of Gibbs, Wimber, George and others. However, we must also recognise that the models of church leadership and church life which the movement puts forward are not drawn directly from Scripture or the Christian tradition (although many of them are justified by appeal to the Old and New Testaments, sometimes convincingly). Instead, they are the core concepts of secular management theory applied to churches as systems and organisations. John Wimber's steps to building a healthy church begins with vision and proceeds to values, strategy and programmes.[16] Wimber is applying here insights identical to those of Peter Drucker and others of 'management by objectives' to ways of being church.[17] This may be a valid and effective way to proceed (and I would argue it has considerable validity) but, again, there is little direct engagement between these management/leadership insights and Christian Scripture and tradition. The local church is (perhaps rightly) seen as systemic, that is, a complex organisation in which each part affects the other.[18] However, the leap is then made to seeing the minister or senior pastor of a large church as the Chief Executive Officer,[19] explicitly by Eddie Gibbs in Table 2.2 illustrating the changing role of a minister as a congregation grows in numbers. As more people join the church, the minister becomes less and less of a pastor to individuals and more and more simply the supervisor and eventually the manager of a network of pastoral carers and other systems.

Having attempted to work this model myself for some time in a

TABLE 2.2

Church Size	Industrial Skill Level
1	Unskilled Worker
2–65	Foreman
66-150	Supervisor
151–450	Middle management
451–1,000	Top management
1,000+	Chairman of the Board

growing church, I am able to testify that to do so meant something of a denial within myself of my calling to be ordained and a deep dissatisfaction with that style of ministry (in addition to a certain amount of justified frustration on the part of church members). I was left struggling for several years between seeing the need to enable and support others in ministry, if the task of pastoral care was to be undertaken adequately; and yet still being called in some sense to exercise pastoral ministry myself, in order not only to fulfil my own calling but also to give integrity to the remainder of my ministry within that place. The inherited language and patterns of ministry no longer fitted the needs of the present day ordained minister. Yet the models offered by the Church Growth Schools were not arising naturally from the Scripture or the tradition but from commercial and industrial models and, largely for that reason, did not fit either.

Leadership as the Defining Quality of Ordained Ministry

The need for enabling and collaborative leadership skills is perceived so acutely by evangelical Churches, ministers and para-church organisations at the end of the 1990s that the word 'leader' is becoming the most commonly used title for a person called to full-time Christian work within the Churches. Conferences and courses are routinely advertised for 'leaders'. Para-church mission agencies in their enabling of the clergy seek to build up, encourage and support 'leaders'. The most recently published and very helpful handbook by David Pytches divides every part of the work of the ordained into one or other aspect of 'leadership'.[20] The word *leader* is now being used not only as a substitute for the Anglican titles *priest* or *presbyter* but also in preference to the much more common expressions of *minister* (meaning 'servant') or *pastor*.

This change of use in the way we describe the ordained should give us pause for thought. There is a danger of a gap opening up between a popular understanding of what ordination is about ('leadership') and the Church's understanding of that ministry captured in its liturgy and especially in the ordinals, which do not use the word. There is a deeper danger of the Church as a whole beginning to use a word to describe the work of the ordained which does not have deep roots in the Scriptures or the tradition. As John Finney points out, one Greek word which is never used to describe Christian ministers in the New Testament is the word *archon*, the normal secular Greek work for a leader in business or politics or industry.[21] The early Church clearly thought very deeply about the different titles used to describe those charged with different responsibilities among the people of God, as we shall see, and was deliberately shy of leadership language and titles taken from the society of the day. Surely, there is a lesson for the contemporary Church.

Management Models and the Non-evangelical Church

If the evangelical world has embraced the insights of leadership and management by adapting them to, and attempting to root them in, the biblical tradition, at least superficially, other streams of Anglican church life have begun to use management insights, as it were, undiluted and unrooted in Scripture. The organisation MODEM (Managerial and Organisation Disciplines for the Enhancement of Ministry) has been set up with the aim that 'by the year 2000 the values and disciplines of those engaged in the management of secular and Christian organisations will be mutually recognised and respected'. MODEM's first publication[22] in 1996 contained a selection of articles on the application of management insights to local church life.[23] The organisation's second book in 1999 comes highly commended by both church leaders and others from the world of management and, again, contains an excellent series of helpful articles. Such insights seem to be gaining ground, particularly at the level of Diocesan and national church life. Stephen Pattison, in a fascinating and cautionary essay on the subject, chronicles the embracing of a management/leadership philosophy by many of the present House of Bishops.[24] Clergy training in management studies is on the increase. Some dioceses are experimenting with management practices either partially or wholesale, as with the Diocese of Ripon's working towards the 'Investors in People' award. Human Resource Management practices are influencing the Church of England's policies on appraisal and review and in-service training and will gradually affect and shape pre-ordination training over the coming years.[25]

Again, many of these developments are good, necessary and in many ways overdue. There is much that the Church can learn from good practice developed over many years in the commercial world or in the public sector. Many of the perceptive thinkers about societies and organisations have a background in management and organisational studies and they have perceptive and prophetic things to say to the whole of society, including the churches. We have both legal and moral obligations to work within employment law and good practice in the appointment and development of staff. Many local churches and even dioceses still have a great deal of catching up to do in this area. It would be arrogant in the extreme for the Church to say it had nothing to learn from the world of management and leadership studies.

But when the insights gained from these worlds are adopted uncritically by the Church, there are dangers. Pendulum swings are not always healthy. Today's underemphasis easily becomes tomorrow's overstatement and broken dream. Uncritical adoption of management insights is not the answer to our need for a new paradigm of Christian ministry. As we shall see in later chapters, there is a great deal in the Scriptures and the Christian tradition about the way in which power should be exercised within the Christian community and by those who would be leaders. In a substantial part of that tradition, we are explicitly told not to model ourselves on society around us in the way that power is used.[26] At the very least, insights flowing from the world of management need to engage with and be checked against the insights of Scripture and tradition before they are incorporated wholesale into the life of the people of God. As Pattison points out, leadership and management ideas are not neutral in terms of values. They carry with them a particular view of the world and of humanity which clashes in significant ways with the a traditional Christian world-view. Their fruits are not universally acknowledged to be good and beneficial, particularly by those who are the 'managed' rather than the managers. Pattison suggests, perceptively, that the Church seems ready to embrace management values in the late 90s just as it too readily embraced secular therapies and counselling techniques in its pastoral care, paying less and less attention to the roots of pastoral practice in the Christian tradition.[27] The secular concepts of 'leader' and 'manager' cannot do justice to the whole of what it means to be ordained nor must we allow them uncritically to shape our understanding of Christian ministry. We need to listen to the lessons of the world around us but we need also to attend to our own inheritance if a new and healthy understanding of what it means to be ordained is to emerge.

Focusing the Problem

Over the past six years I have spoken to many groups of clergy, lay people and ordinands in my capacity as Mission Consultant to the Diocese of Wakefield and, latterly, as someone charged with the responsibility of training clergy in a theological college. It has not been difficult to help people of all traditions to recognise that inherited understandings of the identity and role of the ordained no longer fit the needs of our present situation. Everyone can, as it were, see the problem and understand that some re-thinking is needed, particularly in connection with those new skills required of the clergy, as seen in Chapter 1: enabling and collaborative leadership.

However, once we have moved on from talking about the problem to thinking about solutions and ways forward, two distinct groups have emerged when I have begun to use language and concepts such as 'leadership', 'management' and related insights.

Clergy, lay people and ordinands from an evangelical tradition, with some others from a more central stream, have responded extremely positively. There has been no need to convince them that this kind of area is part of the ministry of the ordained. Their focus has been on learning what will be helpful and applying it immediately. The danger has been that such insights will be taken on board too quickly and uncritically; that they will not be digested theologically and subject to the critique of Scripture and tradition. When this happens, leadership and management insights will prove a false and sterile trail in the longer term.

However, the second group among those I have talked with have responded extremely negatively to concepts such as 'leadership' and, especially, 'management'. This group has included those from a more catholic tradition whose instinctive reaction has been: 'I am called to be a priest, not a manager.' It has also included those who have been the victims and casualties of bold management and leadership ideas either in their workplace or in churches they have been part of. Significantly, it is a group which includes many women of all traditions who find themselves alienated from what they hear as a very male language of management and leadership studies and who are searching for a different vocabulary.[28] Members of this group have been unable to take on insights and ideas about 'leadership' within the life of the churches because there have been so many prior issues to think through and because their own basic theology and model of ministry simply cannot stretch to accommodate the new ideas.

You will have guessed that the author has emerged from the first group and has come to identify with and to appreciate the concerns of the second. My aim in what follows is to revisit the Christian tradition and understanding of ordained ministry and to rework that tradition in the light of the present day needs of the Church in order to develop an understanding of the ordained ministry which is more adequate for the twenty-first century. We begin in the following chapter with an overview of what the Scriptures have to say about leadership and ministry, before beginning to explore what it might mean to see ministry once again in three dimensions.

3

BEGINNING TO SEE IN
THREE DIMENSIONS:
TOWARDS A BIBLICAL THEOLOGY
OF LEADERSHIP

Throughout the centuries the Church has been refreshed, renewed, reformed and re-ordered through its engagement with the Scriptures. The mismatch we have observed and which many reading this book will experience each day of their lives between the traditional view of the ordained minister and the demands of that ministry in contemporary society needs to be taken first to the Bible rather than the secular understanding of leadership emerging from a management culture. What resources can we rediscover in Scripture which will speak to our contemporary situation?

The Right Ordering of Leadership and Ministry to the People of God

One theme which is immediately apparent is that the Bible as a whole is concerned with the healthy ordering of leadership and ministry among God's people from the beginning through to New Testament times. We see the leadership of the emerging nation of Israel change and adapt as the community changes and grows from an extended family, to a collection of tribes enduring slavery, to a redeemed community on a continuous journey, to a people settled in the promised land. Wherever the dominant pattern and style of leadership and ministry changes, the biblical authors take time to pause, to tell the story and to justify what is happening. They often emphasise the degree to which God himself is involved in the transition and the discovery of new patterns of ministry. Often, attention is drawn both to the tradition they have inherited (in previous patterns and styles of leadership) and to the needs of the new situation: there is a balancing which is equivalent to the four sections of the quadrilateral explored above.

So in the transition from the leadership of patriarchs in the extended families of Genesis to the leadership of Moses which was necessary for the liberation from slavery, the writers emphasise carefully the direct call and authority of God which, despite Moses' many excuses, cannot be resisted[1]. The extension and development of Moses' ministry of judging the people following the visit of Jethro is carefully recounted on two occasions in classic texts on the necessity of sharing and delegating the care of a large community.[2] The historians who gathered and edited the books of Joshua, Judges, Samuel and Kings take care to emphasise the transition to kingship which was made by the nation during the time of the prophet Samuel. We are reminded again and again in the later chapters of Judges of the need for a king in Israel;[3] we are taken into the dialogue between the people and Samuel, Samuel and God, and then Samuel and the people again; and then see described the careful calling, choosing and then rejection of Saul, the first king, and the eventual accession of David. Similar attention is paid to the call of the prophets, the setting aside of musicians and temple servants, and the different ways of governing and teaching the people in the period after the exile. Leadership and the forms of leadership matter to God.

Identical concerns can be traced through into the New Testament. As we shall see in a later chapter, Jesus himself places a high priority on the call, training and ministry of the twelve and of a larger group of 70.[4] A major and recurring theme in the Acts of the Apostles is the development of the right forms of ministry within the New Testament churches.[5] The letters of Paul continually return to the way in which ministry is to be exercised and ordered within the body of Christ.[6] Towards the end of the New Testament period, the Pastoral Epistles and the general letters of James and 1 Peter give an increasing emphasis to the conduct and appointment of ministers in the local church.[7] The right ordering of ministry and leadership among the people of God is a central theme of the Old and New Testaments.

A Proper Use of the Biblical Texts on Leadership

However, because there is an abundance of material on leadership and ministry in the Scriptures, there is all the more reason to use and interpret the texts with great care. There are many examples both in recent literature and in sermons and talks on leadership where lessons about how to lead are simply read off, particularly from Old Testament texts, with little attention paid either to the context or to the fact that some of the insights they give may be genuinely pre-Christian. The memoirs of Nehemiah, for example, furnish many 'lessons' in leadership style (prayer, research, clear vision, perseverance against opposition, delegation, decisive action). Many of these lessons are very much in harmony with secular trends in the understanding of leadership and management. However, books and presentations based on Nehemiah rarely emphasise that the governor of Jerusalem is not leading a church attempting to reach a post-Christian society but a small city state in danger of being overwhelmed by its enemies (surely there must be some differences between the two contexts). Similarly there is only rarely any acknowledgement that ministry, death and resurrection of Christ and the gift of the Spirit to the Church might have profound implications for the way in which leadership is exercised and direction given to the people of God.[8] Insights from Nehemiah and other parts of the Old Testament may be valid, but they can hardly be thought to be complete.

Leadership of the People of God in the Old Testament

There are many manifestations of leadership in the Old Testament. However, as the story unfolds, the Old Testament's understanding of leadership among God's people comes to focus more and more clearly in the person and role of the king. Already in Moses and Joshua, and even more so in the Judges, a concept of national leadership is emerging which is looking in two directions. Leaders are called upon, first, to ensure that the people of God are protected from the enemy outside the nation who will regularly seek to conquer and annihilate Israel. They are called upon, secondly, to establish justice and right order in Israel and among its people. So Moses and the judges can be seen in two ways: as protectors and saviours of the nation through their courage and military leadership; and as those who strive to fashion the life of the nation around the laws of the Lord and administer justice within the land. In return, those leaders receive benefits, trust and service from the nation.[9]

The Old Testament's understanding of leadership is linked to its understanding of God. The sovereignty, kingship or leadership of God himself over the nation is seen in similar ways to that of the rulers of the nation. The Psalms proclaim again and again that the Lord is King.[10] God's kingship like the leadership of Moses and the judges faces in two directions. The Lord is a mighty warrior bringing salvation and deliverance from enemies of the nation.[11] The Lord is a righteous judge, ensuring that there is justice within the land, particularly for the poor of society.

This central concept of God's reign and rule naturally feeds into and nourishes the picture of the ideal king of Israel as both a mighty warrior and a righteous judge of the land.[12] The king depends on God for both help in battle and insight in giving judgement. David, the first great king of the united tribes, is portrayed throughout the books of Samuel as one who trusts in God and who is, supremely, the mighty warrior who extends the kingdom and pushes back the enemies of Israel. Solomon, his son, who succeeds him is portrayed, in a balancing way, as the ideal judge of Israel, endowed with the great gift of wisdom, teaching and the interpretation of the law. Israel's experience of David and Solomon, her developing picture of God as king and the ideas about leadership and kingship in the cultures of the ancient Near East all play a part in forming a strong collection of ideas about the king which, again, finds its expression in the psalms. The ideal king, in the prayers of Israel, loves the Lord and is both a mighty warrior and a righteous judge.[13] The shepherd image of the Old Testament is primarily an image of right leadership rather than a therapeutic image of care for individuals in need (although right leadership certainly embraces that function of care for the weak).[14]

The historical books of the Old Testament tell us that Israel's kings did not live up to this developing ideal. Israel herself never regained the glory of the days of Solomon. The rulers of the northern and southern kingdoms were not, by and large, faithful to the worship of the Lord; they were often defeated in battle; they did not uphold justice and the cause of the poor. A tradition of independent, critical commentary on leadership emerges in the preaching and writing of the prophets which continually contrasts the real with the ideal. In the period while there are still kings on the throne, there begins to emerge a longing for the ideal king who will come who will fulfil all that Israel longs for her kings to be.

The northern kingdom of Israel came to an end with the Assyrian conquest in 722 BC and the southern kingdom of Judah ended with the destruction of Jerusalem in 587 BC. For the first time there was no descendant of David enthroned in Zion. Yet still the prophets kept the hope alive that a new ruler and leader would be born who would save the people from their enemies and establish justice in the kingdom and re-establish the reign of God. However, reflection during the desolate years of exile in Babylon began to change Israel's concept of herself in relation to both God and the nations. Her concept of leadership also begins to change in the crucible of intense national suffering as a new identity is formed for the people around the faithful worship of the Lord rather than around a political kingdom.[15] Kings in the ancient world were anointed with oil on their accession. The ideal king would become known in the prophets and later writings as 'the anointed one', which in Hebrew is Messiah and in Greek is the Christ. The entire hope of the nation comes to rest in him.

Around this central strand of the role of the anointed king and Messiah cluster the other concepts of leadership in the Old Testament: not least because most emerge or develop as having some connection with the court and with the temple and all are subject to change and development. The priest is responsible for the right ordering of sacrifice and worship; the wise scribe emerges originally as an administrator of affairs of state; later he develops into the godly teacher and interpreter of the law and so into the Rabbi of Jesus' day; the prophet gives more inspired leadership, often critical of the establishment. All of these have their own traditions, training, sense of call and evolving function in the life of the nation and, after the exile, in the faith community which becomes Judaism clustered around the temple in Jerusalem and, increasingly, dispersed throughout the ancient world. However, each also feeds into Israel's developing understanding of the one who is to come: the Christ.

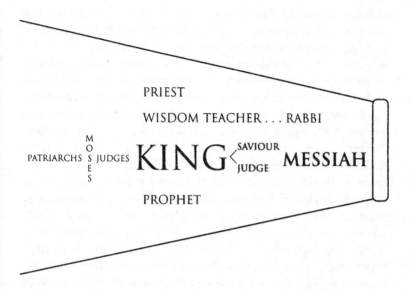

Figure 1: Old Testament patterns of leadership

Jesus the Messiah

If we are to be faithful to the whole of Scripture we must see Jesus against this wider background of the hope of a Messiah who will come both as Saviour and as Judge. Jesus sees himself as both fulfilling and transfiguring the expectations of leaders found in the Old Testament and focused in the hoped-for Messiah. His birth is predicted as that of the coming king.[16] He enters the Gospel story in his maturity, proclaiming the kingdom of God both in word and action.[17] His message is one of salvation: the very name 'Jesus' means 'the one who saves'.[18] The salvation Jesus brings is not the deliverance of Israel from her enemies but the salvation of all people everywhere from their sins. The victory is won not in battle, where David and his heirs won salvation for their people, but through suffering and death on the cross. Jesus' message is also one of justice and judgement and the right ordering of the whole of society, beginning with the new community he calls into being, the Church.

The gospel writers reveal to us a Messiah who intentionally gathers to himself all the strands of the leadership and kingship tradition in the Old Testament but who changes our understanding of those themes as we see them brought together in the Christ. He is designated as the anointed king but his kingdom is not of this world,[19] nor is it established by force. It is a kingdom which belongs to the poor in spirit;[20] which can only be understood in parables and riddles;[21] which begins as a something tiny but grows to fill the whole garden.[22] He is the inheritor of the tradition of the wise teacher, the lawgiver, the Rabbi and scribe, and delivers new laws on the hillside, echoing Moses, yet he is different. He repudiates titles and honour; has harsh warnings for those who consider themselves to be teachers; and 'teaches as one having authority, not as one of the scribes'.[23] He stands in the line of the prophets: speaking messages from God; doing deeds mightier than those of Elijah; rebuking those in power without fear or favour; authenticating his message through suffering. Yet with all of the prophets, the message they bring is more important than the messenger. With Jesus, the opposite applies. He is the message he brings, the living word of God. As a priest he prays for his people yet becomes himself the sacrifice for their sins.[24]

In much of Jesus' ministry he is challenging the use of power among the secular and religious leaders of his age: again and again he repudiates both their attitudes and their methods and some of his strictest censure is reserved for those who misuse authority in the name of religion.[25] As we shall see in the following chapters, Jesus turns the values of the human society upside down. The least important in society is to be the most valued in the kingdom of God: little children, lepers, tax collectors, and sinners. The meek, not the strong and powerful, are to inherit the earth.[26] The values of the kingdom are to apply especially among the community of faith, the church, where there is to be a completely different attitude to leadership: 'Whoever wants to be first must be last of all and servant of all'.[27]

Leadership within the Early Christian Communities

The Old Testament insights about leadership cannot be read across in a simplistic way into our thinking about the Christian Church.

As it were, all of the rainbow rays of light from the Old Testament find their focus in Christ as the lens and prism of God's revelation in Scripture. Within that lens of the person of Jesus, the rays of light are refracted: they are broken down and emerge in different patterns for the new age that has begun. The Church itself is neither a nation nor a corporation but a unique community of faith, hope and love, called to be a community with a distinct heartbeat rhythm of worship and mission and to instruct others in the way of faith.[28] In the earliest days of the Church and, Christians believe, continually since those days, God has poured out the Holy Spirit upon his people. The Spirit is given not to isolated individuals, as in the Old Testament, but on the whole community, from the 'greatest' to the 'least'. The narrative in Acts again continually emphasises the gift of the Spirit to those who are of lowly station and on the outside of faith as well as those within.

'Leadership', 'Kingship' and 'Headship' within the Christian community belong first and foremost to Christ himself, designated within the New Testament, as the head of his body, the Church.[29] The Holy Spirit has given different gifts to different members of the body of Christ, for the common good.[30] The resulting diversity of gifts is to be celebrated and treasured, but is not to be made a cause of division or of showing greater honour to some members of the community in preference to others.

The New Testament letters contain several lists of different gifts of the Spirit, which are in no sense meant to be exhaustive.[31] On the basis of the gifts that had been given, different ministries were exercised within the Christian community for the benefit of the whole. There is no uniform pattern which emerges across the churches that we can discern. Perhaps the clearest list of the early charismatic ministries is that in Ephesians 4.11f: 'The gifts he gave were that some would be apostles, some prophets, some evangelists, some pastors and teachers, to equip the saints for the work of ministry, for building up the body of Christ.' The dynamic here and in similar passages is very much one of Jesus himself anointing and appointing individuals to these ministries and those ministries then receiving recognition from the wider body of the Church. It is worth noting that there is hardly any direct emphasis in any of these lists of the gifts of the Spirit on the qualities which the world around us describes as 'leadership'.[32]

Any understanding of 'leadership' and ministry within the Church which is to be a Christian understanding cannot be derived directly and simply either from society around us or from the Old Testament images and models. Rather, a Christian understanding of what it means to exercise leadership within the Church must take account of, be mediated through and be integrated with

- our understanding of Jesus and his mission
- the gift of the Holy Spirit to the church
- our understanding of the church as the body of Christ

Ministry in Three Dimensions

Alongside these 'charismatic' ministries, given to different individuals by the gift of the Holy Spirit for the building up of the whole body, the early Christian Churches began to evolve a different and parallel structure of ministry to meet the rather different need for the proper ordering and care of local congregations. We find traces of this emerging structure for ministry within the earliest texts of the New Testament, as we shall see in more detail in the following chapters. There is no uniform pattern throughout the different churches which can become a blueprint for ministry in the Church for all ages, but clear principles can be discerned. Nor was there, as we shall see, some kind of age of purity in regard to Christian ministry when the only ministry the Church needed was that of the Spirit mediated through different members of the Church. By the time of the later New Testament documents, this emerging structure is becoming more and more important and more clearly into focus, developed as it is in response to the new context and mission of the church.

The three 'orders' of ministry of *diakonos* (deacon); *presbyter* (sometimes translated 'elder' and sometimes 'priest'); and *episcopos* (most usually translated bishop) trace their roots to New Testament ministries and offices. They are the words which emerge from the New Testament period to carry forward the Church's understanding of three different dimensions of Christian ministry within the congregation and the wider area into the second century and beyond. For almost 2000 years and across the different streams of the Christian tradition, these three orders or dimensions of ministry

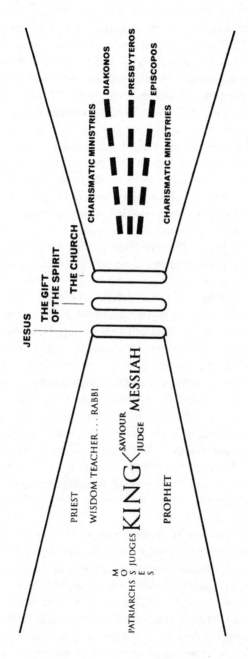

Figure 2: New Testament patterns of leadership

have remained central to the Church's concept of what it means to be ordained and to exercise leadership. Each denomination, as it has emerged, has discovered the need to develop its own expression of these three dimensions of ordained ministry and leadership: the diaconal dimension of service lovingly given within and outside the body of Christ; the presbyteral dimension of ministry centred around the ministry of preaching and of prayer and the sacraments in the local congregation; and the episcopal dimension of keeping watch over the life of both local churches and the wider Church and of commissioning and nurturing others in ministry.[33] The denominations as we see them today have developed many different ways of ordering these three dimensions of ministry and those established more recently have generally avoided the titles of 'Bishop', 'Priest' and 'Deacon'. Even in the new Churches however, there are discernible patterns of servant ministries, teaching ministries, and ministries which are concerned with the well-being of a network of congregations and of those who serve them.

I am not concerned to argue here or in the following pages that a particular form of the threefold ministry can be found in the New Testament which can therefore validate a particular expression of ordained ministry today or, still less, any particular manifestation, stream or tradition of the Christian Church. I would want to argue, as above, that the different contexts in which the Church has found herself down the ages have led to the development of different styles and patterns of ministry and of Church government. This diversity has been needed. The insights of the different traditions today are to be welcomed. There is a need for all of the Churches to be reflecting on and developing their undestanding of the ministry of the whole people of God and how ministry within the body of Christ is to be ordered.

However, I do want to contend that we have in the three dimensions *diakonos*, *presbyteros* and *episkopos* something of a distillation of important insights about Christian ministry and leadership, rooted in Scripture and drawing from a rich tradition in Church history from which we can begin to build a new understanding of ordained ministry. In the Church in England, and especially in the Church of England, ordained ministry has been seen for many years as one-dimensional: the vicar has come to be seen simply as a presbyter or priest with a ministry focused around his or her personal preaching of the word, prayer, administration of the sacraments and care for the needy. As we have seen in previous chapters this one-dimensional view of the ministry of the ordained is no longer adequate either for the missionary task which faces us or for the clergy's own self-understanding. There is a large mismatch between this 'ideal' and what most vicars actually do in practice and feel they need to do in theory.

The place to turn in this mismatch between our understanding and reality is not to the broken cisterns of secular management theory but to our springs of living water;[34] the God who speaks through Scripture and has continued to speak in new ways through Scripture throughout the history of the Church. Drawing our principal understanding of ordained ministry from the leadership traditions simply has the effect of reversing the pattern. Gaps remain between what is practised and what is needed. Instead, the following pages argue, we need to recover and reflect on our tradition of a three-dimensional ordained ministry. The vicar or minister needs to have a diaconal dimension to his or her ministry, so ministry proceeds from an attitude of service and Christian leadership can be seen to involve many basic and practical tasks; a presbyteral dimension focused around the service of the Word and the sacraments; and the dimension of episcopal ministry – the need to guard and to guide the unity of the pilgrim people of God in a particular place and to raise up, commission and nurture others in Christian service.

In the chapters which follow we will explore each of these three dimensions of ministry in turn: first examining their roots in Scripture and the tradition and going on to exploring ways in which the insights gained from each can enrich our understanding of the practice of ministry today. Our goal is an understanding of the ministry and role of the ordained which more closely matches the needs of the whole people of God in the present generation.

PART TWO

DIAKONIA:
MINISTRY IN THE FIRST
DIMENSION

4

DIAKONIA:
MINISTRY IN THE FIRST DIMENSION –
THE EVIDENCE OF SCRIPTURE

The Neglected Dimension of the Ministry of the Ordained

Diakonia is the first dimension of the ministry of the ordained both in terms of sequence and of priority. As we shall see, there is sufficient evidence from within the New Testament documents to argue that *diakonos* was one of the earliest descriptions of the person set aside in ministry by the Church. The attitudes and attributes of *diakonia* need to be acquired before those of the presbyterate or of *episcope* and are the validation and foundation of the second and third dimensions of ministry. In the way the majority of churches have handled the diaconal order, both priests and bishops are ordained deacon as a preliminary to a second ordination to the priesthood and consecration as a bishop.

However, *diakonia*, the ministry of a servant, is also the most important of the three dimensions if ministry and leadership are to be truly Christian and Christ-like. The diaconal tradition within the New Testament can be traced very easily directly to Christ himself and to central strands of Jesus' own self understanding; to the pattern of the incarnation; and to the Old Testament background which helped form Jesus' own identity. Of the three concepts which we will explore and which came to be used as titles for Christian ministers, that of deacon has the richest and the deepest theological tradition of them all.

Principles of *diakonia* ought therefore to be the controlling and guiding principles of all Christian ministry and certainly of the ministry of the ordained. In one sense, certainly, *diakonia* is the inheritance of every baptised Christian. However, to be ordained and set apart as a deacon within the Church of Jesus Christ the Servant is surely to be accounted the deepest and most profound honour and commission which that Church can bestow.

In practice, the reverse can seem to be the case. The majority of ordinands in the Church of England are preparing for ordination both to the diaconate and then, a year later, for ordination as priests or presbyters. In the popular understanding of ordination, the diaconate is a temporary state, passed through on the way to becoming a priest. Little attention is paid, generally, to preparation for the diaconal dimension of ministry either in terms of formation, or to an understanding of what diaconal ministry is or to skills training for that ministry. The ordination of deacons is not celebrated in the same way as the ordination to the priesthood and, in terms of the liturgy, is seen as an inferior ordination. Little, if any, continued thought and reflection is given by most Anglican ordained ministers to this diaconal dimension of their ministry once they have been ordained priest. The language of the call to the diaconate alongside the priesthood does not feature prominently in literature about vocations, processes of selection and training for ordained ministry.[1]

However, when a person is ordained deacon and then priest in the Church of England, the second ordination does not cancel out the first. He or she remains a deacon, set aside for service by the Church of God, for the whole of the rest of their life, unless orders are resigned or withdrawn. The calling to be a servant of others must remain a calling of the person so ordained and a dimension or part of that individual's work and ministry. As a bishop remains a presbyter, so a presbyter remains a deacon. The words 'presbyter' and 'priest' by themselves cannot bear the whole weight of the tradition of ordained ministry in the Church or the whole of the ordained minister's self-understanding. The diaconal dimension to ministry needs to be restated, restored and practised in the churches.[2]

Diakonia and *Diakonos* in the Scriptures

Our examination of the *diakonos* and *diakonia* in the Scriptures will begin at the end: with the use of the term *diakonos* in the New Testament as a title to describe someone who is an identifiable Christian minister within one or more Churches of the New Testament period. We will then look at the term as a general description

TABLE 4.1 Layers of Understanding of *diakonos*

A recognised minister in the NT Church
A general term for Christian ministry
Jesus' understanding of himself
Old Testament roots

of the Christian or Christian service and at contrasting usage in secular Greek; at Jesus as a servant; and at Jesus' own use of the term in descriptions of Christian ministry before looking at some Old Testament roots of the concept.[3]

The term *diakonos* is used in a technical sense, with a capital letter, so to speak, of an office in the church in several passages in the New Testament.

In I Timothy 3:8–13, we have a full description of the office and work of deacons (plural) as envisaged by the writers of this letter which follows immediately on from the description of the office and work of the *episcopos*:[4]

> Deacons likewise must be serious, not double tongued, not indulging in too much wine, not greedy for money; they must hold fast to the mystery of the faith with a clear conscience. And let them first be tested; then, if they prove themselves blameless, let them serve as deacons. Women likewise must be serious, not slanderers but temperate, faithful in all things. Let deacons be married only once and let them manage their children and their households well; for those who serve well as deacons gain a good standing for themselves and great boldness in the faith that is in Christ Jesus.

We gain little insight from this passage into the role of the deacons: I Timothy is focusing on the character and qualifications of those who are to undertake this ministry. One of the general concerns of the letter is the care the Church should take about the character and conduct of its ministers. It is not clear from this passage alone whether men only served as deacons or whether the order was open to women also. The word 'women' in verse 11 is often translated 'wives of the deacons' (see NIV), but more naturally means women who were deacons. Elsewhere, as we shall see, women serve as deacons in the New Testament Churches.

The final verse of the section reads literally: 'Those who deacon well gain a good step for themselves.' The word translated 'step' here (Greek: *bathmos*) is not found elsewhere in the New Testament but in secular Greek carries the meaning 'grade' or 'rank' in the armed forces or civilian life. This word, and the context of the whole passage, implies that to be a deacon was coming to be recognised, at least in part, as a first order of ministry from which some, at least, would go on to other things.

The Pastoral Epistles were written towards the end of the New Testament period. The *Letter to the Philippians* comes from near the beginning and is certainly from the hand of Paul.[5] The letter is addressed as follows:

> Paul and Timothy, slaves [*douloi*] of Christ Jesus
> To all the saints in Christ Jesus who are in Philippi
> with the *episkopoi* and *diakonoi*[6]

Again, we have no hint here of the function of these recognised ministers, other than the meanings of the words themselves. Before the list of greetings in Romans 16 we find a commendation of Phoebe, perhaps one of the bearers of the letter, who is described as follows: 'I commend to you our sister Phoebe, *diakonos* of the Church in Cenchreae, so that you might welcome her in the Lord as is fitting for the saints, and help her in whatever she may require from you, for she has been a benefactor of many and myself as well.' As several commentators point out, the translation 'servant' here is inadequate[7]. Phoebe is a recognised minister of the early church in Cenchreae, which was the port of Corinth. She is visiting Rome for some reason and Paul appeals to the Christians there both to recognise her ministry and to assist her work.

Finally, and more tentatively, Tychicus is described in two places in the Pauline letters by the title *diakonos*, and Epaphras is so described in one:

> Tychicus will tell you everything. He is a dear brother and faithful *diakonos* in the Lord. I am sending him to you for this

very purpose, to let you know how we are, and to encourage your hearts.[8]

Tychicus will tell you all the news about me; he is a beloved brother, a faithful *diakonos*, and a fellow-servant [*sundoulos*] in the Lord. I have sent him to you for this very purpose, so that you may know how we are and that he may encourage your hearts; he is coming with Onesimus, the faithful and beloved brother, who is one of you. They will tell you about everything here.[9]

This you learned from Epaphras, our beloved fellow-servant [*sundoulos*]. He is a faithful *diakonos* of Christ on your behalf, and he has made known to us your love in the Spirit.[10]

It is certainly possible that these three passages are using the word *diakonos* in a general sense of Christian service and not a designated and recognised ministry. However, in two of them the term 'faithful *diakonos*' is used in parallel with 'fellow-servant' (*sundoulos*). If the term is being used generally here, it is hard to see why both descriptions are used together: one or other must be redundant. All three passages, like Romans 16:1–2, are commendations of Christian ministers to the congregations to whom Paul is writing. Tychicus and Epaphras are singled out from others in the lists as having this recognised ministry of *diakonos*. Onesimus, for example, is simply described as a faithful and beloved brother. Once again, the term seems to be used as a description of a recognised ministry, albeit in embryonic form.[11]

The Ministry of the Seven

All through the Acts of the Apostles, Luke pays careful attention to the ordering of the churches' ministry, as we shall see. The most important passage in Acts for understanding the ministry of deacons describes the selection and setting apart of the Seven in Acts 6:1–7. The context is a twofold tension in existing patterns of ministry. On the surface of the text is a problem of numbers: as the church grows so new patterns of ministry are needed to enable the continued care of the whole body of Christ. Just below the surface is the deeper issue of division within the Jerusalem church between the Hellenists and the Hebrews which is to surface in other ways throughout the Acts narrative.

Luke is writing his account for a New Testament church which, as we have seen, knew the ministry of deacons. He does not use the noun *diakonos* to refer to the Seven, or to any other group of ministers or individual in Acts. However, the verb (*diakoneo*, to serve) and the abstract noun (*diakonia*, service) are used several times in striking ways:

> Now during those days, when the disciples were increasing in number, the Hellenists complained against the Hebrews because their widows were being neglected in the daily distribution [*diakonia*] of food. And the twelve called together the whole community of the disciples and said, 'It is not right that we should neglect the word of God in order to wait [*diakoneo*] at tables. Therefore, friends, select from among yourselves seven men of good standing, full of the Spirit and of wisdom whom we may appoint to this task, while we, for our part, will devote ourselves to prayer and to serving [*diakoneo*] the word.

When we consider that these words are only used on six other occasions in the whole 28 chapters of the Acts of the Apostles,[12] it seems that the author is saying something quite deliberate. For the first time, ministry and leadership in the Church is expanding and developing away from and beyond the ministry of the Twelve. All ministry, both the practical and the spiritual, is to have the primary foundation of service.[13] Neither the service to the needy nor the service of the word is to be neglected. Nor are they to be rigidly separated, if the passage is to be truly taken in context. The apostles clearly have been waiting at tables as well as serving the word. They sense the time is right to change the balance of their ministry although not necessarily completely. The Seven who are appointed to ministry are portrayed in later chapters as being used in the service of the word also. One dimension of ministry complements and gives integrity to the other. The means of appointment (statement of qualifications; selection of candidates; public commissioning with prayer and laying on of hands) is reflected elsewhere in Acts and in the Pastoral Epistles and, we may surmise, reflects the ordered practice of the Church in Luke's own day. The passage continues to shape the process of setting apart new ministers in the Church today. In linking the diaconal dimension of ministry with practical care for those in need and care of the finances, Luke is probably reflecting not only the situation of the early Church as he perceived it but the situation in his own day. The financial aspects of the deacons' ministry was continued into the following centuries and endures today in some traditions.

Elsewhere in Acts and in the whole of his gospel, Luke studiously avoids using the term *diakonos*. On one occasion in the gospels, where Matthew and Mark both use the term *diakonos*, Luke deliberately changes the word to use the participle not the noun.[14] Later in Acts, in describing Timothy and Erastus, we might have expected *diakonoi*. Again the participle is used.[15] The most obvious reason for Luke's reticence seems to be that *diakonos* had become a common 'technical' term for a person set aside for a particular ministry for the churches for whom Acts and Luke's gospel were written. Luke is wanting to make some connections and trace the roots of diaconal ministry back into the earliest period of the Church but avoids superimposing the pattern of his own day onto the emerging shape of the ministry.

A Generic Term for Christian Ministry

Underlying the specific and evolving use of the term *diakonos* for a Christian minister is a much more general and more common meaning of 'ministry' to which any and every Christian might be called. The word *diakonos* and its related words are particularly common in Paul's writings as a description of his own ministry and the ministry of others. *Diakonia* is also used in several passages as a description of Christian giving and therefore of practical help to the needy.[16] The noun *diakonos* occurs 21 times in the epistles of Paul and refers in at least half of those references to the ministry of Paul and his associates.[17] Paul frequently uses the related but similar word *doulos*, meaning 'slave' or 'servant', to describe his own ministry in addition to *diakonos*. His normal way of introducing himself at the beginning of the epistles is as an apostle. However in Romans and Titus he writes as *doulos*: a slave or servant of God first and an apostle second and Philippians is written from Paul and Timothy, servants (*douloi*) of Christ Jesus.

A collection of passages from the letters to the Corinthians illustrate well how fundamental this diaconal foundation to ministry is to Paul's service of God and leadership of the Church. Throughout 1 and 2 Corinthians, Paul is asserting the validity of his own authority and ministry over against that of other leaders and teachers who are attempting to divide the church in Corinth or to lead people astray. The strongest thread in Paul's validation of his own ministry throughout the letter and the ground of his appeal is the servant nature of his life and work.

What then is Apollos? What is Paul? Servants [*diakonoi*] through whom you came to believe, as the Lord assigned to each.[18]

Think of us this way, as servants of Christ and stewards of God's mysteries.[19]

For I think that God has exhibited us apostles as last of all, as though sentenced to death, because we have become a spectacle to the world, to angels and mortals.[20]

For we do not proclaim ourselves: we proclaim Jesus Christ as Lord and ourselves as your slaves [*douloi*] for Jesus' sake.[21]

We are putting no obstacle in anyone's way, so that no fault may be found with our ministry [*diakonia*], but as servants [*diakonoi*] of God we have commended ourselves in every way: through great endurance, in afflictions, hardships, calamities, beatings, imprisonments, riots, labours, sleepless nights, hunger; by purity, knowledge, patience, kindness, holiness of spirit, genuine love, truthful speech and the power of God; with the weapons of righteousness in the right hand and the left; in honour and dishonour; in ill repute and good repute. We are treated as imposters and yet are true; as unknown and yet are well known; as dying and see – we are alive; as punished and yet not killed; as sorrowful, yet always rejoicing; as poor, yet making many rich; as having nothing, and yet possessing everything.[22]

Different Words for 'Servant'

The language of the New Testament is a rich language and, as we have seen already, there is not simply one word for 'servant' but several in common use. All carry slightly different meanings and connotations in the Greek of the New Testament period. *Doulos* carries the meaning of 'slave'; one who is owned by his or her lord and master. Where *doulos* is used the emphasis is upon obedience. *Hyperatos* is the one who toils at the oars to row the ship or who assists in the lowly work of the household. The emphasis here is on the help given. The *diakonos* is the one who serves and waits at table in secular Greek. Literally the word means 'one who comes through the dust'. The emphasis is on personal service freely and lovingly given to the recipient. As far as we know, *diakonos* was not used in any extensive way outside of the Christian Church to describe ministry or public service: the word was not one which members of the ancient world would willingly apply to themselves. The early Christians were not able to adopt the word *doulos* for their own ministers although they use the term frequently to describe their own relationship to Christ and to one another. The word had too many public and legal connotations. And so it is the term *diakonos* which emerges as expressing the foundation for all Christian service and specifically the first dimension of ministry among the Christian communities and which gradually becomes one of the key words in the Christian tradition for those set aside in the service of the Church.

Jesus as a Servant

Paul's understanding of his own ministry and relationship to Christ is not only rooted in his thinking about himself but also in his thinking about Christ. One of his most basic and formative categories for exploring the person of Jesus is that of servant. As we have seen, he uses the term *diakonos* of Christ on several occasions, but, more often, Jesus is described as *doulos* in his relationship to God. Our understanding of ministry as *diakonia* finds much deeper roots than the patterns of ministry which emerged in the early Church: service expresses something essential of the character and nature of Christ and of the incarnation:

Let each of you look not to your own interests, but to the interests of others. Let the same mind be in you that was in Christ Jesus,

who, though he was in the form of God,
did not regard equality with God
as something to be exploited,
but emptied himself,
taking the form of a slave [*doulos*],
being born in human likeness.
And being found in human form,
he humbled himself
and became obedient to the point of death –
even death on a cross.[23]

A similar and powerful understanding of Jesus as servant is, of course, found in the different gospels both in the words of Jesus and in his actions. In two passages in the synoptic gospels Jesus links his own understanding of himself as a servant with the attitude and ministry of his disciples. It is significant that both occur in the context of disagreements and disputes among the disciples about 'leadership' and who is to be the greatest.

Then they came to Capernaum; and when he was in the house he asked them, 'What were you arguing about on the way?' But they were silent, for on the way they had argued with one another about who was the greatest. He sat down, called the twelve, and said to them, 'Whoever wants to be first must be last of all and servant [*diakonos*] of all.'[24]

When the ten heard this, they began to be angry with James and John. So Jesus called them and said to them, 'You know that among the Gentiles those whom they recognize as their rulers lord it over them and their great ones are tyrants over them. But it is not so among you; but whoever wishes to become great among you must be your servant [*diakonos*], and whoever wishes to be first among you must be slave [*doulos*] of all. For the Son of Man came not to be served [*diakoneo*] but to serve [*diakoneo*] and to give his life as a ransom for many.'[25]

54

Something vital and important is being said here by Jesus to his church not simply about Christian ministry but about the way power and leadership are exercised among the people of God: we are to be different – 'But it is not so among you.' We are to adopt a radically different approach to leadership and to greatness which is founded upon *diakonia*. We are to adopt this different approach not because it works or is more effective or is more life-giving to those among whom we exercise a ministry (although it is all of these). We are to adopt this approach because this is the ministry of Jesus himself, the pattern of both his life and his death: 'The Son of Man came not to be served but to serve and to give his life as a ransom for many.'

Matthew's version of the dispute with James and John is very similar to Mark's. However, he gives a different emphasis to Jesus' sayings about *diakonia* in the great woes against the scribes and Pharisees two chapters later. The sayings here must be taken as warnings to the emerging Christian ministry as well as condemnation of the Pharisees of Jesus' day:

> 'They love to have the place of honour at banquets and the best seats in the synagogues, and to be greeted with respect in the market-places, and to have people call them *rabbi*. But you are not to be called *rabbi*, for you have one teacher, and you are all students. And call no one your father on earth, for you have one Father – the one in heaven. Nor are you to be called instructors, for you have one instructor – the Messiah. The greatest among you will be your servant [*diakonos*]. All who exalt themselves will be humbled, and all who humble themselves will be exalted.'[26]

Salutary warnings indeed from Matthew about special seats and titles and greetings for those who would aspire to be teachers and leaders within the Church of Christ the servant. Luke places an even greater emphasis on the disputes about greatness and the exercise of power by reflecting the tradition that there were even disputes about greatness at the Last Supper, not unexpectedly as decisions were taken about who would sit next to Jesus at the Passover meal:

> A dispute also arose among them as to which one of them was to be regarded as the greatest. But he said to them, 'The kings

of the Gentiles lord it over them; and those in authority over them are called benefactors. But not so with you; rather the greatest among you must become like the youngest, and the leader like one who serves [*ho diakonon*].[27] For who is greater, the one who is at the table or the one who serves [*ho diakonon*]? But I am among you as one who serves [*ho diakonon*].'

Among Jesus' final words to his disciples before his death are a warning that power is not to be exercised within the Christian community in the same way as power is exercised among the gentile kings. Secular society is not to be our model for leadership practices. We are to be a radically different community in the way in which we order our life and ministry. Power exercised within the gentile kingdoms creates dependance and patronage; people are brought into subjection to other people, diminishing their humanity and their calling. The only safe subjection is to Christ the Servant. The only safe model for the exercise of Christian leadership is to follow the one who serves.

John's gospel is the last of the four to be written and reflects a period in the life of the church when *diakonos* had almost certainly become a technical term.[28] John can hardly give more prominence than he does to the theme of service in Christian ministry and leadership in his description of Jesus' washing the disciples' feet in John 13. Again the setting is the Last Supper. Again the connection is made with Jesus' understanding of himself and his ministry and death. Again the appeal is made that this is the attitude which needs to be modelled among those who are Jesus' own people and especially among those who are to exercise leadership in the new community.

> And during supper Jesus, knowing that the Father had given all things into his hands, and that he had come from God and was going to God, got up from the table, took off his outer robe, and tied a towel around himself. Then he poured water into a basin and began to wash the disciples' feet and to wipe them with the towel that was tied around him.[29]
>
> After he had washed their feet, had put on his robe and had returned to the table he said to them, 'Do you know what I have done to you? You call me Teacher and Lord – and you are right, for that is what I am. So if I, your Lord and Teacher, have

washed your feet, you also ought to wash one another's feet. For I have set you an example, that you also should do as I have done to you. Very truly I tell you, servants [*doulos*] are not greater than their master, nor are messengers greater than the one who sent them. If you know these things, you are blessed if you do them.'[30]

Old Testament Roots

The importance of the idea of the servant in Jesus' own understanding of his ministry and suffering does not emerge, as it were, from nowhere in the pages of the New Testament. Jesus himself is drawing from the Old Testament tradition of the servant of God which runs from Moses through Elijah to Jeremiah and into the portrayal of the nation of Israel as the suffering servant in the beautiful Servant Songs of Isaiah 40–55.[31] According to the Exodus traditions, Moses begins his exercise of leadership according to the ways he has learned as a prince of Egypt and yet has to be schooled for forty years in the wilderness keeping sheep in order to learn to be truly a servant of God.[32] Later in the narrative, after immense sufferings and labour in the service of God's people, Moses is the only person in the Old Testament described by the singular of the Hebrew word *'anaw'*, meaning meek or humble: 'Now the man Moses was very humble, more so than anyone on the face of the earth.'[33]

A characteristic of David's leadership of the people, taken up into the traditions of the ideal king in Israel, is that of humility before God and before others. Often, for those in positions of leadership in Israel, that humility and the sense of being the servant of God is refined through immense suffering arising from their response to the call of God. The same image is applied to the nation in the Songs of the Servant:

'Here is my servant, whom I uphold,
my chosen, in whom my soul delights;
I have put my spirit upon him;
he will bring forth justice to the nations.
He will not cry or lift up his voice,
or make it heard in the street;

a bruised reed he will not break,
and a dimly burning wick he will not quench.'[34]

It is this concept of servanthood which forms the character of Mary in her assent to the angel's announcement: 'Behold, I am the servant of the Lord; let it be to me according to your word.' 'He has brought down the powerful from their thrones and lifted up the lowly.'[35] It is this diaconal dimension to the leadership of the people of God in the Old Testament which becomes the defining strand of Jesus' own self understanding and of his ministry and death: the service and the suffering of the servant becomes the means of redemption, healing and salvation not only for Israel, but for the whole world. The concept of salvation and righteousness coming through the servant of God is indeed central to the Christian scriptures and to Christian ministry today.

5

DIAKONIA
IN THE TRADITION

Our understanding of the shape, purpose and function of ministry today needs to be informed not only by the Scriptures but also by almost 2000 years of Christian history which precedes our own. Many generations of Christian people have grappled with questions of how best to order the life of the Church locally and in a wider way. Their struggles and solutions will have both positive and negative lessons for us as we engage with similar questions in a different context. The way ministry has been shaped in the past also affects our own starting points in respect of legal frameworks; services of ordination and, more subtly, perceptions of the ordained ministry both in Church and society. This brief chapter will examine first the history of the ministry of deacons in the Church, some models of *diakonia* in practice from history and today, and the way in which the diaconal ministry is seen in our own generation. My purpose, again, is not to argue for the restoring of a permanent diaconate, although I happen to believe that the theological arguments for this are convincing.[1] I am arguing here that a full, three-dimensional concept of the ordained ministry needs to embrace *diakonia*, Christian service. For that reason we need to understand the different ways in which this dimension of ordained ministry has been expressed in the history of the Church.

The Deacons' Story[2]

The ministry of deacons continues to grow and develop beyond the New Testament period for around five hundred years, a period called by one writer 'the golden age of the diaconate'. There are a range of references to the role and ministry of the deacons and the evolving and changing relationships between deacons, presbyters

59

and bishops. The secular Roman writer Pliny, governor of Bythinia, writes to the Emperor Trajan in AD 112 about the customs of the Christians and mentions 'two women who are called ministers'. The Greek word underlying the Latin *ministrae* is almost certainly *diakonoi*.[3] The letters of Ignatius of Antioch, dated a few years earlier in AD 107, written on his way to martyrdom in Rome, attest to a ministry of bishops, presbyters and deacons within each local church. The deacons are seen by Ignatius as representing Jesus Christ in their ministry: 'Correspondingly, everyone must show the deacons respect. They represent Jesus Christ, just as the bishop has the role of the Father and the presbyters are like God's council and an apostolic band. You cannot have a Church without these.'[4] The deacons represent Jesus, we presume, because the nature of their role is to be a servant as Christ is servant to all. The shape of the deacons' ministry revolves and evolves around the service of both God and the wider community, expressed in practical acts of love and in a role within the public worship or liturgy of the churches.

The practical acts of love, as with the Seven in Acts, embrace a care for the finances of the congregation, particularly the distribution of the money given for the poor, a substantial responsibility in a large urban church. As the Church began to own its own property and buildings, the deacons' role was naturally extended to this aspect of service as well. 'The Epistle of Clement to James' speaks of a pastoral role for the deacons. They are to be 'as eyes to the bishops', not only observing individuals with a view to their correction but feeding back information to those who will preach on appropriate subjects to be addressed within the preaching of the Church. They are to have a particular role in following up those who are falling away from the congregation and 'desist from assembling to hear the discourses'. They are also to have a particular role in relation to care of the sick: 'And let them learn who are suffering under bodily disease, and let them bring to the notice of the multitude who do not know of them, that they may visit them, and supply their wants according to the judgement of the president. Yea, though they do this without his knowledge they do nothing amiss.'[5]

The Epistle has here an excellent job description for a lay pastoral team in a large congregation. The bishop here functions as the leader of a congregation or group of congregations, not a diocese. Those who assist him in the work of care are to have a threefold function of service: to help maintain a two-way communication between bishop and people; to have a particular care for those who are falling away; and, in the case of the sick, to report needs to the entire congregation. The work of caring for one another, and especially those who are ill, is not the preserve of the clergy alone but the work of the whole body of Christ.

The service of the deacons within the public worship of the Church centres around the reading of the gospel, the *diakonia* of the word; the presenting of the offering of the people, the *diakonia* of practical giving; assisting the bishop (the normal president at the eucharist for much of this period) by waiting at table; administering the chalice and, in some traditions, making announcements during the service such as inviting the intercessory prayers; requiring the unbaptised to depart after the ministry of the word and the concluding invitation to 'Depart in peace'.[6] As early as the time of Justin Martyr (c. 100–165), deacons were taking the consecrated bread to Church members who were sick or in prison.[7] At baptisms, deacons and deaconesses assist in practical ways and have the responsibility for anointing candidates before the baptism and continuing to care for and instruct new converts in the days afterwards: 'When she who is being baptised has come up from the water, let the woman deacon receive her, and teach her how the seal of baptism ought to be kept unbroken in purity and holiness.'[8]

Up until the time of the conversion of the Emperor Constantine, therefore, the deacons were given a significant and major role within the life of the churches. It was not uncommon for one of the deacons in a district to be appointed bishop rather than one of the existing presbyters. However, there was significant change in the relationships between all three orders following the entrance of large numbers into the Church after the adoption by the Roman Empire of the policy of toleration for Christians and equality for all religions.[9] As bishops have care for larger areas beyond the local congregations, so the role of the presbyters within the local churches assumes a greater significance. 'As the presbyters take the place of the bishop in the churches of the "diocese", the deacons become their assistants as well.'[10] There has been a change from organic structures in which the different orders of ministry embody different aspects of the ministry of the whole Church, to a vertical or

hierarchical structure with the deacons seen as embodying a sub-
sidiary ministry to that of bishops and presbyters. Although the
story unfolds in a slightly different way in the East compared to
the West, the ministry of deacon becomes by AD 600 increasingly
seen as a transitional order: an apprenticeship passed through on
the way to becoming a presbyter or priest. The idea of the 'priest'
has swallowed up the diaconal and episcopal dimensions of ministry
in the local church, to the detriment of the Church's overall mission
to society.

At the Reformation a number of attempts were made to revive
the diaconal dimension of ordained ministry. The Church of England
retained the diaconal order although Cranmer abolished other minor
orders which had evolved in the intervening years. However, the
diaconate remained in reality a stage to be passed through on
the way to ordination as a priest. In Strasbourg, following the teach-
ings of Bucer, deacons became parish officers concerned with charity,
visiting the sick and relieving the poor. Lutheran churches either
abolished deacons or reduced them to a lay function as parish clerks
or vergers. Calvin confines their work to charity: 'In most Calvinistic
countries, the diaconate was regarded as a hard and laborious work
concerned with poorhouses, hospitals and orphanages.'[11] In the
years since the Reformation, Non-conformist churches have commonly used the term deacon to refer to senior and usually elected
lay officials within a local congregation who share in the administration of church property and finances and, at least in theory, in
the pastoral care of the congregation.

From the end of the sixteenth century until the mid-twentieth
century the ministry of the deacon has either become a lay
expression of Christian service in the Protestant tradition or, in the
Catholic tradition, a transitional minor order of ministry to be passed
through on the way to priesthood. The combined effect of this
twofold shift has been to separate *diakonia* from the mature ordained
ministry of the churches when, in reality and of necessity, *diakonia*
should be the foundation of that ministry. The Church has created
a situation in which those who are given increased responsibility
are seen as graduating out of the need to express their ministry in
acts of practical service and Christian love: to be representatives of
Christ.

Fresh thinking about the diaconate began in the eighteenth and nineteenth centuries and has continued into the twentieth century, largely stimulated by the need to consider the ministry of women in the Church. The Anglican ordinal in the ASB 1980 contains a much fuller understanding of ordination to the diaconate, picking up many different strands of the tradition which is more clearly differentiated from ordination as priest or presbyter. The epistle and gospel readings emphasise the role of being a servant.[12] The charge to deacons, although very brief when compared to the parallel charge to priests, evokes the *diakonia* of the New Testament and the early Christian tradition:

> 'A deacon is called to serve the Church of God, and to work with its members in caring for the poor, the needy, the sick, and all who are in trouble. He is to strengthen the faithful, search out the careless and indifferent, and to preach the word of God in the place to which he is licensed. A deacon assists the priest under whom he serves in leading the worship of the people, especially in the administration of the Holy Communion. He may baptise when required to do so. It is his general duty to do such pastoral work as is entrusted to him.'[13]

The preface to the ordination prayer links the ministry of the deacons with the ministry and death of Christ, drawing not only on Mark 10:45 and parallels but also on Philippians 2:5–11:

> 'We praise and glorify you, most merciful Father, because in your great love of mankind you sent your only Son Jesus Christ to take the form of a servant; he came to serve and not to be served; and taught us that he who would be great among us must be the servant of all; he humbled himself for our sake, and in obedience accepted death, even death on a cross; therefore you have highly exalted him and gave him the name which is above every name. And now we give you thanks that you have called these your servants, whom we ordain in your name, to share this ministry entrusted to your Church.'[14]

The fresh thinking on *diakonia* is in evidence ecumenically as well as within the Anglican tradition. The Roman Catholic Church has re-established the Diaconal order as an order in its own right of those who assist the priest within the parish ministry as well as part of the preparation for priesthood. The Methodist Church has re-established the diaconal order which was founded by John Wesley as an order for deaconesses but which had lapsed. Men as well as women train and are licensed to be deacons within circuits. The Anglican report on the diaconate quoted within this chapter recommended in 1988 the establishing of a permanent diaconate.[15] This recommendation was not carried forward by General Synod and the House of Bishops as the Church of England subsequently entered a decade of debate about the ordination of women to the priesthood. However, following a General Synod debate in November 1998, a working party has recently been established to begin thinking again about diaconal ministry.

The World Council of Churches' Lima text, *Baptism, Eucharist and Ministry*, again uses the now familiar language of *diakonia* to sum up the role of deacons:

'Deacons represent to the Church its calling as servant in the world. By struggling in Christ's name with the myriad needs of societies and persons, deacons exemplify the interdependence of worship and service in the Church's life. They exercise responsibility in the worship of the congregation: for example, by reading the scriptures, preaching and leading the people in prayer. They help in the teaching of the congregation. They exercise a ministry of love within the community. They fulfil certain administrative tasks and may be elected to responsibilities for governance.'[16]

Diakonia in the Whole Tradition of the Church

The principles of *diakonia* are found in a much wider perspective than the ordained ministry or the story of the diaconal order. Examples of *diakonia* are to be found in abundance in the whole history of the Church and in every generation in the lives of God's saints – both those who are publicly recognised as such and those who are not. Saint Francis and the Franciscan and Poor Clare orders embody much of what it means to be a servant and to embrace the lower path. The poet and Anglican priest George Herbert expresses *diakonia* in much of his verse and, crucially, in the pattern of his life and ministry. William Booth, the founder of the Salvation Army, embodies *diakonia* in his concern for the poor of society beyond the reach of the conventional churches and his expression of practical service. Pope John XXIII embraced as his lifetime motto the diaconal text: 'Strive to be unknown.'[17] Mother Theresa has inspired and moved the entire world, it seems, and certainly the subcontinent of India through her Christian commitment to service of the poorest of the poor and those who are dying.

Yet *diakonia* by its very nature is also a hidden and secret ministry. The best examples we can find will probably not be ones recorded in history or reported in the media but examples which we stumble across and which humble us in the ordinary circumstances of our lives: the person who commits much of their life to the care of elderly relatives or a grown-up but mentally handicapped child; the teacher committed to a school in a needy part of the community when there are better jobs and more prestige elsewhere; the church treasurer prayerfully serving and guiding the needs of the local church over several decades of his life; the volunteer toddler group leader getting up early to set out toys for the sake of building community in the midst of the city; the man who empties the bins and sweeps the floors of the church halls each day in his retirement; the couple who covenant a large part of their income to Christian Aid; the prison visitor befriending and being committed to those excluded from society; the hospice volunteer and Cruse counsellor sitting with the dying and the bereaved.

> 'For I was hungry and you gave me food, I was thirsty and you gave me something to drink, I was a stranger and you welcomed me, I was naked and you gave me clothing, I was sick and you took care of me, I was in prison and you visited me . . . Truly I tell you, just as you did it to one of the least of these who are members of my family, you did it to me.'[18]

Diakonia is the ministry of Jesus in serving and loving his world. *Diakonia* must be a vital dimension of the ministry of the ordained in the context both of the world and of the church:

'In baptism every disciple is called to make Jesus known as Saviour and Lord and to share his work in renewing the world. Some by ordination are given particular tasks. A deacon shares with the bishop and his presbyters in the ministry of word and sacrament and in works of love. In a distinctive way the deacon is a sign of that humility which marks all service offered in the name of Christ. He bears witness to his Lord who laid aside all claims of dignity, assumed the nature of a slave and accepted death on a cross. In the name of the Church, he is to care for those in need, serving God and his creation after the pattern of Christ our Master. To fulfil such a task is not in human power but depends upon the grace of God who alone can give us that mind which was in Christ Jesus through whom we now pray.'[19]

6

DIAKONIA AND
THE ORDAINED MINISTRY TODAY

We have seen that this first dimension of Christian ministry has a distinguished pedigree both in Scripture and in Christian tradition and Church history. The term 'deacon' is used as one of the earliest titles for the Christian minister. Underlying the term is a rich theological seam of biblical ideas embracing the Church's understanding of Christ and Jesus' own understanding of his ministry which traces its roots back into the Old Testament tradition. This diaconal dimension of ministry has played a significant role in the history and development of the church in different periods both in those formally recognised and set apart as deacons, and in the examples of the great saints of the past and those in whom we see this aspect of Christ's ministry reflected today.

Diakonia or Christian service, as we have seen, is the calling of every baptised Christian, not simply those who are ordained. Yet it must also be the particular calling of those who are ordained if they are to express the ministry and character of Christ through their ordination, if they are to act as a focus and example for the service of all the baptised, and if they are to be true to their ordination as deacon which, in the majority of churches, precedes their ordination as priest or presbyter. In the minds of many, it seems, being set aside as a minister of the word and sacrament, the heart of presbyteral ministry, means graduation from the more menial tasks of the Christian life. This sense of graduating from the routine, mundane acts of service finds support in the management models which many clergy have been led to adopt. The legitimate appeal of the apostles in Acts 6.2 to restore the balance of their ministry has become the rationale for avoiding a series of tasks which are vital not only for their own sake but for the health of a person's whole ministry, particularly if that ministry involves the exercise of leadership or authority.

This chapter explores both the vital nature and the meaning of the diaconal dimension to ministry in contemporary society. As the apostles set aside seven to assist them in different aspects of their ministry, so we will explore seven facets of what it means to be a deacon in the ordinary run of local church ministry today: to borrow the language of the management gurus, we might call them the seven habits of highly effective deacons.

Simple, Hidden, Practical Acts of Service

Everyone who is ordained in the ministry of the Church comes into that ministry with a set of expectations about what day-to-day work is involved. Those expectations are formed from a certain amount of contact with those who are ordained through a whole lifetime; perhaps from books or films; perhaps from models taken from Scripture or Church history; or from experiences during ordination training. Expectations can be both positive and negative.

Every person's expectations will be inaccurate to some degree. The map of our hopes and fears of ministry will not match the terrain exactly. Sometimes that will be because something is 'wrong' with the church in this particular place in this area of its understanding of ministry. Sometimes the reason for the mismatch will be because the map is wrongly and, perhaps, romantically drawn. Part of the process of adjusting to any new task or environment is one of allowing expectations and reality to interact and working through the places where there is a radical mismatch in a creative way. Not to do this is to run the risk of continual frustration, disappointment and, eventually, cynicism.

One of the areas of greatest mismatch in my own experience and that of many clergy I have known was in this area of practical acts of service. I somehow swallowed the idea that ordination meant graduation from tasks such as moving chairs, setting up for meetings, washing up and providing refreshments and emptying dustbins. 'It is not right that we should neglect the word of God in order to wait at tables', I would grumble to myself time and again during my curacy as I found myself shifting tables, chairs and crockery for a church social event; washing up alone after a meeting when everyone had gone home; typing, duplicating and folding leaflets for distribution; or dragging table-tennis tables across the floor for the youth group I was charged with leading. My somewhat romantic ideas of ministry had convinced me that the majority of the time I would be engaged in study for and preparation of sermons and the pastoral care of individuals, or else exercising dynamic leadership in one way or another, and that I should therefore resent the more obvious forms of *diakonia* as intrusions into this primary commitment.

In reality, as everyone reading this who is already ordained will instantly acknowledge, practical tasks such as these are an inseparable part of the ministry of the clergy. We never graduate and we never will. It is certainly possible to have a wrong balance between the different dimensions of ministry and for this balance to need to be corrected. Our vocation may change through different periods of our lives to put the major weight on one or other dimension of ministry. But, surely, as representatives of Jesus the servant, we should never want to lose this aspect of our *diakonia*. The task of the curate, vicar or minister will always include unblocking the loos for the toddler group; sweeping up the glass after another broken window; trying to unjam the photocopier; drying up in the kitchen after the harvest festival; helping to paint and decorate the church hall. In one sense, these tasks are not prominent in our job description. We may often find ourselves saying: 'Was this what I was ordained for?' In another sense, we profess to follow someone who washed feet, became a slave, waited at tables, who said that if we want to be leaders we must become the least.

Acts of service are important for their own sake and for the sake of faithfulness to Christ. They are also important, however, for the sake of relationships with those among whom we are called to serve and for our own health in ministry. Good, lasting relationships are forged when people work side by side on a common task in which both are equal partners. Washing up together or raking grass will serve to build a relationship better than a superficial conversation over coffee or a confrontation in a PCC meeting. The minister who studiously avoids all the washing up, cleaning and gardening will find a gap may grow between themselves and their parish.

An essential part of motivating others is an active demonstration that we are willing to undertake the most dirty and difficult tasks in order to move things along. One of my earliest experiences of working for the Diocese of Wakefield was organising a very large day conference in the hall of a local secondary school. Around six hundred people attended for what was an effective but demanding day. At five o'clock in the evening three people were left in the school hall moving chairs and sweeping up the mess: myself and my colleague (who both had to be there); and the diocesan bishop, who could by this time have been at home resting and preparing for his next engagement. The action was instinctive rather than deliberate yet its effect was powerful both as an example and as a means of building a relationship of trust and co-operation.

One of the dangers in ordained ministry, particularly if we are seen to be 'successful' in the work to which we have been called or if we are entrusted with significant responsibility within the life of the Church, is that other Christians will put us on a pedestal and begin to exaggerate our gifts and our significance. There are parallel syndromes in most walks of life. Power and patronage distort relationships. There is always a danger that we come to accept the assessment of those who see our strengths but not our weaknesses, particularly if we are seduced into a state of self-importance in which others are committed to serving us but not vice versa. Simple, practical acts of service are the vital and continual antidote we need to this subtle self-aggrandisement.

Service to the Community

Churches can be centrifugal organisations: that is, they have a tendency to draw in and to consume the energy of those who are members of them and serve in them, both clergy and committed lay people. All the ordained will feel this pressure, particularly if the congregation they serve begins to grow. There will be a strong pull from the priestly or presbyteral dimension of ministry to focus more and more energy on the ministry of Word, sacrament and the pastoral care of individuals and groups, perhaps to the exclusion of all else.

Should this pull be resisted or accepted and on what grounds? My own practice as incumbent of a growing church was to accept this trend as right and inevitable. As the church of which I was vicar grew in size and numbers there came a point when it was very, very hard to sustain all the commitments and meet all of the needs which were arising within the Christian community. It seemed a logical and necessary step therefore to reduce the commitments and interests I had taken on outside the Church and to leave the lay members of the body of Christ to exercise that kind of ministry. So, over time, I reduced my links with the local NACRO group;[1] came off a secondary school governing body and reduced my commitment to a primary school; discontinued regular meetings with social workers and other caring professionals in the area; stopped visiting the social services day care centres; and so on. Time and energies became focused increasingly upon the growing congregation.

In retrospect, I believe, for myself and for the Church's ministry in that parish, these were wrong decisions, although they were honestly made. The presbyteral dimension of ministry was gaining ground over and above the diaconal. Part of my vocation as a Christian minister was and is to build the kingdom of God and to serve the wider community, not simply to build up the Christian congregation. My hope and expectation that an increasing number of lay Christians would seek to express their discipleship through service within the community as I withdrew was never realised (with some notable exceptions). Looking back, this was not surprising. The model for ministry which I was providing, and which others then emulated, was one of gradually withdrawing from community involvement in order to focus upon building up the body of Christ. The very difficult calling I was faced with was the modelling of a whole, three-dimensional ministry, which must include some elements of service to the wider community – to building the kingdom of God beyond the confines of the Christian community.

All clergy wrestle with this conflict between the diaconal and presbyteral aspects of ministry. Models of ministry within the liberal tradition of the Church have focused on the diaconal aspect of the mission and calling of the ordained. The vicar will spend much of his or her time and energy serving community projects in schools; with the homeless or unemployed; helping to guide economic regeneration of a community. Very little energy is devoted to building up the body of Christ, growing new Christians, ensuring that there is a lively and committed Christian presence within an area to pass on the good news to the next generation. Conversely, models of ministry within the evangelical and more recent catholic tradition have focused on the presbyteral dimension of ministry, the need to minister to and to build up the body of Christ. So the vicar's energy and time are given to the tasks of evangelism, nurture, pastoral care, preaching and teaching within the Christian community. The larger the church (or, the more the smaller churches and parishes are combined), the less time the clergy have available for service of the wider community. The truth is that both traditions need one another. The vocation of the ordained must find its expression both outside and within the Christian community if that vocation is to reflect the ministry and mission of Christ. A clergyman or woman who does not minister in one or other of these two areas will instinctively feel something is missing from their ministry. Over time, the Church's attempts to preach the Gospel and to call men and women to saving faith in Christ will be undermined without a living tradition of Christian service to the communities around us.[2]

Eric Treacy was a former Bishop of Wakefield. One of the most striking passages in his biography is the description of the way in which *diakonia* continued to find expression at the time in his life when *episcope* had become his main concern. Each Saturday found Bishop Treacy and his wife visiting the inmates on the high security wing of Wakefield prison. His actions did not serve directly to build up the Church. Yet they speak powerfully of Christ's love and of his mission to the whole of society and they lent an integrity to the remainder of the Bishop's ministry which is still remembered and respected.

Competent and Careful Administration

In both the Scriptures and the tradition a significant part of *diakonia*, as we have seen, is the administration of finance and buildings, and particularly the relief of the poor. All clergy in local church ministry find themselves investing significant time and energy in administration. In the survey quoted in the Chapter 1 for many this can be over 20 hours each week: over a third of their working time. For many it is their least enjoyable task.

Most clergy, with the presbyteral dimension of ministry uppermost in their minds, are frustrated by administration, finance and buildings. Many find it difficult to see how these administrative tasks match their vocation to priesthood and, perhaps in consequence, do not spend time and energy thinking through how these tasks can best be tackled or acquiring the relevant skills and training to do them well. The results are that some clergy spend too little time on essential administration, which undercuts the remainder of their ministry. Others, because of inefficiency and lack of clarity about what they should be doing, invest too much time here, and paperwork and buildings consume all available energy. Gordon MacDonald has an excellent analysis of the way in which un-budgeted time and energy flows towards our areas of greatest natural weakness. In areas where we are naturally gifted, for example the preparation of sermons and services, we are able to do tasks quickly and take short cuts, resulting in adequate sermons although not our best work. But in areas in which we struggle to be competent the simplest tasks can take a great deal of our time.[3]

Effective administration is enabling of other aspects of ministry; ineffective administration is disabling. All of the ordained need a basic level of competence in this aspect of *diakonia* in terms of planning, answering correspondence and returning telephone calls, keeping records and registers, reading a balance sheet and under-standing church finances, and ordering and chairing business meetings. Similarly, as those charged, with others, with the care of buildings, a basic level of competence in dealing with architects and builders, knowing where to go for help, and the ability to think through the proper ordering of buildings for worship and for service is essential. These things are not some Anglican or denominational adjunct to the ministry of leadership in the local church which existed in some purer form in New Testament times. They are part and parcel of the calling to serve the Christian community. Many of them can and should be shared with others. Most clergy will want to delegate most administration most of the time. But some will remain and it needs to be tackled competently and well, not as a nuisance or distraction from the heart of ministry but as part of the essence of what it means to serve.

Listening to Others

Diakonia involves the discipline of learning to listen to others as a vital tool in understanding both people and complex communities and situations both within and outside the churches. The model of ministry demonstrated by the risen Christ on the road to Emmaus shows us *diakonia* in action in relationships with people: even those who are heading in the wrong direction.[4] Jesus does not confront them in power and order them to turn around. He draws alongside them in a hidden and secret way, in such a way that they do not know who he is. He listens, and listens with some depth and with perceptive questions, both to their story and to their pain before the way is opened for him to teach them, to instruct them and for them to see who it is who is meeting with them.

One of the many genuinely useful insights into the way in which organisations work from the discipline of management studies is the importance of listening and learning within every level of any large community. Both companies and voluntary organisations will often evolve structures which separate those who make decisions from those who have accurate information about the situation on the shop floor or in the field. The company's life and performance suffers in consequence particularly in respect of its ability to adapt to change. Peter Senge has coined the phrase 'The Learning Organisation' to describe a new and evolving kind of company which attempts to grow a culture of listening and learning and connecting decision makers with accurate information.[5] At one level developing a learning organisation is about incarnating *diakonia* into its culture. There has been significant interest in the relevance of learning organisation theory to the life of churches.[6] A number of writers on management thinking also stress the importance of any organisation cherishing the voices of dissent. Again, any community including a church can easily develop a culture in which dissent and constructive criticism (the prophetic voice, in theological language) is discouraged and suppressed. Among the people to cherish in any organisation are the ones who will dare to say that something isn't working. Only then will the problems be recognised and addressed.[7]

An ordained minister needs to act in this first dimension of *diakonia* in many different contexts. In individual pastoral situations, a primary challenge is to learn to listen carefully to another person's pain or situation. Listening can be healing in and of itself but is certainly a first stage in establishing any relationship of care and restoration. In the ministry of evangelism and nurture, listening plays a key role. Each person's story and journey with God is different. By hearing different people's impressions and stories of what God has been doing in their lives we avoid trying to fit them into our own narrow categories. Tuning in to the needs of both the wider society and the local church is a necessary preliminary to preaching and the proclamation of the Gospel. Listening is vital whenever a new minister, curate, vicar or parish priest arrives in a circuit or parish. Every community is different. A vital part of *the induction process* is to sit down and listen to the story of the church in that place as told by a cross-section of different people from within the community of faith. To do this is to lay a very necessary foundation for any common vision which may arise.

Listening to the whole community needs to be central to the process of guiding a community through a period of change. St Benedict insists, in his rule for community life which has inspired the Church through fifteen centuries: 'Whenever anything important has to be done in the monastery, the Abbott must assemble the whole community and explain what is under consideration ... It is often to a younger brother that the Lord reveals the best course.'[8] Listening to and trying not to alienate the voice of criticism and dissent is also vital, although probably the hardest part of listening. More times than not, I have found my relationship with someone strengthened if they have been able to tell me why they think I have failed them or what they have against me. Sometimes I have agreed with their assessment and done my best to be changed. Occasionally, on taking soundings with other people, I have disagreed. But it has been better to have an honest conversation than for one of us to simmer or to sulk and for the relationship to be fractured. Listening both to God and to other people is the foundation for responsible and godly leadership. Listening begins with acknowledging that we are servants and have so much more to learn.[9]

Attitude and Integrity

Who among you would say to your slave who has just come in from ploughing or tending sheep in the field, 'Come here at once and take your place at the table?'. Would you not rather say to him, 'Prepare supper for me, put on your apron and serve me while I eat and drink; later you may eat and drink'? Do you thank the slave for doing what was commanded? So you also, when you have done all that you were ordered to do, say, 'We are worthless slaves; we have done only what we ought to have done!'[10]

These hard sounding words of Jesus are addressed to the apostles in the context of the Gospel and therefore addressed to every Christian but particularly to those who are ministers and servants in the Church of Christ. They describe an ethic of *diakonia* which is to run through everything that is done in our ministry. It is not to be done for reward or gain. It is not to be done for the sake of winning attention or acclaim or position. The slave has surrendered his or her rights in order to serve. At the end, when we have undertaken our tasks faithfully and well, and more besides, we are commanded to say to ourselves: 'We are worthless slaves; we have only done what we ought to have done.'

But if these are hard words, they are also markers on a path of great if severe mercy. Those who attempt to live as ordained ministers of the Church of Jesus Christ face numerous temptations. The more subtle and dangerous of these focus around the sense that we are owed many things for our 'selfless acts of service' and for all that we have given: money, status, recognition, notice, love, promotion, influence. If we allow the desire for these things to grow within us, when they do not materialise the resulting disappointment can grow into cynicism and bitterness which are the enemy of faith and love. It is as though our acts of service to God, the Church and the community are accumulating an imaginary balance of payments in our favour. After several years of ministry, God, the Church and society, we feel, owe us a significant debt. Yet the debt is not paid in any obvious way. Any further service we might give, then, is grudgingly and grumpily given.

Harder but better, more life-giving and life-saving is the way of *diakonia*. We enter this ministry as volunteers, as servants. Because we are called to *diakonia* then we do all that is asked of us and more besides: we aim for personal service lovingly given. As long as we have food and clothing, we aim to be content.[11] And at the end of the day, when we have done all that we were asked to do, we say: 'We are worthless slaves; we have done only what we ought to have done.'

The ordained ministry is an excellent, hard, demanding way of living, providing many opportunities for service and sacrifice. Because it is founded on *diakonia* it should not be seen as a career in the conventional sense. The proper unfolding of each person's vocation and ministry before God ought to involve development and new opportunities and tasks undertaken being matched to individual gifts. The proper exercise of *diakonia* on the part of the ordained herself or himself needs to be matched and balanced by the proper exercise of *episcope* both by that same individual and by the wider Church community. Yet the foundational and guiding attitude is one of service. At the heart of becoming a *Christian* leader is integrity: a wholeness of life and consistency between the faith we profess and the lives we lead. Integrity is more important than any gifts or skills that we might have been given. WYSIWYG is an acronym used in personal computing. It stands for 'What You See Is What You Get'. Diakonia is at least a WYSIWIG quality in the ordained. If we are to observe and practise Jesus' teaching in the Sermon on the Mount then in many areas there will be more going on below the surface of our lives than is apparent to those who see us in action. Our activity, such as it is, will rest on a deep foundation of secret and personal prayer, giving of minds and an imagination which can be open to the scrutiny of others.

Spirituality

Our spirituality is our way of praying but more than a way of praying. It describes the way we see God but also the way in which we relate to him and communicate with him. The heartland of our spirituality influences and is influenced by our understanding of mission and ministry and the life of the Church. The spirituality of *diakonia* is a spirituality of trust and listening: looking to God for provision but also for guidance and for direction:

> As the eyes of servants look to the hand of their master,
> as the eyes of a maid to the hand of her mistress,
> so our eyes look to the Lord our God,
> until he has mercy upon us.[12]

> O Lord, my heart is not lifted up,
> my eyes are not raised too high;
> I do not occupy myself with things
> too great and too marvellous for me.
> But I have calmed and quieted my soul,

like a weaned child with its mother;
my soul is like the weaned child that is with me.[13]

Listening for the Church

An essential part of the New Testament picture of the life of the Church is the firm belief and conviction that God is guiding his people in an immediate and direct way through both outward events, prophetic words and particular answers to prayer. The witness of Acts is clear. From the very beginning the apostles are not deciding for themselves what to do: they are obeying the instructions of the risen Christ as his servants. In one sense the whole of Acts is an unfolding of Jesus' instruction to preach the Gospel through Jerusalem and all Judea, in Samaria and to the ends of the earth. The apostles wait in the city for the promise of the Father, following the instructions of Jesus. At key events in the life of the early Church they come together to seek God in prayer. At others, God himself intervenes through visions, prophetic words or through speaking directly to the life of the believer.[14]

This understanding of the involvement of the risen Christ in the life and development of his Church is carried through in the epistles with, as we have seen, the doctrine of the Church as the body of Christ and Christ as the head of the body,[15] and in allusions in Paul's letters to his following God's guidance in the direction of his mission and ministry.[16] In the Book of Revelation, Christ is pictured as walking among the lampstands of the local and regional churches. He has specific things to say to each of them through the letters to the seven Churches: different things to commend and to condemn; different and specific instructions to be followed.

Those who would exercise ordained ministry and leadership within a local congregation have an urgent and great need for this diaconal spirituality which waits upon God and listens to God for his priorities and his way forward for a particular local church or part of a local church's ministry. Sometimes the situation will seem impossible, like a complex tangle. There will be a need to wait upon God simply to discern where to begin the unravelling. Often we will need to think through who may be the right people to share in a particular task. Sometimes we will reduce the options to a choice between alternatives. We will need to weigh those up carefully and prayerfully, trying to discern God's call and God's guidance. On other occasions the way ahead will seem obvious. We will still need to bring our proposed course of action back to God: to seek his blessing upon what we do. Waiting upon God is not unlike waiting at table: bringing to him each option in turn until we find one with which he is pleased.

Listening to God as his servants will often need to be corporate as well as individual, as was the pattern for the Church in Antioch and elsewhere. The discipline of the parish I served as vicar over many years before I arrived was to set aside the first week of each year as a week of prayer. Normal activities were suspended and as many of the congregation as could be there gathered each evening to worship and to pray. The focus of the week was only partly on intercession. Mainly we came together to centre the life of our Christian community around the life of God at the beginning of the new year. Often as different people met together over the course of a week, clear themes would emerge for our life and worship and witness together in the coming twelve months, through Bible passages which were shared, through pictures which were given, and sometimes through more direct words in which individuals perceived and the community recognised the guidance of God for our common life. Looking back over a distance of several years, we didn't always get the listening right – but more often than not, initiatives or insights gained as a result of those weeks of prayer bore significant fruit in the years to come.

Listening in the Direction and Details of Ministry
Together with waiting upon God for the life of the Church and for individual situations within it, goes waiting upon God and seeking his guidance for the direction of one's own ministry and the balance between different tasks which will change and develop according to an individual's gifts and the needs of the particular situation. Conversation, appraisal and support networks will form part of this process for the Christian minister but they will not be the whole story. Equally vital is time spent in disciplined listening and reflection upon one's own pattern of ministry and life direction.

Time, Space and Discernment in Listening
Time must be set aside for this dimension of prayer and ministry. This will include time for quiet and reflection each day to weigh

before God the events of the last 24 hours and the plans for the next. It will involve the discipline of learning to bring different situations and dilemmas to God in prayer in the course of a pastoral interview, or a meeting – sometimes overtly but often in silent prayer for guidance. Sermon preparation will include waiting on God for inspiration and direction. It will mean developing the habit of careful reflection and listening to God about where to go and whom to see: referring each decision back to the Lord of the Church. And it will mean time set aside more regularly to listen to and attend to God for the future of the whole Church and areas of it and to review the direction of one's own ministry.

Different ways and models will be appropriate for different stages of life and responsibility. The best pattern for me over a number of years as an incumbent was to take a day out every six weeks or so to go away to a retreat house and reflect through the day both upon the shape of my ministry and upon the direction and development of the parish. Many dilemmas of ministry were resolved walking around the cricket pitch at the Community of the Resurrection in Mirfield. In the years in which I neglected that basic discipline of listening and reflection there was less creativity, less clear direction in the leadership I was able to give, and less fruit in the life of the Church.

Time and space to listen are one essential for the spirituality of *diakonia*. The other is to learn to attend, to recognise, to weigh and to discern when the Holy Spirit is speaking to an individual or to a congregation and what is being said. All those who are ordained have at least some experience of this in the discernment and weighing of their own vocation. Different streams of the Church's life down the centuries will be helpful here. The charismatic tradition more than any other has helped the Church to recover the need for and the means to listen to God together and this aspect of the prophetic ministry. Wise principles have been adduced for discerning what God may be saying to his people in the midst of a host of Scriptures, pictures and words which may be shared.[17]

The Ignatian stream of the spiritual tradition, I would argue, is essentially diaconal. It emerged out of Ignatius' own seeking of God for his own vocation and calling to which he was to devote his whole life and energies. Within the Ignatian tradition are ways of learning the discipline of listening to God through Scripture and through careful reflection upon our lives in the presence of the Holy Spirit. These ways of learning are called 'Spiritual Exercises' by Ignatius. The two best known are imaginative meditation upon passages from the gospels and the 'Awareness Examen', or thanksgiving and reflection upon the previous day. They are ways of building habits and attitudes of *diakonia*. We learn from Ignatius not only to listen to God for more insights about the life of the Trinity but about our own lives in relation to his call. Over time, we learn to recognise the voice of the shepherd or guide of our lives[18] and we learn tests for distinguishing that voice from others which may be speaking.[19]

Serving and Being Served

The seventh diaconal habit is perhaps the hardest for those who feel themselves called to serve others, that of allowing mutual service; but it is a vital component in *diakonia*. As many writers have recognised, unless the habit of serving others is complemented by a willingness to allow other people to care for us, 'service' can become in its own way a means of manipulating others to our own ends. 'She was the kind of woman who was always doing things for others', writes C. S. Lewis in the *Screwtape Letters*, 'You could always tell the others by their hunted look.' The picture of the clergyperson who gives their whole lives to selflessly serving others but refuses to disclose any areas of vulnerability to their faith community is a familiar one from popular stereotypes of ministers but does not sit well with the needs of the present generation or with the true spirit of diaconal ministry. In the story of the footwashing, Peter is rebuked when he refuses to allow Jesus to wash his feet. If Christians are called to wash one another's feet following Christ's example, mutual service is what is implied. Without mutuality of service and support, and therefore some degree of vulnerability in leadership, there can be little forming of friendship and of community.[20]

All of these habits of *diakonia* are one attempt to work out what the diaconal dimension of ordained ministry means in practice. In different ways they will be expressed and focused in the diaconal role in worship: welcoming the people; reading the Gospel; receiving the offerings; assisting the celebrant; and sending the congregation out in their mission to the world.[21] The liturgical expression and focus of diaconal ministry however, is not the essence of *diakonia* which remains the service both of the Christian community and of the kingdom of God in society.

PART THREE

SERVICE AS A PRESBYTER: MINISTRY IN THE SECOND DIMENSION

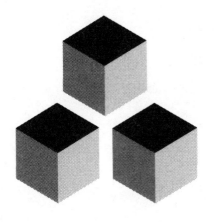

PRESBYTERS
IN SCRIPTURE

The Old Testament and Secular Sources

Diakonos, as we have seen, has no real background as the title of a specific office holder either in the Old Testament or in other ancient writings, although the wider notion of servant is, of course, rich in meaning. The same cannot be said of the title *presbyteros* which was extensively used in a variety of ways both in Jewish scriptures and practice and more widely in the ancient world. We know that *presbyteros* is used as a term for a local official in Sparta, a city of ancient Greece, and in similar ways in ancient Egypt.[1] The word is a comparative term of the adjective *'presbus'*, which means old, and simply and literally means *'elder'*.

The elders of Israel are found all the way through the Old Testament from the Exodus onwards, as any concordance will reveal.[2] They form an informal group with which Moses consults both before and after the Exodus from Egypt.[3] According to Numbers, they act as a kind of shared leadership for the people when the task becomes too much for one person.[4] After the settlement of the land through the time of the judges the elders are a kind of local community leadership within the tribes, villages and towns, speaking on behalf of the people to the wider rulers and also settling disputes and witnessing legal exchanges.[5] Non-Israelite tribes and cities also have elders who appear to have exercised a similar function. The elders play a key role in the establishment of the monarchy during the time of Samuel[6] and with the acceptance of David as king over the northern tribes.[7] From time to time they are mentioned in the history of the Israelite and Judean kingdoms as leaders of the people in the towns and cities of the land and representatives of the people in Jerusalem.[8]

During and after the exile the elders remain prominent both in

Jerusalem and through the diaspora, the dispersion of the Jews throughout the ancient world. Ezra works closely with groups of elders in Jerusalem on his return there[9] although their function adapts and changes as Israel has changed from a nation confined to a particular territory and governed by a king to a religious community increasingly dispersed throughout the ancient world. Opinion is divided as to the role the elders played within the synagogues as they were established and developed in different areas. According to some scholars, elders formed a governing group within the synagogue; according to others their function was much less formal. Elders were the people of influence within the community who did not themselves direct the life of the synagogue but appointed those who did.[10] By the time of Jesus we find two groups of Jewish *presbyteroi* mentioned in the New Testament: the elders who are lay members of the Sanhedrin in Jerusalem, often grouped with the scribes and the Pharisees in Jesus' teaching, and the occasional presbyters who is linked to one of the synagogues in the smaller communities.[11] Matthew focuses on the elders as participants in the trial of Jesus.[12] The elders of the Sanhedrin also play a part in the persecution of the early Church.[13] The phrase 'the teaching of the elders' is also used in the gospels to refer to Rabbinic tradition in contrast to Jesus' own teaching.[14]

Christian Presbyters in the Acts of the Apostles

We find two groups of people represented by the term *presbyteros* in the Acts of the Apostles, corresponding to the two groups in Judaism in the Sanhedrin and in local synagogues. Luke uses the term *presbyteros* to denote the corporate leaders of the Christian church in Jerusalem acting in council. There appears again to be a very deliberate use of terms to signify a gradual handing over of power and authority within the church in Jerusalem from the apostles to the apostles and presbyters acting together and finally to James the brother of Jesus with the presbyters. At the beginning of the narrative, decisions are taken collectively by the apostles.[15] The presbyters alone are mentioned as representatives of the Christian community in Jerusalem as recipients of the gifts from Antioch in 11.30. At the Council of Jerusalem, the apostles and presbyters consult together[16] and the letter goes out to the gentile churches with the heading: 'The brothers, both the apostles and the presbyters to the believers of Gentile origin in Antioch and Syria and Cilicia'[17] and the decision is reported to have been reached jointly by both groups.[18]

After Acts 16:4 the apostles are no longer mentioned as acting with authority either in the Jerusalem church or for the Church as a whole. Paul speaks to a formal assembly of the brothers in Jerusalem in Acts 21. Luke simply reports that 'James, and all the presbyters, were present.'[19]

The other place we find Christian presbyters in Acts is as a collective term to describe local leadership of the gentile churches instituted by Paul and his companions, leadership clearly influenced in some way by the pattern of leadership found in synagogues, from which the initial converts came, and the presbyters of the Jerusalem congregations. Here we come across a difficulty in interpretation of the evidence. According to Acts, the establishing of groups of elders represents Paul's practice. However, in the main Pauline epistles outside the Pastoral Letters we find no mention at all of this office, in contrast to several *diakonoi* and at least one group of *episcopoi*. It may be that Paul's omission of the term means that he did not call local church leaders *presbyteroi* and that Luke is reading back later practice or terminology into the Acts narrative. It is more likely that the omission of the term from Paul's letters is simply accidental, given the great care with which Luke uses titles for ministry in the whole of his writings.[20] In any event, the latest practice reflected in Acts is that of the date at which Luke is writing, normally reckoned to be in the second generation of Christianity (the eighties AD[21]).

Assuming then that the institution of presbyters reflects the sequence of events which actually happened, Luke portrays their institution in the gentile church as a response to the needs of newly established Christian communities. We simply do not know whether the church in Antioch which sent out Barnabas and Saul in response to the prompting of the Spirit had elders. The indications in Acts 13 are that the church there was led by 'prophets and teachers' and had no formal structure of *presbyteroi*. Nor is there any indication that Paul and Barnabas paid attention to any structure for local church ministry or government on their first mission until they come to make a return journey to each place they have visited to encourage the new disciples. There have been many converts who are sustained, initially, through their great joy, through the presence of the Holy Spirit in their midst[22] and, no doubt, through continued contact with the apostles who are still in the region until:

> After they had proclaimed the good news to Derbe and had made many disciples, they returned to Lystra, then on to Iconium and Antioch. There they strengthened the souls of the disciples and encouraged them to continue in the faith, saying, 'It is through many persecutions that we must enter the kingdom of God.' And after they had appointed *presbyteroi* for them in each church, with prayer and fasting they entrusted them to the Lord in whom they had come to believe.[23]

Note that the presbyters are here appointed by the apostles, not by the first congregations. The words 'with prayer and fasting' refer in the original Greek most naturally to the act of appointing presbyters rather than to the entrusting them to the Lord. We must assume that there is a similar service of commissioning in each city and that this appointing of presbyters for the new churches becomes standard practice.

One of the subthemes running through both Luke's gospel and the Acts of the Apostles is the adjustment the Church is making to a delay in the return of Christ as King. The first disciples in the years following the resurrection, it seems, expected the return of Christ to be in their own lifetime. Mark's gospel was in all probability written for a Church anticipating such an early return of the Messiah. In such a state of expectancy, little thought needed to be given by the Church to its internal structures and the ordering of ministry. As time elapsed however, and the apostles could not look after every congregation, other structures had to be devised appropriate to the context and the needs of the congregations. In Acts 14 we see part of this transition in microcosm as churches are established without any thought for ministry and then the apostles put a structure in place to enable the continued growth and development of a congregation over a period of time. Ministry emerges in response to the needs of a community in mission.

The Speech to the Ephesian Presbyters

Acts leaves us to assume that the practice of appointing presbyters in the newly established congregations remains normative throughout the second missionary journey. By the time of Paul's great city-wide mission of Ephesus the procedure is well established. Luke uses the occasion of a return visit by Paul to the city in Acts 20 to encapsulate his understanding of Christian presbyteral ministry for the generation who followed the apostles in the great speech to the Ephesian elders, which has become a foundational text for every generation in understanding ministry and is echoed today in the ordinals.

All three dimensions of ministry which we are exploring together are represented in the address not as separate orders of ministers but as different strands in the ministry of both Paul and those who listen to him. Luke surely uses all three roots of *diakonia*, *presbyteros* and *episcopeo* intentionally and deliberately, knowing the developing patterns of ministry of his own day. The principle which underlies the speech is one of *imitation*: the ministry of the presbyters is to take as its model the ministry of the apostle.[24] In this, the speech is faithful to the principles of imitation encapsulated in the main Pauline epistles.[25] Paul places himself and his own pattern of life and ministry at the beginning and end of the speech as the pattern for those to whom he is speaking. His own ministry is diaconal. The implication is that their ministry is also to be one of service.

> You yourselves know how I lived among you the entire time from the first day that I set foot in Asia, serving the Lord [*douleo*] with all humility and with tears.[26]

> But I do not count my life of any value to myself, if only I may finish my course and the ministry [*diakonia*] that I received from the Lord Jesus, to testify to the good news of God's grace.[27]

> You know for yourselves that I worked with my own hands to support myself and my companions. In all this I have given you an example that by such work we must support the weak, remembering the words of the Lord Jesus, for he himself said, 'It is more blessed to give than to receive.'[28]

At the central point of the speech, Paul challenges the presbyters to: 'Keep watch over yourselves and over all the flock of which the Holy Spirit has made you overseers [episkopoi], to shepherd the church of God.' The presbyters are to have an episcopal dimension to their ministry: keeping watch over the flock. For the first time in the passages we have examined the shepherding metaphor is used to describe Christian service. As we shall see, the metaphor is one which is used in the later New Testament writings and is particularly linked with the ministry of the presbyters. The image draws upon the shepherd traditions of the Old Testament and also Jesus' application of the term and image of shepherd to himself in both the Synoptic Gospels and the Johannine tradition.[29] Its primary and general reference in the Old Testament, as we have seen, is to the image of a ruler and guide who, as part of his leading of the people, pays particular attention to the sick and the weak among the flock. In linking the picture with the function of being episcopos, Acts 20 stands in the same tradition.

Great emphasis is placed in the speech upon the teaching ministry of Paul, both public and private, and, by extension, on the teaching ministry which belongs to the presbyteroi: 'I did not shrink from doing anything helpful, proclaiming the message to you and teaching publicly and from house to house, as I testified to both Jews and Greeks about repentance towards God and faith towards our Lord Jesus.'[30] Richard Baxter was to make much of the this verse and verse 28 as the foundation of his ministry in Kidderminster in the sixteenth century and of his classic writing on the pastoral ministry, 'The Puritan Pastor', in which he emphasises catachesis in the home as much as preaching as a means of teaching the people.[31] This ministry of teaching is a major responsibility both for Paul and for the presbyters, for which they will give account for the way in which they have exercised their ministry: 'Therefore I declare this day that I am not responsible for the blood of any of you, for I did not shrink from declaring to you the whole purpose of God.'[32]

This doctrine of accountability in ministry draws on the prophetic traditions of the Old Testament, particularly Ezekiel 3, and in turn continued to inform the charge to priests in the ordinal:

> The Church and Congregation whom you must serve is his Spouse, and his Body. And if it shall happen the same Church,

or any Member thereof, to take any hurt or hindrance by reason of your negligence, ye know the greatness of the fault and also the horrible punishment that will ensue.[33]

The presbyters of Ephesus are, we presume, not stipendiary or, therefore, full time if they follow Paul's example.[34] As good shepherds they are to have a particular concern for the weak.[35] Their ministry is not to be one of impassive efficiency but of great love and tenderness towards those in their care. The passage is structured around three instances of tears: the tears of a servant-evangelist shed by Paul as he commends himself to the Ephesian Christians in the beginning; the tears of a pastor as for three years he has not ceased to warn everyone (v.31); and the tears, finally, of Christian fellowship and of bonds of love created when lives are shared: 'When he had finished speaking, he knelt down with them all and prayed. There was much weeping among them all; they embraced Paul and kissed him, grieving especially because of what he had said, that they would not see his face again.'[36]

Presbyters in the New Testament Letters

The nature and functions of presbyteral ministry as expounded in Acts 20 are underlined and reinforced by the references to presbyters in the general epistles. 1 Peter[37] contains a long exhortation to the presbyters of the churches of Pontus, Galatian, Cappadocia, Asia and Bythinia:

> Now as an elder [sumpresbyteros] myself and a witness of the sufferings of Christ, as well as one who shares in the glory to be revealed, I exhort the elders [presbyteroi] among you to tend the flock that is in your charge, exercising the oversight [episcopeo] not under compulsion but willingly, as God would have you do it – not for sordid gain but eagerly. Do not lord it over those in your charge but be examples to the flock. And when the chief shepherd appears, you will win the crown of glory which never fades away. In the same way, you who are younger must accept the authority of the elders [presbyteroi]. And all of you must clothe yourselves in humility in your dealings with one another for 'God opposes the proud but gives grace to the

humble'. Humble yourselves therefore under the mighty hand of God so that he may exalt you in due time.[38]

Again, as in Acts 20, we have the three dimensions of ministry mentioned together in the same passage and in relation to the same pastoral office. The root *diakonia* is not used but the presbyters are exhorted not to 'lord it over' the flock – the same word is used in the gospel passages about *diakonia*.[39] The *presbyteroi* are encouraged to 'clothe themselves in humility' along with the rest of the congregation. And as in Acts 20.28 they are called to exercise oversight (*episcope*) as part of their presbyteral ministry. There is a similar emphasis on accountability at the day of judgement (v. 4) and, of course, the metaphor of the shepherd reappears with a specific link made to Christ the shepherd. The ministry and function of the presbyters appears to be similar to that of the Ephesian elders, in so far as we can tell. The injunction to minister 'not for sordid gain but eagerly' perhaps reflects a situation in which some presbyters at least are beginning to be supported by their congregations and to devote themselves to full time ministry instead of providing for their own needs.

In the second and third letters of John the author writes as the *presbyteros*, the elder, claiming a title which, again, we must assume, was in common use in the churches. And in James 5 the elders are mentioned again, this time as exercising a ministry of healing on behalf of the congregation:

> Are any among you sick? They should call for the elders [*presbyteroi*] of the church and have them pray over them, anointing them with oil in the name of the Lord. The prayer of faith will save the sick, and the Lord will raise them up; anyone who has committed sins will be forgiven.[40]

The elders here exercise a ministry equivalent to that of the twelve disciples in the gospels on behalf of the whole Church. Prayer for others, including listening to the confession of sins and pronouncing them forgiven, was clearly part of presbyteral ministry from the beginning of the Church.

In the letter to Titus the situation reflected is one in which Titus himself has been left behind in Crete by Paul, in a situation similar to that in Acts 14, 'that you should put in order what remained to be done and should appoint elders [*presbyteroi*] in every town as I directed you.' We then have a list of qualities to look for in such elders: 'someone who is blameless, married only once, whose children are believers, not accused of debauchery and not rebellious.'[41] There is then mention of a second office (*episkopos*) – singular as opposed to plural – with a further list of qualities:

> For a bishop [*episkopos*] as God's steward, must be blameless; he must not be arrogant or quick tempered or addicted to wine or violent or greedy for gain; but he must be hospitable, a lover of goodness, prudent, upright, devout and self-controlled. He must have a firm grasp of the word that is trustworthy in accordance with the teaching, so that he may be able to preach with sound doctrine and to refute those who contradict it.[42]

It is possible, as we have seen in Acts and 1 Peter, that these two lists refer to the same group of people: the *presbyteros* is also called here *episcopos*. This is the way the passage is read by almost all commentators. However, it is also possible, given the way in which the different dimensions of ministry begin to separate into distinct orders in 1 Timothy, that originally we had two lists here: one of qualifications for the *presbyteroi* (plural) and a second and more demanding list of qualifications for the *episcopos* (singular), parallel to the criteria for appointing deacons and bishops in 1 Timothy 2. At least one of the criteria (to be blameless) is duplicated between the two lists.[43]

In 1 Timothy 3, as we have already seen, we have a detailed list of qualifications for those who would be appointed *episcopos* and *diakonos*.[44] Yet the letter also knows of the ministry of the *presbyteros*.[45] How are the three related? The most obvious explanation would suggest that the letter is addressed to Christians who are already familiar with the ministry of *presbyteros*. The letter is addressed to Timothy as he wrestles with problems of false teaching and church life within the congregation at Ephesus at a later stage than that which provides the background to Acts 20. The new instructions and the details concern the appointment of an *episcopos* (described in the singular although perhaps more are intended) and *diakonoi* (described in the plural), suggesting that these may be new developments in this situation. If this is the case, we can see that they have developed in response to particular needs in the life of the churches.

False teachers have indeed arisen, as described in Acts 20 and throughout I Timothy, presumably from among the Ephesian presbyters themselves. And so the Epistle commends the development of two more ministries in the Ephesian situation, drawn from the emerging picture within the Mediterranean churches. The *diakonoi* have a distinct ministry in their own right. They are to be tested before they are allowed to serve. They do not, as far as we can gather, exercise a ministry of teaching or hospitality on behalf of the congregation. Their office also serves as a testing ground for those who are to move on to serve the congregation as presbyters and exercise a teaching and preaching ministry. The ministry of the *episcopos* develops as the Church discovers the need for those who will exercise authority over the inevitably diverse group of presbyters, particularly in respect of sound doctrine, as that authority can no longer be exercised by the apostles. The three dimensions of ministry are beginning to separate out in I Timothy into the embryo of the three distinct orders which we find in Ignatius of Antioch.

According to the Epistle, Timothy himself has been appointed for ministry by the laying on of hands of the council of elders (*presbyterion*) giving us a fascinating glimpse of the way in which the early Church publicly prayed for and authorised those who would exercise a ministry: 'Do not neglect the gift that is in you, which was given to you through prophecy with the laying on of hands by the council of elders.'[46] The same word for laying on of hands is used in Chapter 5 with advice which again reflects the need, for those who would exercise ministry on behalf of the Church, to be tried and tested: 'Do not ordain anyone hastily and do not participate in the sins of others; keep yourself pure.'[47]

Earlier in the chapter we have further instructions about and insights into the developing role of the presbyters:

> Let the elders [*presbyteroi*] who rule well be considered worthy of double honour, especially those who labour in preaching and teaching; for the scripture says, 'You shall not muzzle and ox while it is treading out the grain' and 'The labourer deserves to be paid'. Never accept any accusation against an elder [*presbyteros*] except on the evidence of two or three witnesses. As for those who persist in sin, rebuke them in the presence of all so that the rest also may stand in fear.[48]

The role of the presbyter here is lovingly and faithfully to govern and direct the life of the congregation and, for some at least, to labour, literally, 'in word and teaching'. The situation of the presbyters has moved on from Acts 20 and I Peter. Clearly the expectation now is that those who are appointed to this office will receive the means of support and be entitled to their reward. Perhaps because of their vulnerable position, the presbyter is also entitled to particular protection against false accusation. Because of their increased responsibility, those elders who persist in sin are to be rebuked publicly, not privately, a verse which implies that there are those whose responsibility it is to watch over the conduct of the presbyters.

Jesus and Presbyteral Ministry

The ministry of presbyters emerges from Acts and the New Testament letters as the recognised and authoritative ministry of public and personal teaching, preaching and care of individuals and of congregations, including prayer for their healing.

It is not hard to see this pattern and this dimension of ministry modelled in the ministry of Jesus. The gospels bear witness to the time and priority Jesus gave to the ministry of preaching and teaching throughout Israel, addressing both the crowds but also small groups and, on occasion, individuals. Jesus' own styles of teaching have continued to provide a model and inspiration for Christian preachers in every generation. Jesus models the exercise of authority combined with love and compassion as the gospels systematically portray his dealings with those at the centre of communities and those on the edge; with the elderly and with children; with women and with men. The ministry of both teaching and preaching and healing is passed on to the disciples as the pattern for ministry within the Christian communities, as is reflected in Acts and in the remainder of the New Testament. Jesus takes to himself, as we have seen, the imagery of the Shepherd as ruler and guide of the new Israel, linked in Acts and the Epistles with presbyteral ministry:

> I am the good shepherd. The good shepherd lays down his life for the sheep. The hired hand, who is not the shepherd and does not own the sheep, sees the wolf coming and leaves the

sheep and runs away – and the wolf snatches them and scatters them. The hired hand runs away because a hired hand does not care for the sheep. I am the good shepherd. I know my own and my own know me, just as the Father knows me and I know the Father. And I lay down my life for the sheep. I have other sheep that do not belong to this fold. I must bring them in also, and they will listen to my voice. So there will be one flock, one shepherd.[49]

To be a good shepherd, and by implication a good presbyter, involves self-sacrifice and the laying down of one's own life. Like the Old Testament pictures of kingship, it involves the protection of the community against threats from outside and the right and just ordering of life within the congregation. It involves providing the flock with the right food and pasture in the right season. Most of all, it involves personal knowledge, understanding and love of those for whom the presbyter is called to care. There is no escaping this dimension of the ordained ministry; no reducing of the task of the ordained to that of manager; no separation of the pastoral and teaching office.

A Cautionary Word

As we have seen on a number of occasions to date, Luke is deliberate and precise in his use of terms describing ministry. On only one occasion in his gospel does he use the term *presbyteros* other than to describe Jewish elders in the Sanhedrin or the synagogue. The passage is in Luke 15; the context is the story of the father and two sons: 'Now his elder son [literally, his son the *presbyteros*] was in the field; and when he came in he heard music and dancing.' Luke is using the term *presbyteros* primarily as an adjective here, contrasting the elder son with the younger. Yet the part of the story which concerns the elder brother is strangely relevant to those called to be presbyters in the life of the church. One of the recurring dangers in ministry is that our desire to be faithful and to do God's work, as we see it, obscures our vision of the mercy and grace and love of God and our own relationship of love with the Father. If we attempt to be presbyters without remembering *diakonia* then we quickly begin to be resentful; comparing and contrasting ourselves with others, in the effort we have made for God, in the sacrifices under-taken, in the lack of reward received. In the end, instead of being the ones who are active in welcoming home the lost, we become resentful of the intrusion they make into the sterile order of our working lives.

It is at least possible that Luke has framed the story in a context in which the Church knew the ministry of presbyters, so as to speak at least in passing of some of the dangers of presbyteral ministry to those called to the task. It is by no means easy learning to live as an elder brother or sister.

8

PRESBYTERS AND PRIESTS
IN THE CHRISTIAN TRADITION

' . . . while we for our part will devote ourselves to prayer and to serving the word'[1]

At the heart of the presbyteral dimension of ministry in Scripture and the tradition is the call to preach and to pray. The call to prayer embraces the ministry of intercession; leading the prayers of God's people in public worship, particularly in the eucharist; and personal prayer with and for individuals, particular those in need of reconciliation and healing. The call to preach and to serve the word includes not only public proclamation in the context of worship but the teaching and instruction of individuals and small groups; the announcing of the good news outside of the Christian congregation; and, particularly, the preparation of both children and adults for church membership expressed in baptism and confirmation. The general exercise of pastoral ministry which is the daily experience of those called to be presbyters or priests flows out from this call to pray and to preach. Christian pastoral ministry is more than a vague desire to demonstrate the love of Christ to all humanity. At its heart is a desire to fulfil the great commission, to make disciples of all nations[2]; to labour to present each person mature in Christ[3] and to that end to work for the strengthening of the Christian community, the Church. The two central means of this making of disciples, this enabling of growth to maturity and the upbuilding of the Church, are the ministries of prayer and of the word: the heart of presbyteral or priestly ministry.

Presbyters and Bishops

The unfolding and developing role and title of the presbyter throughout the history of the Church moves and changes so as to emphasise one or other of these aspects of presbyteral ministry at different times. The history of the ministry is one which has been the subject of a great deal of study and reflection throughout the history of the Church and, sadly, the function and title of those ordained for this ministry has been and remains the cause of much division.

Presbyters, as we have seen, form part of the emerging pattern of ministry in the New Testament churches according to both Acts and the Epistles. Their ministry is attested as one of prayer and of preaching and is, so far as we can tell, a collegial ministry. In the second century, the presbyters find their place within what is becoming a settled pattern of threefold ministry as assistants to the bishop within the local congregation both in the liturgy, expressing the dimension of prayer, and in preaching, teaching and catechising, the service of the Word.

As we have seen, the nature and function of the three orders begins to change as bishops begin to assume responsibility for more than one congregation and ultimately for geographical areas in the third and fourth centuries and beyond. The presbyters begin then to assume the role which had belonged to the bishop in the second-century Church of presiding at the eucharist when the Church came together, and forming the focus and centre for the life of the local Christian community in congregations and places where the bishop did not reside. Their ministry, over time, becomes therefore less collegial and more individual, although they are still regularly spoken of in the sources in the plural.

The overlap which is present in between *presbyteroi* and *episcopoi* in the New Testament is carried over into the first five centuries of the Church. Presbyters continue to exercise episcopal ministry in the context of the local congregation. Bishops certainly continue to exercise the presbyteral ministries of presiding at worship and of preaching. John Chrysostom (c. 347–407), bishop in Constantinople, was renowned as a preacher in his cathedral church, as was Augustine (354–430) in North Africa. Often in Lent those who were to be baptised on Easter Day would make extended pilgrimages to the church of the bishop to receive daily instruction both in the form of preaching and special services and individual conversation and prayers.

Language of Priesthood

Towards the end of the second century, in the writings of Tertullian, Cyprian and others, we begin to encounter a second stream of the biblical tradition informing reflection and thinking about the role first of bishops but also of presbyters: that of the cultic priesthood of the Old Testament, which existed to offer sacrifice on behalf of the people as a means of reconciliation, intercession and thanksgiving. The New Testament, of course, uses this language and imagery of Old Testament priesthood to refer to Christ both as the sacrifice bringing reconciliation with God and, in the most developed way in the Epistle to the Hebrews, as High Priest:

> Therefore he has become like his brothers in every respect, so that he might be a merciful and faithful high priest in the service of God, to make a sacrifice of atonement for the sins of the people.[4]

> Since then, we have a great high priest who has passed through the heavens, Jesus the Son of God, let us hold fast to our confession. For we do not have a high priest who is unable to sympathise with us in our weaknesses, but we have one who in every respect has been tested, as we are, yet without sin.[5]

The theme of Christ the High Priest is a major theme in Hebrews as the writers strive to encourage Christians with a Jewish background that Christ himself is the fulfilment of all that came before him under the old covenant and a sufficient Saviour. However the same theme recurs in other New Testament writers.

The whole people of God are also described as a priesthood in 1 Peter and in Revelation and are called to offer themselves as living sacrifices by Paul in Romans: 'like living stones, let yourselves be built into a spiritual house, to be a holy priesthood, to offer spiritual sacrifices acceptable to God through Jesus Christ'.[6]

> You were slaughtered and by your blood you ransomed for God saints from every tribe and language and people and nation; you have made them to be a kingdom and priests serving our God and they will reign on earth.[7]

> I appeal to you therefore, brothers and sisters, by the mercies

of God, to present your bodies as a living sacrifice, holy and acceptable to God, which is your spiritual worship.[8]

The Greek word which underlies all of the references to Christ as High Priest and to the priesthood of all believers is *hiereus* and the Hebrew word which it translates and draws from is *cohen*. In the New Testament there are only hints of these words used to refer to or describe Christian ministers, either by extension as part of the priestly people of God or in the intriguing reference to the metaphor of the cultic priesthood towards the end of Romans: 'because of the grace given to me by God to be a minister of Christ Jesus to the Gentiles in the priestly service of the gospel of God, so that the offering of the Gentiles may be acceptable, sanctified by the Holy Spirit.'[9]

However, by the end of the second century as the Church continued to reflect on the nature of ministry, this language of the Old Testament cult, of Christ as High Priest and of the priesthood of all believers, begins to be used in a new way of the ministry of those ordained within the Church. The eucharist is seen as a focusing of the prayer and worship offered on behalf of the Church, appealing to Christ's sacrifice of himself. Therefore the person presiding at the eucharist, offering thanksgiving and intercession, is described in priestly and cultic language. At the same time, the role of the presbyter in pronouncing absolution on behalf of the Church for the forgiveness of sins is also strengthened, particularly in the writings of Cyprian (d. 258) who had to wrestle with the proper discipline to follow in restoring many who had lapsed during a great wave of persecution.

The concept of New Testament *presbyteros* thus begins to take on some of the attributes and language used of the Old Testament *hierus* and of Christ as *hierus*, by virtue of his being part of the priesthood (*hieratuma*) of the whole people of God. Emphasis is placed upon both bishop and presbyter as intermediaries between God and the people in offering prayers, the 'sacrifice' of the eucharist and pronouncing absolution. The English word 'priest' is actually derived from *presbyteros*, not from *hierus*. Nevertheless it represents a fusion of these two streams of meaning which has led to caution and unease about using it as a term for Christian ministers among many streams of the Christian tradition since the Reformation.

Sacrament and Word

There is a steady shift in the balance of the priest's ministry away from the ministry of the Word and towards the ministry of the sacrament and prayer offered on behalf of the Church throughout the thousand years from Augustine to the Reformation. Priests come to be ordained to a state or an order and not to a particular place or 'cure of souls'. There is thus a stronger and stronger emphasis on priesthood as *being* (the ontological aspects) as opposed to priesthood as *doing* (the functional aspect). Being set apart meant to be celibate and therefore, increasingly, different in kind from the lay people or congregation of the Church. One or both of the elements at holy communion are consumed only by the priests, not by the people. The priest faces away from the congregation at the celebration of the eucharist, emphasising his role as intermediary. Confession became obligatory in the Church in the West, and thus the priest became as much a representative of God to the people as of the people to God.

At the Reformation, many of these imbalances and distortions were corrected by the Protestant Reformers and some have been corrected, subsequently, by the Roman Catholic Church. The Reformers emphasised once again the priesthood of all believers rather than of a distinctive and different group set aside for ministry. Most of all they emphasised once again the importance of the ministry of the Word in presbyteral ministry and pastoral practice as flowing from prayer and preaching. The main continental reformers abandoned the title priest altogether. The three orders of deacon, priest and bishop were retained at the English Reformation but the concept of the nature of priesthood was changed, with some of those changes being expressed in and through the services of ordination: 'In essence, the Anglican ordinals call into question the notion of a sacrificial priesthood focused on the eucharistic offering, in favour of a pastoral and didactic model of the ministry centring on public proclamation, the orderly administration of the sacraments, and private exhortation.'[10]

From the Reformation onwards it became impossible in the Church of England to be ordained other than to a title, a geographical parish, emphasising again a close connection between the ministry of the ordained and the whole people of God. It was impossible thereafter to simply 'be' a priest. Care is taken to ensure that ordinations take place publicly and before the congregation. Candidates are to be 'first called, tried, examined and known to have such qualities as were requisite'. The practice of handing over the chalice and paten as symbols of the priestly office was at first supplemented and then replaced by the practice of the handing over of a Bible with the words: 'Take thou authority to preach the word of God and to minister the holy sacraments in the congregation.'

The bishop's charge to those about to be ordained stresses over and over again the centrality of the Scriptures in the ministry which they are about to exercise: 'consider how studious ye ought to be in reading and learning the Scriptures, and in the framing the manners both of yourselves and of them that specially pertain unto you, according to the rules of the same Scriptures; and for this self-same cause, how ye ought to forsake and set aside (as much as you may) all worldly cares and studies.'[11] There are also frequent references within the service to the need for the anointing of the Holy Spirit for the work to which the candidates are called including, at the centre of the service, the singing by the congregation of 'Come Holy Ghost our souls inspire'.

The following centuries saw much bitter debate on the nature of the eucharist and therefore on the nature of priestly ministry both within the Church of England and across Europe. Anglicans found themselves defending their understanding of ministry against Roman Catholic claims that it was invalid, on the one hand, and Puritan and Reformed claims that it allowed too much of an expression to the cultic-priestly language, on the other. The evangelical revivals of the eighteenth century which saw the birth of Methodism influenced the debate in one direction; the Oxford Movement in the nineteenth century in the other.

The argument and disagreement have continued until the present day[12] although there have been encouraging signs in the recent ecumenical dialogues of a consensus emerging. The Lima text, Baptism, Eucharist and Ministry, describes the ministry of presbyters as follows, returning to the bifocal ministry discernible in the New Testament and the tradition:

> Presbyters serve as pastoral ministers of Word and sacraments in a local eucharistic community. They are preachers and teachers of the faith, exercise pastoral care, and bear responsibility for the discipline of the congregation to the end that the world may believe and that the entire membership of the Church may be renewed, strengthened and equipped in ministry. Presbyters have particular responsibility for the preparation of members for Christian life and ministry.[13]

The Charge to Priests in the Alternative Service Book

In the light of this great history of debate, the charge to priests/ presbyters in the Alternative Service Book ordination service must be reckoned extremely effective in many aspects of catching the spirit of presbyteral or priestly ministry, both in the Scriptures and in the tradition in language which is acceptable to the whole spectrum of the Church of England. The service itself draws heavily on the liturgical revision undertaken for the Church of South India[14] and acknowledges the variant titles used in its heading: The Ordination of Priests also called Presbyters. The charge itself draws on the language of the Prayer Book Ordinal, itself drawing on Martin Bucer, but the tone is one of joyful service rather than sombre responsibility.

> 'Priests are called by God to work with the bishop and with their fellow-priests as servants and shepherds among the people to whom they are sent. They are to proclaim the word of the Lord, to call their hearers to repentance, and in Christ's name, to absolve, and to declare the forgiveness of sins. They are to baptize, and prepare the baptized for confirmation. They are to preside at the service of Holy Communion. They are to lead their people in prayer and worship, to intercede for them, to bless them in the name of the Lord, and to teach and encourage by word and example. They are to minister to the sick, and prepare the dying for their death. They must set the Good Shepherd always before them as the pattern of their calling, caring for the people committed to their charge, and joining with them in a common witness to the world.'[15]

The charge will be used as a basis for exploring this second dimension of ministry in more detail in the following two chapters. The opening paragraph describing the duties of the priest has a structure based around the two-fold ministry of word and sacrament. The priest is to 'proclaim the word of the Lord' leading to the reconciliation of the people to God and in turn to baptism and preparation for Confirmation. She or he is to preside at the celebration of Holy Communion and this in turn is a centre of and leads into leadership in prayer and worship, intercession, and general pastoral ministry. The shepherd imagery which is clearly linked to the ministry of presbyters in the New Testament runs through the prayer and indeed through the whole service.

The charge contains several references to *diakonia* as a dimension of priestly ministry. Priests are to be servants and shepherds; they are to 'serve with joy'. As in the Prayer Book ordinals there is an emphasis both on the need for the Holy Spirit to fulfil this ministry and upon the strength and grace which come through the daily study of the Scriptures which finds its outworking in the shaping of the life and ministry of priests and people.

However, the primary weakness of the charge to priests and of the ordination service as it now stands is that the third dimension of *episcope* is absent. In this, the text is untrue to the biblical witness in which presbyters clearly did share in the ministry of oversight and to the actual experience of all those called to parish ministry. There is some reference at the beginning of the prayer to the priests working collaboratively and collegially with the bishop and with fellow priests but no reference whatsoever to collegial working with the whole people of God. There is no reference to the building of wholesome communities as well as individual care; of the necessity of enabling, supporting and encouraging the ministry of the congregation; protecting it from error; or of guiding, with others, its common life and mission other than, possibly, in the two undeveloped terms 'watchers' and 'stewards'. The picture of Jesus as Shepherd and the priest as shepherd which is retained has been by implication divested of its biblical meaning of guiding and leading a community, with the twin focus of protection from external threat and the right ordering of its inner life, and has become a ministry exercised by an individual towards other individuals.

Priests need to exercise and be proficient in the second, presbyteral dimension of ministry yet on its own, as we have seen, the ministry of Word and sacrament and the pastoral care of individuals and families which flows from this ministry is not enough. There must be the enabling, energising and leading forward of the Christian community which finds its expression in the episcopal dimension of ministry.

Sacrament and Word – Being and Doing

Debates about priestly or presbyteral ministry throughout history have wrestled with two major questions. First, should priority in presbyteral ministry be given to the sacrament or to the ministry of the Word? Catholic understandings of ministry emphasise its sacramental dimension; protestant and evangelical understandings have given priority to the ministry of the Word. My argument here and in the chapters that follow is that both are necessary and important in the second dimension of ministry. The ministry of a priest does not consist of only that which a priest and no-one else can do. To argue this is to shrink priestly ministry only to presiding at the eucharist and pronouncing absolution. Rather, priestly ministry is better seen as a particular combination of ministries, clustered around the ministry of the Word and of the sacrament. This is an understanding of presbyteral ministry which is rooted in the Scriptures and in the tradition of the Church and which is caught, as we shall see, in the ordinals. As the Church of England enters the twenty-first century, it is surely a time to attempt to leave behind us some of the debates and divisions which have marred our common life in the recent and distant past. The ministry of both word and sacrament are vital to the health of the body of Christ and to our mission in the present generation.

The second question has been the way in which priestly or presbyteral ministry has been seen either primarily as *being* or as *doing*. Again the Catholic tradition has emphasised the concept of what ministers are or become, while the Protestant and evangelical emphasis has been upon what ministers do. In Catholic models of preparation for ministry the emphasis has been upon the *formation* of life and character with the assumption that the skills for ministry are relatively easily learned. The Protestant tradition in its models of preparation has focused in contrast upon *training* for ministry, assuming that the character for that ministry is easily acquired. Once again we need urgently to bring together the two sides of the dichotomy. Ministry is both being and doing. Preparation embraces both the formation of character and the acquisition of learning and skills.

9

MINISTRY IN THE
SECOND DIMENSION
(1): THE SERVICE OF THE WORD

We have seen even in the brief survey of the last chapter that the concept of priest or presbyter has a complex history although an honourable one in every Christian tradition: from earliest times, in all of their different manifestations, churches have continued to set aside individuals for this kind of ministry through a process of selection and prayer with the laying-on of hands. The common thread in the tradition of this priestly or presbyteral dimension of ministry is the centrality of prayer and the service of the Word which develops into the ministry of Word and sacrament. However, as was argued above, in some of the more recent debates and discussions of 'priesthood' it has seemed as though this single concept is being asked to bear too much weight and to embrace so many diverse concepts of what it means to exercise ordained ministry in contemporary society. In the process, the common thread from the Scriptures and the tradition of what it means to exercise this dimension of ministry is lost from view.

Think for a moment of the variety of tasks and ministries which those who are ordained are called to exercise. The man or woman called to be a hospital chaplain or to prison or armed services chaplaincy is engaged in very different work from the person who is licensed as vicar of an urban parish. The person ordained priest and exercising non-stipendiary ministry whilst continuing to earn their living and express their Christian service also through their work as a teacher, a probation officer or a bus driver has something but not everything in common with the country vicar seeking to serve Christ, congregation and community over several villages and a very large rural area. The archdeacon or Diocesan Education Officer may find their working day taken up with meetings and

108

administrative tasks or else tackling extremely difficult and demanding problems far removed from the work of the curate asked to focus on building up the young peoples' groups in a suburban parish. The ordained local minister, generally exercising his or her ministry as part of a team of ministers in the parish where they have worshipped for many years, expresses and embodies a different ministry from the ordained but itinerant evangelist who may work across a whole diocese or a wider region of the country.

All of these people have been ordained priest. All are called to express priestly or presbyteral ministry as a part of who they are and a part of what they do. But 'priest' or 'presbyter' are inadequate as a complete description of either person or task. If we attempt to make words mean everything, in the end they mean nothing. The ministry of each involves in different measure both *diakonia* and *episcope* to different degrees and in different ways. A three-dimensional concept of ministry is needed to enable us to describe this rich and God-given diversity of callings.

However, in order to think clearly about the diakonal and episcopal dimensions of ministry, we need also to be able to define clearly this presbyteral dimension as it has been expressed in Scripture, tradition and experience and to assert once again that the two areas of prayer and service of the Word, or the ministries of Word and sacrament, remain a vital part of the ministry of the ordained. We saw in the earlier chapters that so great is the confusion about the identity of the ordained and so great the mismatch between the traditional 'priestly' role and the task of an incumbent that many have been drawn to leadership models drawn either from the church growth movement or from secular management philisophy. Little work seems to be done where this happens to integrate the insights about what it means to be an ordained priest or presbyter within these leadership models.[1] To be a leader becomes more central than to exercise a priestly or presbyteral model of prayer, preaching and pastoral care. One of several dangers which follow is that prayer and preaching can become little more than servants of the leaders' vision. The continual temptation is for sermons to become exhortations towards a particular goal and prayer to become more and more directed to a similar end.

We see in the recent and distant history of the Church the tendency we have to follow pendulum swings of fashion to extremes and to throw babies out with the bath water. The recognition that part of the calling of the ordained is to exercise responsible Christian leadership within a community must not negate, obscure or control the equally vital calling to preach and to pray, itself a necessary expression of the particular kind of leadership which is called for among the people of God.[2] The purpose of this chapter and the next is to explore a little more what it means to exercise this presbyteral ministry within the context of the contemporary Church whatever the overall vocation and task of the ordained person. We will take as our guide the central part of the charge to priests in the ASB ordinal, addressing first the service of the Word before the call to pray and administer the sacraments.

The Service of the Word

> The Spirit of the Lord God is upon me
> because the Lord has anointed me;
> he has sent me to bring good news to the humble.[3]

> For the lips of a priest should guard knowledge, and men should seek instruction from his mouth, for he is the messenger of the Lord of hosts.[4]

> God was in Christ reconciling the world to himself, no longer holding men's misdeeds against them, and . . . he has entrusted us with the message of reconciliation.[5]

> Priests are to proclaim the word of the Lord, to call their hearers to repentance. Pray that [the Holy Spirit] will each day enlarge and enlighten your understanding of the Scriptures, so that you may grow stronger and more mature in your ministry, as you fashion your life and the lives of your people on the word of God.[6]

> Will you be diligent in prayer, in reading holy Scripture, and in all studies that will deepen your faith and fit you to uphold the truth of the Gospel against error?[7]

> Receive this Book, as a sign of the authority which God has

given you this day to preach the gospel of Christ and to minister his Holy Sacraments.[8]

The Call to Study

The first duty of those who are called to the diaconate of the word is to build faithful and lifelong habits of study and reflection around and upon and within and under the text of the Scriptures. The call to presbyteral or priestly ministry in whatever form is a call to this kind of disciplined study and engagement. One of the primary purposes of the theological college model of preparatory training for ministry remains the setting aside of time and energy to lay a foundation for a lifetime of serious and reflective study of the Scriptures which will inform and nurture every dimension of ministry. One of the privileges of being set apart for full-time stipendiary ordained ministry is the time which can be claimed and which needs to be claimed for this demanding task of continued learning and engagement with Scripture. Those called to train through non-residential courses and/or exercise ordained ministry whilst holding down a full-time job are heirs to a long and honourable tradition which goes back to St Paul and, most probably, to Christ himself. However, one of the continual tensions of that calling is time for both preparatory and continual study.

In my own experience and in my observation of others' habits, ministries and bookshelves, the habit of disciplined study of the word of God all too easily slips and is neglected in the midst of other competing and conflicting demands of ministry and work. The demands of the pastoral care either of a numerically large congregation or of a small number of very needy individuals or else the seeking of significance and identity in church or society all too often take precedence. If biblical and other kinds of study survive at all, it can all too easily become 'hand to mouth' reading directed simply towards the preaching of the next sermon or leading of the next meeting and not the kind of life-giving, consistent and rich quarrying of the text envisaged either by the apostles or by the bishop's questions in the ordination service.

Different rhythms and methods and patterns of study will be appropriate to different individuals and in different seasons of life. John Stott's maxim of an hour set aside for study each day, a day set aside each month and a week set aside each year[9] will suit many. Gordon MacDonald helpfully recognised in his own ministry that some months of the year were very demanding in terms of pastoral care needed by his congregation, typically in the wintertime. However, the summer demands were correspondingly lighter and therefore this was the better time to set aside part of each day for more concentrated and deeper reading for the purposes of self-renewal and progress in study and reflection.[10] Many clergy benefit from belonging to a reading or study group organised on a deanery or fraternal basis which provides the stimulus they need to undertake the necessary work. Where clergy work together, studying a biblical or theological book together as a regular part of a staff meeting can be equally helpful. Some training incumbents model study and reflection by taking their colleagues away for a reading day at a retreat centre once every four to six weeks where time can be set aside both for reading and reflection together. An essential question to be asked (and to ask oneself) in any periodic retreat, appraisal or review situation is: 'What are my patterns of study and, particularly, study of the Scriptures?' for so much else in the ministry of the Word depends upon this.

One of the benefits of a regular pattern of biblical study is undoubtedly that of continual emotional and spiritual renewal which comes from the study of Scriptures. Ministry is demanding. Proper rhythms of work, rest and relaxation are important and we shall examine these in the context of *episcope*. But there is also need for nurture, sustenance and renewal which are provided in deeper reading and study of the scriptures. Both the psalmists and the tradition of Jeremiah use the image of trees planted by streams of water 'which yield their fruit in due season' as the picture of the person who is diligent in attending to and meditation upon the word of God.[11] The promise given in Isaiah 40 is for the tremendous renewal of strength given to those who wait on God: 'they shall mount up with wings like eagles, they shall run and not be weary, they shall walk and not faint.'

In one of the most influential secular leadership texts of the 1990s, Stephen Covey has as his seventh habit for effective living the acquiring of the discipline of 'sharpening the saw'. He tells the story of one man watching another attempting to cut down a large tree with an exceptionally blunt saw but making negligible progress.

'Why don't you stop and sharpen the saw?' he asks. 'There is no time to sharpen the saw,' comes the reply, 'I have to cut down this tree.'[12] Both the Scriptures, our own tradition, the ordinal and received popular wisdom unite to tell us that the discipline of study is essential for continued self-renewal, for the sharpening of the saw, yet so often and so easily that discipline is squeezed out by other demands.

However, the purpose of study is not only or chiefly that of self-renewal but 'the fashioning of your own life and the lives of your people upon the Word of God'. Scripture is to be continually studied with a view to the continual formation and reformation of the lives of both presbyter and people. The continual study of the biblical text which is the first and necessary part of the service of the word bears fruit most obviously in the second part: the public proclamation of the Gospel through preaching.

The Call to Preach

According to the whole of the biblical tradition, there is massive and creative power in the Word of God. According to the opening chapter of Genesis, the universe itself comes into being through the living word spoken by God and pregnant with life. The central theme of Deuteronomy and the deuteronomic tradition of the Old Testament is that life is to be found in the law and the word of Yahweh. The preaching of Jeremiah is shot through with cries of both anguish and judgement that God's people have neglected to listen to him, so bringing disaster upon themselves. In the context of the end of exile and the hope of return, the prophet of Isaiah 40–55 again expresses the wonderful creativity and life-giving power of the Word of God:

> For as the rain and the snow come down from heaven,
> and do not return there until they have watered the earth,
> making it bring forth and sprout,
> giving seed to the sower and bread to the eater,
> so shall my word be that goes out from my mouth;
> it shall not return to me empty,
> but it shall accomplish that which I purpose,
> and succeed in the thing for which I sent it.[13]

The New Testament testifies in similar ways to the life-giving, creative power of the Word of God. The Johannine tradition identifies Jesus himself with the Logos, the incarnate Word of God.[14] The Pastoral Epistles describe Scripture as 'God-breathed' and 'useful for teaching, for reproof, for correction and for training in righteousness, so that everyone who belongs to God may be proficient, equipped for every good work'.[15] The writer to the Hebrews describes the Word of God as 'living and active, sharper than any two-edged sword, piercing until it divides soul from spirit, joints from marrow; it is able to judge the thoughts and intentions of the heart'.[16]

A central part of the vocation to be a priest or presbyter is to bring a congregation into contact with that living word of God; and the word of God into contact with the congregation through regular, biblically centred preaching. In many, many contexts, others will share in and consequently enrich that ministry. Yet it remains a central part of the priestly calling, within every part of the Anglican tradition. The conservative evangelical tradition has done much in recent years to keep alive a high view of the preaching ministry. Yet it is not necessary to take a fundamentalist or conservative view of the Scriptures in order to give a high place to preaching and the ministry of the word.

The purpose of preaching is to nourish, sustain, inspire, correct and equip the people of God for the mission of God in the world but it is particularly to proclaim the good news of Christ. We are commissioned to tell the story of his birth, life and ministry and especially of his death and resurrection and to call those who listen to repentance, faith and new life. All true priestly ministry is therefore evangelical in its character: centred around the Gospel of Jesus Christ; charismatic in that it will seek to be inspired and empowered by the Holy Spirit; and catholic in that it seeks the building up and sustaining of the whole body of Christ.[17]

Preaching which is centred upon the Word of God changes lives and causes Christian communities to be built up and, very often, to grow, because life cannot be contained. Many voices have been raised in recent years both lamenting the decline in preaching and seeking to build up and equip the preaching ministry. Those who write in this way from the conservative or reformed wing of the evangelical movement are surely right to emphasise the need for word-centred preaching as foundational in ordained ministry and in the leadership of local churches, and right to address a neglect of the discipline; but surely wrong when they seem to claim that preaching is the whole and the sum even of presbyteral ministry, let alone the whole ministry of the ordained either in Scripture or the tradition.[18]

The Direction of Preaching

More often than not, preaching will take place within a church building in the context of Christian worship and to a congregation which seems to consist of faithful Christian people. For these reasons it might seem natural to direct the vast majority of preaching towards issues of concern chiefly to these 'faithful Christians'. To follow this trend is to make both a theological and a pastoral mistake. Preaching which is addressed to faithful Christians tends to shrink in its scope. Its concerns drift away from the great issues of life and of living which are common to all people. Sermons become too detailed and theological (in the wrong sense) as if the preacher is addressing a group of theologians, or else very detailed exegesis as if written as part of a biblical commentary. They tend to focus more and more on a narrow range of issues to do with the Christian life (such as prayer, the sacraments, the gifts of the Spirit, sharing our faith). Bill Hybels, Senior Pastor of Willow Creek Community Church in Chicago, has said that the message behind the majority of sermons in the majority of churches boils down to 'pray more; do more in church; give more; come to more meetings'.

In the biblical tradition, preaching is directed towards the whole of creation, not just the faithful and not just those who will listen. The Old Testament prophets do not address their sermons to the faithful in Israel. In practice, most of their regular preaching was done in the Temple and at other sacred sites at the time of the great festivals and pilgrimages when people came together for worship. Therefore, their congregations were, by and large, the equivalent of those who attend church on Sundays. Yet the issues the prophets are addressing are the issues facing the whole community, not just the faithful. Similarly, a large proportion even of their preaching which has survived consists of oracles addressed to the international community.[19] Jeremiah is appointed a prophet to the nations, not simply to Israel.[20]

The public preaching of Jesus, by and large, is directed towards the whole community and not simply those who are faithful. From time to time we see him drawing apart with his disciples. However, his most radical and profound words are addressed to the whole of society not to any particular group, as in the Sermon on the Mount and throughout the gospels. In similar ways the Apostles in Acts direct their preaching not to the communities of the faithful, by and large, but to the issues and concerns of the wider society. In the context of those concerns they strive again and again to tell the story of Jesus and to proclaim his life, death and resurrection seeking the response of repentance and faith.[21] Even where the epistles address the specific concerns of the new churches (itself a very different task from preaching) Paul in particular draws the congregations back again and again to the death and resurrection of Christ and the Gospel message both in matters of doctrine and of Christian conduct in the whole of life.[22]

We are called to minister in a mission context. For that reason we dare not assume that every person in every congregation is a converted and committed Christian. There will be those in many churches every Sunday and in other churches at least some Sundays who are agnostics, interested enquirers, even atheists, as well as lapsed Christians and those unsure about what they believe. Those of us who are Christians need to be drawn back regularly to the centrality of the Christian Gospel. We also need to hear that Gospel applied to the issues facing our communities, our nation and the international community. As Christians living out our lives in a secular environment we need to hear a regular reasoned defence of the Christian faith in the midst of that society. Apologetics has become a neglected discipline both in theology and in sermons. The experience of Willow Creek community church and other churches around the world is that preaching which addresses the whole of society is a necessary companion to preaching which addresses the needs of the church.

My own experience and that of others who have attempted to address issues relevant to the whole of society and not simply to the Church is that the world around us wants to listen. In 1993, I publicised a short sermon series based around the hit Meatloaf album

Bat out of Hell II, to be held in a hotel in the centre of Halifax. The album is essentially about loss of meaning, regrets, questions and memories in mid-life crisis and was being bought and listened to by the generation who remembered the original album from their youth. The series attracted a modest congregation of up to 60 people, some of whom had very little church connection. The media response to the series however, was astonishing and involved local and national press articles, national television and radio, and over 20 live and recorded radio interviews, broadcast as far away as New Zealand. The stories went beyond the 'Vicar off his rocker' level, although there were some of these. The response from the vast majority of reporters and camera crews was extremely positive: the Church is addressing popular culture in thoughtful ways; give us more.

Preaching is a dynamic transaction in which the congregation plays a part as well as the preacher and the Holy Spirit. Those preparing for the presbyteral dimension of ministry need adequate training both in an understanding of what preaching is and its place within the ministry of the ordained[23] and of the skills involved in the preparation and delivery of sermons.[24] Those who are ordained to this ministry already need to review regularly their development as preachers. An increasing number of agencies now provide re-sourcing and courses to help both new preachers and those who are more experienced. Regular and honest feedback on preaching is an essential part of that development. To grow in preaching is to grow in the presbyteral dimension of ministry.

The Call to Catechise

Catechesis is the technical term for teaching the Christian faith to enquirers and new believers. It comes from the Greek meaning 'to teach' (unsurprisingly). We have seen from Paul's modelling in Ephesus, in the life of the Church in the first three centuries, Richard Baxter's urging, and the ordinals, that the ministry has traditionally been part of the calling of the presbyter's service of the Word.

Few would doubt that there is a great need for this ministry in our present context: perhaps greater than for many centuries. As a Church we are in the midst of an enormous transition. Our model of mission for centuries has been based upon teaching the Christian faith to children. Next to most of the Anglican and Non-conformist churches built by the Victorians was a large Sunday School genuinely filled week by week with the majority of the children of the local community. It is estimated that at the turn of the century something like 85 per cent of the population was in contact with a church or Sunday School and learned their faith there. Massive resources were poured into the task. However, by the century's end, that statistic has been reversed. Only 14 per cent of children and young people are now in any kind of contact with the churches.

We therefore have to make the enormous transition to teaching Christian faith once again to adults who are often beginning with very little background knowledge. Many under forty have had little contact with a Christian community either as children or adults and many have learned only a small amount about Christian faith from their state education. Even those adults who have been part of congregations for the whole of their lives may not have engaged with the themes of faith in a learning context since their own childhood.

At the same time, we live in a generation in which many adults have begun or are open to beginning a spiritual search. There are tremendous responsibilities upon the Church to teach the Christian faith to adults and to teach imaginatively and well. That teaching will be go hand in hand with incorporation of new members into the body of Christ and will be for many, their preparation for baptism or else, if they were baptised as infants, for confirmation.

The Church has rediscovered during the decade of evangelism that adults come to faith as part of a journey or process.[25] As part of that journey, and as an essential stage for most people, the Church needs to provide an opportunity for systematic teaching about Christian faith in a context where relationships can be formed and people can ask questions and learn at their own pace. Every church needs some kind of nurture group to which those who are enquirers, or finding their feet in the congregation after a gap of a number of years can come. Established church members ready to go over the basics of their faith again may also find the group helpful.

During the last few years different resources have become available to help churches to engage with this task, including the Alpha course, which consists of a ten-session course, and the Emmaus material, which provides a fifteen-session nurture course followed by fifteen short courses for small groups to enable growth in the Christian faith over a number of years. Clearly the ordained minister cannot be involved in all of the different groups which a church might run to facilitate adult learning and the teaching of the Christian faith. To insist on this would be to deny the reality of collaborative ministry, stifle the gifts of others, and put a stranglehold on the growth of the Church in every way. We will look in the chapters on *episcope* at the necessity of commissioning and supporting others to this ministry. In some situations, the ordained minister may only be able to be involved at all through supporting and enabling the ministry of others. However, if it is possible to play a part, the place to be active and 'hands on' is in the nurture groups of the congregation where people are learning the basics of the Christian faith.

Paul writes to the church in Corinth: 'Like a skilled master builder I laid a foundation and someone else is building on it.'[26] The apostle differentiates between the task of laying a foundation of the faith which, as with a building, is the task for the highly skilled master builder wherever possible; and continuing to build on that foundation, once the corners have been set and the main design is in place, a task which on the building site might be left to the apprentices or the less experienced. Leading a nurture group for enquirers and new Christians requires, ideally, a certain amount of theological training and experience, partly because the questions which come from the group will range over any and every subject. It will not be necessary in every situation for the leader of every group to have received formal training and to have been ordained priest, but those who are ordained will want to have a particular care for and involvement in this ministry.

My own practice as an incumbent in a parish which had experienced gifted and able lay ministry over many years was to be involved in a 'hands on' way in just one area: that of leading the nurture groups, along with others. For just over eight years, one evening a week every week and occasional afternoons, I was involved in teaching and leading the course which was developed for that parish and which grew into, eventually, the Emmaus nurture material. As one group ended, another would begin. The groups varied in size from half a dozen to over 30. Over the course of eight years around 300-400 people took part in different ways, including many who were already members of the congregation. There were always others involved in leading the group with me and sharing in the befriending and care and work with individuals which always came out of the meetings and in some of the teaching. Very often, these co-leaders would take the bulk of the group on at the end of the nurture course as it became a home group; the members would take on responsibility for caring for one another and encouraging one another in faith and mission, whilst I began work with new co-leaders and a new group of enquirers. The nurture groups gave me a chance to have some contact with almost all those who were drawn to faith or into the life of the Church and to build the beginnings of a meaningful relationship, which I could never have done through visiting or through superficial conversations after church services. Continual engagement with those on the outside of faith looking in played an enormous part in keeping my perspective fixed on mission and outside of the congregation.

Looking back with the perspective of several years, that continuous involvement in the ministry of nurture and catechesis was as much a backbone of my priestly and presbyteral ministry within that parish as the ministry of preaching and the sacraments, and as vital to the growth and development of community. I say again that those who are not ordained are well able to lead excellent nurture groups. But those who are called to presbyteral and priestly ministry must have the gifts and skills in this mission context in which we serve to teach the Christian faith to enquirers and to facilitate community through small groups.

10

MINISTRY IN THE SECOND DIMENSION (2): THE MINISTRY OF THE SACRAMENTS AND OF PRAYER

Among the many gifts entrusted to the Church by God are the sacraments: outward and physical signs of inward and spiritual reality, precious tokens of the love of God and channels by which that love is appropriated and received. In the development of ministry within the Church, the ministry of presbyters has become particularly concerned with the orderly and right and loving ministry of these signs of love, which belong to the whole body of Christ and are given for the blessing of the whole body of Christ. For the most part this ministry of the sacraments finds its roots and origins in prayer with or on behalf of individuals and the whole community on different occasions to which the apostles promise to give themselves in Acts 6.

Through the centuries the Church has debated the nature of the sacraments exhaustively. All traditions are united in giving overwhelming prominence to Baptism and Holy Communion as clearly commanded and instituted by Christ himself. The Protestant tradition has restricted the term 'sacrament' to these two alone. The Catholic tradition has expanded the number of sacraments to seven to include Penance, Ordination, Anointing or Unction, Marriage, and Confirmation. The Anglican way has been to give due prominence to Baptism and Holy Communion and to allow place for but a diversity of interpretation of the significance of other parts of the sacramental tradition.[1]

Those who are ordained priest and those who are preparing for ordination are ordained to serve the whole Church and not simply that tradition in which they themselves have been nurtured. Increasingly, congregations are less monochrome in their tradition and will include church members who have a range of quite different understandings of the sacraments and their place in the Christian life and a similar range of different expectations of the role of the ordained. At the very least therefore, all those who are ordained need to be aware of different understandings of the sacraments and to have thought through their own theology and practice.

We are also called to minister increasingly in the midst of a secular society and a mission context in which people are beginning to look beyond the rational modernist world-view which has prevailed for so long. Signs, symbols, colour and texture in worship and an appeal to the senses is becoming more important in every tradition. Those nurtured in an evangelical tradition are finding that there are tremendous resources within the catholic heritage of the Church on which they can draw within this mission context. The whole of the sacramental tradition has emerged as the Church has sought to find enabling ways of prayer, celebration and signs of grace into which all can enter and take part which transcend the gifts of a particular person, time, community or place. As such this tradition is particularly important in the context of mission.

Baptism

> Receive the Holy Spirit. If you forgive the sins of any, they are forgiven; if you retain the sins of any, they are retained.[2]

> Priests are to call hearers to repentance, and in Christ's name to absolve, and to declare the forgiveness of sins. They are to baptise and to prepare the baptised for confirmation.[3]

Baptism is the great Christian symbol of radical new beginnings; the sign and the sacrament of washing and cleansing, of death and resurrection, of new birth and of new creation. Its roots are in the symbolism of the Old Testament scriptures. Christ himself was baptised by John in the Jordan river and from the first disciples onwards, baptism in water has been the almost universal sacrament of incorporation into the body of Christ.

In recent years the Church has reflected in different ways on the nature of baptism as we move away from a society in which less people are baptised as infants and grow up within the family of the Church, to a Church and society which sees adults coming to faith and needing support and help upon that journey. Thinking about baptism has therefore become part of our thinking about catechesis: the instruction of new believers in the faith.[4] The renewal of baptismal practice has been recognised by the Anglican Church worldwide as an integral part of mission and evangelism. Baptism is for people of all ages, both adults and infants. 'Baptism is administered after preparation and instruction of the candidates, or where they are unable to answer for themselves, of their parent(s) or guardian(s).'[5]

For the priest or presbyter this shift in thinking about baptism has profound implications. Thought needs to be given to the different ways in which both children and adults can be welcomed into the life of the congregation and accompanied on their journey of faith. The most helpful and right place for baptism within each person's journey needs to be thought through in the context of a parish policy. That same policy will need to embrace, in consultation with the diocese, the point at which children who are baptised should begin to receive Holy Communion and the most helpful point at which those baptised as children should be presented to the bishop for confirmation and to make their baptismal vows and promises for themselves.

Thinking the issues through in relation to parents presenting their children for baptism will mean sensitive reflection on what kind of learning opportunities are most helpfully offered both for the children and for those parents who are not already part of the Christian community. Responsibilities of welcome need to be balanced against those of education and teaching. If there are too many 'requirements' when a parent initially brings their child for baptism these can seem like an insurmountable barrier. Too few, and the danger is that parents and godparents commit themselves and their children to something which they only partly understand. Each parish will want to think through the opportunities for the children, who are fully part of the Church, to take part in worship, to be accompanied on their journey in appropriate ways and to grow up to maturity in Christ. The provision of crèche facilities, parent and toddler groups,[6] incorporation of children into the liturgy, groups for children and teenagers of different ages all flow from this ministry of initiation: building the road of faith.

Thinking though the issues surrounding baptism and

confirmation in relation to adults will present different questions. Are different liturgies helpful to mark different stages of the journey of faith, arising from and complementing baptism itself?[7] Many parishes find sponsors or companions helpful for adults who are preparing to be baptised and confirmed. How will the newly baptised continue to grow in faith and live out their discipleship and ministry?

None of these questions or policies are ones which can be answered or put into practice by the priest alone. Although the ordained minister will normally be the person who baptises a child, young person or adult, the whole community of the Church will need to be involved in the formulation of policies, the ministry of welcome, and the walking alongside those who are growing in faith. Once again we see a move away from individual ministry to a collaborative style, worked out in different ways in different contexts. Although the minister has a presbyteral role in the sacrament of baptism, there is need also in the exercise of episcope in leading the Church's mission; in drawing together and enabling teams of people to care for different aspects of this ministry and in oversight of the whole.

All of this, in turn, leads us back to the truth that baptism itself is not simply initiation into the Christian way but a call and commission for the whole people of God for Christian service and to participate in God's mission to the world. In important ways, a key focus for ministry in the second dimension is the enabling and building up of the people of God so that they are able to live out their baptism to the full as mature Christian disciples active in Christ's service both in society and within the Church.

The *ministry of reconciliation* like baptism, flows out of the service of the Word, particularly the ministry of preaching and catechesis. As the Gospel is proclaimed regularly and faithfully, 'publicly and from house to house', the fruit of this ministry will be individuals and communities becoming aware of their need of reconciliation with God. Part of presbyteral ministry is the willingness to receive the authority entrusted by Christ to the Church and by the Church to its ordained ministers to minister reconciliation and to declare the forgiveness of sins. This will most often be a public declaration in the context of worship using the formal words provided in the liturgy. However, particularly in the mission context in which we live, prayer for reconciliation with individuals will also be part of the priestly or presbyteral role.

Those who share in the leadership of groups for enquirers and new Christians need as part of that ministry both to explain the way in which men and women can be reconciled to God and to model that reconciliation. Often that will include offering to individuals the opportunity to make a commitment to Christ in the presence of another person. This is a precious ministry and one which belongs to the whole body of Christ. There is no need for it to be restricted to those who are ordained. However, at the very least the person who is ordained priest or presbyter needs to have thought through the way in which they would pray with someone at a point at which they feel ready to make a personal act of commitment to Christ and be prepared for this ministry.[8]

As an incumbent working with those who were coming to the Christian faith for the first time as a grown adult, I often found that individuals were helped enormously by the making of a personal confession to an authorised minister of the Church and hearing the personal declaration that their sins are forgiven in and through Christ's death on the cross. For many this is not appropriate, but for some it will be helpful. Very often people come to faith with major and significant sins on their consciences which they will need to talk through and to move on from. The ministry of reconciliation becomes to them a vital and precious ministry, expressing the heart of the mission of God to the world. These conversations are able to take place in complete confidence. The person is able to articulate to God in the presence of another their repentance and renunciation of that sin and to hear the words of absolution addressed to them.

On other occasions the priest or presbyter will find themselves dealing with individuals whose consciences are troubled by particular events or besetting sins where personal confession may be appropriate and helpful, or those returning to faith after a long time away with many things on their conscience.

The Scriptures give both permission and encouragement to the whole body of Christ to 'confess your sins to one another'; in one sense any Christian may be able to exercise this ministry of reconciliation. In another, the Church's wisdom down the years has been that particular grace, preparation and discipline are needed to exercise this ministry regularly; to listen to the outpourings of another's heart and not condemn them externally or internally; to retain the confidence completely; to have the wisdom to say little but the right thing in moments when others are extremely vulnerable; and to be entrusted with the authority to declare sins forgiven.[9]

The other dimension to the ministry of reconciliation with God is the ministry of enabling individuals to be reconciled with each other and to forgive those who have hurt and injured them from the present or from the past. Again, the need for this ministry of prayer with others is often focused particularly around the time of an adult's first coming to faith. Jesus commands us to pray: 'Forgive us our sins as we forgive those who sin against us.' In both the Lord's Prayer and the parable of the unmerciful servant a very close link is made between our own reconciliation to God and our willingness to forgive those who have wronged us. This ministry of enabling others to come to the point of forgiveness of those who have wronged them through prayer is the heart of what has become known in charismatic circles as the ministry of inner healing. In the classical pastoral tradition it is undoubtedly a central part of the 'cure of souls'. Men and women come to faith often with their lives scarred and damaged by huge wounds caused by broken relationships, family feuds, divorce or abuse of different kinds. In order for them to leave those events behind and move on into the new life they have found in Christ, there must be forgiveness. Both the preaching and the prayer ministry of the ordained must seek to enable this ministry.[10] The regular exercise of this ministry of reconciliation has its own formative and shaping effect on the life and character of the ordained person in a constant awareness of one's own frailty; of the great love and mercy of God; of the need to forgive 'seventy times seven'; and of the constant vacillations of the human heart.

Holy Communion

Priests are to preside at the celebration of the Holy Communion. They are to lead their people in prayer and worship, to intercede for them, to bless them in the name of the Lord and to teach and encourage by word and example.[11]

Set them among your people to offer with them spiritual sacrifices acceptable in your sight and to minister the sacraments of the new covenant.[12]

At the centre of Christian worship, by the command of Christ, is the remembering together of the death and resurrection of Christ through the taking and setting apart of ordinary bread and wine to be effective signs and symbols of God's love in Holy Communion.

The celebration of the Eucharist, again, is an act of the whole people of God, not the action of an individual on behalf of a community. Those who are ordained priest and presbyter however have been given by the common wisdom and tradition of the Church down the centuries a particular responsibility both for the ordering of this celebration and common meal and for presiding at this particular act of worship.[13] It may be that in the years to come the Church of England will depart from this received tradition and, in a new mission context, develop new forms of lay presidency to supplement and stand alongside the role of the ordained. However, for the priest or presbyter this is a responsibility which must be taken seriously for the health of the whole body of Christ.

Again, the Church and its ministers have become sadly divided over this most precious of gifts and meals and its relationship to ordination. For those in the Catholic tradition, the celebration of the eucharist has become the centre; the high point and the purpose of ordained ministry towards which everything tends and away from which everything leads. Enormous energy is focused therefore on preparation for this aspect of ordained ministry and, sometimes, on the minutest details of preparation, posture and inflection. In such a depth of concentration on the eucharist there is a danger in missing the bifocal nature of presbyteral and priestly ministry as ministry of both word and sacrament or of subordinating the former to the latter. There is also, in practice, a danger of concentrating the whole role of ordained ministry too exclusively in that which only the ordained can do.

However, if the Catholic tradition has given too much prominence to presiding at Holy Communion, those from the evangelical wing of the Church have often made the opposite error and have seen themselves and have been prepared for ministry as ministers of the Word but not necessarily as ministers of prayer and of the sacraments.

Which aspects of this dimension of ministry remain the most important in a context of both the nurture of an existing congregation and the opportunity for mission?

Preparation for the common meal of the community is vital. Although it will often be entrusted to others, as in the gospel account of the Last Supper, and can legitimately be seen as a diaconal ministry, it remains part of the responsibility of the one who is to preside to ensure that proper preparations have been made and that all is in order. This role and ministry includes very simple tasks such as ensuring that the building is tidy and heated to an appropriate temperature; that the right service sheets and books have been set aside; that the building is as helpfully ordered as it can be to enable the worship of the people of God.[14]

The proper preparation for leading worship and particularly for presiding at the service of Holy Communion will include the preparation of oneself. All too often, vestries are busy places before a morning service: clergy are sorting out notices and details of the service or trying to catch people about this and that; devotional prayers before the service are perfunctory. Not enough time is allowed for a stillness and settling and focus upon the worship to come. The ASB rubrics to the Communion service commend 'careful devotional preparation for every communicant'. A similar discipline of preparation is essential for those who will lead that celebration.

Welcome is vital. The one who presides is also the host. It is essential that those who come to the meal are warmly welcomed into the community; both those who are part of the Church and those who are visitors or enquirers. The welcome is the welcome of the whole people of God, the openness and friendliness of the congregation expressed formally in the service at the peace, in the greeting given by the stewards, and less formally in many different ways. The welcome is one which is extended to strangers as well as those who are part of the community; to the poor as well as to the rich;[15] and to children and young people as well as adults. It may begin with something as simple as ensuring the right time of the service is clearly displayed on a notice board.

The person leading the service has a particular responsibility to ensure that the liturgy is accessible, both that it can be followed and that adequate printed or verbal explanation is given for what is taking place. Churches who welcome a great many visitors are wise to include a short explanation of what the Holy Communion service means to the Christian community at the beginning of the service booklet used. In most congregations, printed sheets are easier to follow than a prayer book. If they are changed according to the Church year, there is the opportunity to include seasonal variations in the liturgy. Special care needs to be taken to welcome those who attend a communion service but who are not able to receive communion either because they are children or because they are newcomers to the congregation.

The right ordering of the service again will involve consultation and the wisdom of many different people within the congregation but will also be the particular responsibility of the president. There is an established rhythm to the way in which any congregation worships – however formal or informal their worship style. That rhythm needs to be one which has been thought through and reflected upon regularly rather than one which simply emerges through default or inherited sloppy practice. The time and space given within the service to songs, to the ministry of the Word, to the prayers, the number of alternatives and to the notices all need to be considered.

The priest in particular needs to acquire a feel and a sense of the liturgy of the service: of its pace, movement, style and language. The prayers used in the communion service are texts which have been lovingly and prayerfully distilled by the contemporary Church from 2000 years of the tradition. That process continues still through contemporary liturgical revision. Those whose responsibility it is to use them in public worship need to have studied them and to understand their different levels of meaning, their origins and their shape in order to use them well. The liturgy, as it were, needs to have become part of the priest or presbyter and to be spoken from within; passing through the heart and life and not simply the eyes and the mind of the one who presides. Language and diction, wher-ever possible, need to be clear and accessible. Gestures of the hands and arms, like language, need to have been thought through both in respect of the tradition in which we stand and their relevance or otherwise to our worship today.

The **involvement of others** in the worship will need to be a particular concern of the one who presides. The very word 'liturgy' means in its origins 'the work of the people (*laos*)'. There may need to be some occasions in which the only person who says and does anything in the service is the one who presides but these are very far from the ideal in expressing that this is the celebration of and by the whole people of God. The whole pattern of the Church's life will be modelled by and set by its central celebrations of worship and particularly by the eucharist. If the model given is that of 'everything is done by the priest' (other than behind-the-scenes preparations) then a powerful message is sent out to the whole community for the rest of that Church's ministry: all the important 'spiritual' tasks are to be performed by one person on behalf of the community. If, on the other hand, the eucharist models the genuine gifts of different members of the body of Christ being used to the glory of God, then that ethos will spill over into and affect the life of the Church from Monday to Saturday.

In the service of Holy Communion the president, on behalf of the congregation, takes ordinary bread and wine, gives thanks to God, breaks the bread and shares the elements with the congregation as a remembering and making present of the death of Christ for the sins of the world. Ordinary elements are consecrated, set apart, invested with meaning and significance for the whole community whose story flows from the death and resurrection of Christ. The Church has recognised down the centuries that the normal and regular right ordering of its sacramental life requires that those who are to perform these simple but profound actions and words of consecration are themselves in great need of the grace of God to equip them for this ministry. This need for the grace of God is expressed in the service of ordination as priest and in the continued prayers of the whole people of God for those who are ordained.

This does not mean in any sense that the priest or presbyter is a special person in some way or a special kind of person. It means the opposite: that a person who is in every respect very ordinary has been called by God to this particular ministry; that the Church as well as the individual has recognised the call as genuine; and that they have been set apart through the grace of God for this special purpose within the community.

The priest will be called to celebrate Holy Communion in many different contexts in the course of a lifetime of Christian service: from great festival gatherings in the midst of a large congregations to many occasions in homes with small groups or with individuals who are infirm, housebound or near the end of their life. Enabling the prayer and worship of the whole people of God in this way is an enormous privilege and a lifelong vocation. As we share Holy Communion together we are remembering and making present the death and resurrection of Jesus as the beginning and the continuing centre of our Christian lives. This will be true for the congregation, but also true for the ordained person who will find that their own life is shaped and moulded by this sacrament into the patterns of death and resurrection which give it such power in the life of the Church.

Pastoral Ministry and Prayer for the Sick

> Priests are 'to minister to the sick and prepare the dying for the death. They must set the Good Shepherd always before them as the pattern of their calling, caring for the people committed to their charge and joining with them in a common witness to the world.'

The particular calling of presbyteral ministry towards ministry to the sick and the dying finds its roots first in the care and compassion of God for all his people. Although the shepherd metaphor in Scripture is primarily a metaphor about giving guidance and leadership to the whole community, part of the expression of that leadership is a particular care for the weak, the sick and the lost. Secondly, the ministry to the sick springs from Jesus' own ministry of healing which forms such a significant proportion of the Gospel narrative. Third, as we have seen in the New Testament, there are very early traditions in Scripture which witness to a role for the presbyters in effective prayer for those who are sick within the community, acting as representatives of the whole people of God. In the whole of the Christian tradition the heart of ordained ministry has been distilled into the phrase 'the cure of souls', language still used in services of induction and institution as the priest receives a licence from the hands of the bishop.

As we have seen in other areas of presbyteral ministry, in a church where the congregation is of any size, it will be impossible for the single person ordained priest (with, at best, one or two colleagues) to keep in touch with every family or individual and to minister to every person's needs. Some models of Church life, as we have seen, therefore suggest that the minister should somehow 'graduate' away from this presbyteral dimension of care for individuals and invest the whole of their time and energy into training and enabling others to ensure that the care of the whole community is enabled by that community. This does need to happen. But it should not be at the expense of the pastoral ministry exercised by the ordained.

Anyone called to ordained ministry is likely to have the desire to care for people, especially those who are vulnerable, somewhere near the heart of their calling. To deny that part of one's own vocation simply in order to manage the care of a congregation is not likely to be fruitful. Conversely, congregations have a right to expect that those who serve them as ordained ministers will continue to have a strong and effective pastoral dimension to their ministry. A large congregation or group of congregations can normally grasp the necessity for pastoral care to be shared and devolved from the ordained to the whole people of God; they find it much harder to comprehend an ordained minister for whom management and oversight of the care of others has completely replaced a 'hands on' caring role. We are shaped, over time, by the way we ourselves shape our lives.

As the Scriptures and the ordinal demonstrate, there is a clear relationship between the pastoral ministry and the ministry of prayer and the sacraments. At the heart of pastoral ministry is a desire to bring the grace of God lovingly and sensitively into the lives of men and women and children, often in times of great need. This will involve, often, not only prayer for people through intercession but prayer with people, often involving laying on of hands or anointing for strength and for healing in different contexts. A particular priority in this ministry will be given by the ordained to those who are seriously ill and to those who are dying and to the bereaved. This ministry is more than a human response to difficult situations but the call to become a channel of the peace and love of Christ to the lives of others.[16]

Intercessory Prayer and Blessing: Spirituality in the Second Dimension

Public prayer and the leadership of public worship, particularly the administration of the sacraments, form one part of the second focus of presbyteral ministry. The second part will be hidden from view and will be the element of intercession on behalf of the community which is the calling of every Christian but which will find a focus in the ministry of the ordained. Listening, as we have seen, is the hallmark of diaconal spirituality. Intercession, prayer on behalf of others, can be seen in a corresponding way as the hallmark of the second dimension of ministry.

The tradition of those who are exercising leadership among the people also interceding on their behalf to God is one which is deep in the Old Testament scriptures. Abraham is portrayed in Genesis as one who intercedes and debates deeply with God, appealing for mercy for the cities of the plain on the grounds of God's justice and fair dealing.[17] Moses is called to intercede on behalf of his people not only before Pharoah but, in the wilderness, before God himself.[18] The office of the High Priest was concerned with intercession on behalf of the people of Israel: Aaron's vestments include the ephod on which are inscribed the names of the Israelite tribes 'for remembrance'.[19] The whole of the prophetic tradition emphasises intercession as the normal role of the prophet: both prayer for individuals and prayer for the nation from Samuel through Elijah and Elisha to the prophets of the canonical books. Jeremiah is commanded at different points to no longer intercede and pray for Jerusalem, so great is her sinfulness.[20] The great models for leaders in the post-exilic period, Daniel, Ezra and Nehemiah, all are leaders who take seriously this ministry of prayer.

This same quality of intercession is modelled in the ministry and life of Jesus and in the lives and letters of the apostles. Jesus himself prays often on behalf of others. The beautiful and stirring high priestly prayer of John 17 is that all his disciples might be sanctified and made holy in truth. These ideas of Jesus as High Priest are further developed, as we have seen, by the Epistle to the Hebrews, which gives us a vision of Christ as the fulfilment of the Old Testament priesthood, making intercession for us. The apostles' declaration in Acts that they will give themselves to prayer is modelled for us in the way the narrative unfolds and the different insights we receive through the epistles. Paul was clearly someone who spent not only his time but his emotions and his very self in prayer as an integral part of his ministry of seeing Christ formed in others.[21] His prayers for the different churches and for individuals

at the beginning of the epistles are not general but specific thanks-
givings and intercessions on behalf of very different communities,
born out of time spent before God and on behalf of people. Other
ministers in the Epistles are commended as 'agonising' or 'wrestling'
in prayer for those they have ministered to in Christ: 'Epaphras,
who is one of you, a servant [*diakonos*] of Christ Jesus, greets you.
He is always wrestling in his prayers on your behalf, so that you may
stand mature and fully assured in everything that God wills.'[22]

What is present in Scripture is witnessed to also in the tradition.
In every generation and in every country around the world today,
wherever there has been or is a significant breakthrough for the
kingdom of God in terms of social justice or of evangelism, at its
root is a ministry of intercessory prayer.

Again, we must say, intercession is the calling of every Christian
and a particular vocation and gift to some at different times of
their lives. However, in an age in which the pursuit of different
spiritualities is in danger of becoming simply another part of the
quest for self-fulfilment, we need to assert that this aspect of prayer
which is the giving of oneself secretly on behalf of others is a vital
discipline and tool in presbyteral or priestly ministry. It is one
which receives little if any public acclaim or even acknowledgement.
Almost always intercession is a very pedestrian activity: lifting
people, situations, nations to God in prayer faithfully and regularly.
Yet it represents the foundation and core of any ministry which is
concerned with seeing individual people reconciled to God,
churches established and made strong, and society transformed.

Those who are ordained to Anglican ministry have a responsibility
and privilege laid upon them to spend time each day in the Daily
Office. To say Morning or Evening Prayer (or both) either alone or
with others is not only a tremendous support and strength to ministry and a means of attending to Scripture daily but is also a
very appropriate vehicle for developing a disciplined pattern of
intercession. Such a pattern will include prayer for individuals
closest to us; prayer for those who are our colleagues in different
ways; prayer for those whom we are serving in different ways and
those whom we have served in the past. It will also include, most
helpfully, following frameworks and guidelines for prayer produced
by our diocese or denomination or by different Christian groups
whom we may want to support.

Exercising a faithful and fruitful ministry as a priest or presbyter in the Church of Christ is not, in the first instance, a matter of techniques, gifts or skills but is founded upon learning this discipline of prayer for others. This is no ordinary calling.

Blessing

'... to bless them in the name of the Lord'

Blessing is about far more than pronouncing a particular prayer at the end of the service 'in the name of the Father and of the Son and of the Holy Spirit'. To seek to bless others and to be a blessing to them is to seek to devote oneself to the good of others, in whatever way that might happen is the wider meaning. Gary Smalley and John Trent in their book *The Blessing* have drawn attention to the tremendous hunger for affirmation and a sense of others commending what we do (or not) in modern society. They draw out four characteristics of what it means to bless others through our lives: 'A family blessing begins with *meaningful touching*. It continues with a *spoken message of high value*, a message that pictures *a special future* for the individual being blessed, and one that is based on an *active commitment* to see the blessing come to pass.'[23]

A Call to Holiness

The key theme of the diaconal dimension of ministry is integrity. Simple acts of service to others, listening both to God and to others, the attitude of a servant, care over detail and a willingness to be available to the wider community, combine to give an integrity to ordained ministry which effects and empowers the wider ministry of leadership which they may be called upon to exercise. All ministry is both being and doing. However, one is not prior to the other. Who we are and who we are becoming affects the choices we make, the way in which we undertake our task, and the direction in which we focus our energies. Conversely, the way in which we order and direct our time, the activities we engage in, the priorities we make for the week to week exercise of ministry steadily affect and shape the people we become. Living out ministry as a servant builds integrity.

The parallel key theme of the priestly or presbyteral dimension of ministry is holiness. Very few of the themes and areas of ministry in this chapter or the preceding one are exclusively the preserve or calling of those who are ordained priest. Some are the calling of every Christian. Others are the calling of lay ministers alongside those who are ordained. Our understanding of priesthood should not be restricted or contracted simply to those tasks which only a person ordained priest can perform on behalf of the church. Nor should it be expanded to include other necessary aspects of the ministry with the result that it can mean anything and everything. The particular combination of ministries of Word and sacrament described in these two chapters – as exercised by those whose vocation to this ministry has been recognised by the Church and whose ministry is exercised in the midst of and within the community of faith and which itself enables the mission of that community – is the presbyteral or priestly ministry.

From its earliest beginnings to the present time, the Church has recognised that for its own health and well-being, this combination of ministries called presbyteral or priestly has needed people who have themselves been 'set apart' for the task. The sense of being set apart, is, of course, the root meaning of the biblical concept of holiness. As with integrity and *diakonia*, there is a twofold interaction between what it means to be holy and the exercise of priestly ministry. The exercise of that ministry, whether that be preaching, presiding at Holy Communion or prayer with someone who is sick, needs to flow from and out of our whole person. It takes a whole lifetime to prepare to preach a sermon. The grace of holiness which we have been given and which God has forged in us through our different experiences of joy and suffering, including our experience of being called and set apart for this task all contribute to that ministry. At a very basic level a major, deliberate and persistent departure from the standards which Scripture and the Christian tradition have set for the Church's ministry, in truthfulness, sexual practice, financial dishonesty, abuse of power or any other area will have a profound effect on a person's ministry even where it remains undiscovered.

In a similar but converse way, the experience over many years of sharing in the ministries of reconciliation, preaching, teaching, prayer and the sacraments have the capacity (slowly and, it often seems, imperceptibly) to form character and to lead to that particular quality of holiness which we find in Christ: joyful yet long-suffering and compassionate; righteous yet not judgemental; free yet disciplined; accessible yet profound.

PART FOUR

EPISCOPE:
MINISTRY IN THE THIRD DIMENSION

11

EPISCOPE IN
SCRIPTURE AND TRADITION

The Nature of *Episcope*

We have seen how the two concepts of diaconal and presbyteral ministry remain vital for describing and understanding the ministry of the ordained in the context of the ministry of the whole people of God. The root of *diakonia* is in every sense the foundation of all ministry which is truly Christian, including the exercise of leadership. *Diakonia* also describes very genuinely much of the ordinary, day-to-day work of the ordained. Presbyteral or priestly ministry, seen as the ministry of Word and sacrament and by extension that of prayer with others and personal care for them is also foundational. Those who are ordained need to be competent, diligent and gifted in these areas. Whatever the context of their ministry and whatever demands might be made of them, they will never reach the point where they are no longer deacons or priests. The whole of the ministry of the ordained cannot be subsumed into the notion of 'leadership'.

However, it is also true, as we have seen, that the whole task of the ordained minister cannot be fully embraced either by these first two dimensions of ministry. There is much which is vital which has not yet been described. As we saw in the opening chapters, the mission context in which the Church now finds itself is calling for a shift in the balance between the different dimensions of ministry. Gifts which have not been traditionally part of the diaconal or priestly calling are increasingly demanded of the clergy: the gifts of intentionally enabling and building community; the gifts of discernment in identifying the charisms of others and enabling them in ministry; gifts of collaboration, of vision; and of guiding a Christian Church through a period of change.

It is possible to argue that these aspects of ministry are legitimate

141

extensions of the presbyteral dimension – but the danger then is
that the terms priest and presbyter come to mean anything and
everything and lose their twin focus of ministry of Word and sacrament. It is also possible to turn to secular models and
understandings of leadership and management both for insights
into how these tasks are best done and for our basic categories of
understanding of this aspect of ministry. However, as we have seen,
secular language about leadership and management not only alienates many clergy and lay people from what are essential concepts
for the life of the Church in this and the next generation; it also
leads to the danger of our importing into the heart of the way we
do Church and ministry, values which are close to the opposite of
our values about service and the ordained.

There is in the Scripture and the churches' own tradition a third
cluster of concepts related to Christian ministry which exactly fills
the gap we have identified in our understanding of what it means
to be ordained: the concepts summed up by the Greek word *episcope.*
From *episcope* we derive the word *episcopos* and from that we derive
the word 'bishop'. It is not my purpose in this chapter and the
following to talk in a narrow sense about the ministry of bishops
(although there may be some points of relevance). Bishops remain
first and foremost, like all of the ordained, deacons and priests.
They have the title '*episcopos*' because their ministry is meant to be
weighted much more towards this third dimension of ministry; just
as the ministry of a deacon should be weighted towards the first
dimension. Rather, it is my intention to explore here the ministry of
oversight and leadership as it relates to and is part of the ministry
of every ordained person. The missionary needs of the Church in
the present generation call for the restoring of this third dimension
of ministry to the whole of the ordained, especially those charged
with the task of the care and oversight of one or more local churches
as vicars, rectors or as priest in charge.

This chapter therefore explores the roots of the term and concept
of *episcope* in Scripture and the Tradition, as in the preceding sections.
The following chapters then unpack the concept for ordained ministry today. To anticipate the conclusions of the present chapter at
the beginning, the dimension of ministry which is *episcope* has been
focused in Scripture and historically around three great themes.

The first is that of the person exercising episcope as a *focus for the unity* of the people of God. But what kind of unity do we mean? The people of God must never be seen as a static entity, safely settled in one place for ever. We have here no continuing city. The people of God are a people on the move. Building, guarding and preserving the unity of God's people involves therefore the nurturing of community and relationships not simply with individuals but among small groups, informal networks and larger congregations on the one hand. One the other it means enabling the whole Church and community to move forward and to move together. This in turn means that *episcope* embraces the dimension of ministry which includes discerning and articulating a vision for a local congregation; enabling and bringing about change in communities; identifying restraints and dangers; resolving conflict and so on. The person exercising *episcope* does not do so simply by virtue of her or his office, simply by being there. This dimension of ministry is hands-on work requiring the development of a particular set of skills in which many clergy have not been intentionally formed and trained.

The second area is that of *enabling, developing and sustaining the ministry of others*. One of the great symbolic tasks of the bishop in a diocese is to ordain new ministers. At local church or sector ministry level, a vital role for the clergy is to set free and enable the ministry of the whole people of God. This in turn means exercising discernment about the gifts and abilities of others; developing the skills needed to clarify tasks and roles and to enable others both to begin a ministry and to continue in it through the provision of the necessary support and review. However high a church's view of lay ministry, and however gifted the lay people in a particular congregation, that ministry will not be used to very great effect unless the ordained are actively seeking to enable their gifts. As someone who is regularly asked to lead workshops for lay people in dioceses, I can testify to a fair degree of frustration among those lay people who invest their time in training courses only to find that their gifts and skills are neither recognised nor used by their incumbent.

And the third area of *episcope*, foundational to each of the others, is the ability to keep watch: over one's own ministry, over the lives and ministries of others, and over the whole congregation. Amidst the competing demands and pressures of what can be an unclear and difficult role, the clergy themselves are in great need of continued and high quality support as well as of giving that support to others.

Episcope in the Scriptures

Roots in the Old Testament and in Secular Greek

In classical Greek *episcopos* is a word used to describe both the gods and individual people. The root of the word means 'one who watches over'. In Homer the gods are described as those who 'witness and watch over' treaties and the affairs of nations.[1] The word is used of men and women who have the task of watching over, guiding, protecting and caring for others.[2] In Athens in the fourth and fifth centuries BC, the *episcopos* was a state official charged with the preservation of public order; and the title is used elsewhere in the ancient world for minor officials or the officers of societies. There is not a great deal of evidence to suggest its use in a religious connection outside of Judaism and Christianity.

The Greek translation of the Old Testament, the Septuagint, following classical Greek usage, also uses the term *episcopos* of both God and human beings. The noun *episcope* is employed to translate the Hebrew meaning 'visitation' of God both to bring grace but also judgement. People are described as *episcopoi* in a variety of contexts as minor officials who look after others or over different parts of the temple.[3]

New Testament Usage

As we have seen in earlier chapters, the term *episcopos* and related words begin to be used from a relatively early stage to describe ministers of the New Testament Church. Philippians, as we have seen, is addressed to the whole congregation 'with *episcopoi* and *diakonoi*'.[4] In Acts, the Ephesians elders are also described as '*episcopoi*': 'Keep watch over yourselves and over all the flock, of which the Holy Spirit has made you overseers [*episkopoi*], to shepherd the church of God that he obtained with the blood of his own Son.'[5]

In 1 Peter the elders are urged, in very similar language, 'to tend the flock of God that is in your charge, exercising the oversight [*episkopeo*]'.[6] By the end of the New Testament the previously overlapping roles of the *presbyteros* and *episcopos* are beginning to separate out. The verses specifically referring to the role of the *episcopos* in Titus read:

> For a bishop [*episkopos*] as God's steward must be blameless; he must not be arrogant or quick tempered or addicted to wine or violent or greedy for gain; but he must be hospitable, a lover of goodness, prudent, upright, devout and self-controlled. He must have a firm grasp of the word that is trustworthy in accordance with the teaching, so that he may be able both to preach with sound doctrine and to refute those who contradict it.[7]

And in 1 Timothy we read:

> The saying is sure: whoever aspires to the office of a bishop [*episkopos*] desires a noble task. Now a bishop must be above reproach, married only once, temperate, sensible, respectable, hospitable, an apt teacher, not a drunkard, not violent but gentle, not quarrelsome, and not a lover of money. He must manage his own household well, keeping his children sub-missive and respectful in every way – for if someone does not know how to manage his own household, how can he take care of God's church? He must not be a recent convert, or he may be puffed up with conceit and fall into the condemnation of the devil. Moreover, he must be well thought of by outsiders, so that he may not fall into disgrace and the snare of the devil.[8]

We learn a great deal from these passages about the qualities looked for in an *episcopos* in the church envisaged by the Pastoral Epistles and something about the function the person called to this office is to fulfil. There is a high degree of overlap, as we should expect, between the role of the *episcopos* and that of the *presbyteros* in that the *episcopos* is to tend the flock, to preach and to teach and, particu-larly, to refute error. If the view is followed that the *episcopos* emerged in Ephesus as the person who was to watch over and to lead the presbyters then we can see that from an early stage the call to preserve the unity of the Church in a particular region was integral to the office. The (often uncomfortable) image and picture of the father caring for his household is used in 1 Timothy as a picture of the role and office of *episcopos*. The picture suggests again that the *episcopos* is to be concerned for unity; that his is to lead and preside over the Church as a father presides over a family; and that he is particularly charged with the exercise of discipline.[9] The concern that he must be well thought of by outsiders is not simply applied as a test of character but presumably is evidence that the *episcopos* was to have some representative role on behalf of the Church in dealing with those beyond its limits.

Jesus and Episcope

The fragmentary New Testament evidence about the office of *episcopos* and the development of that office in the history of the Church draws on the pattern and model of Christ, as do the first and second dimensions of ministry. We have seen clearly in the gospels the way in which Jesus is both *diakonos* and *presbyteros*. He also acts as *episcopos* in **watching over the unity, vision and progress of the small community** which he forms. Often the direction he suggests is exactly opposite to that advocated by the disciples. In Mark 1, for example, Simon and the crowds pursue Jesus to bring him back to Capernaum. Jesus himself has a different vision: to go on to other towns and to preach there, 'for that is why I came out'.[10] Out of the crowd who follow him, Jesus intentionally forms and builds a community which includes the Twelve; a smaller and more intimate group of Peter, James and John, as well as larger groups from time to time. Jesus is not pushed, deflected or distracted from his mission by the pressures around him. The turning point in Luke's narrative comes in 9:52 when Jesus 'set his face towards Jerusalem'. The seemingly random wanderings around Galilee are replaced by a purposeful progress towards the Holy City and towards the passion.

Alongside this clear sense of vision, direction and purpose that guides Jesus' ministry and which he shares and communicates with the community formed around him, we see throughout the Gospel a continuous emphasis on Christ **commissioning and enabling others** to ministry and equipping them for that ministry. The Twelve are drawn together not simply to be with him but to be sent out to preach.[11] Many of the new names which Jesus gives to his disciples are concerned with their ministry and the role they will play within the new community, supremely the renaming of Simon as Peter. We read of the disciples, both men and women, accompanying Jesus and watching him at work.[12] Then twice in Luke's gospel we are given formal accounts of the sending out first of the Twelve and then of the Seventy[13] and of the process of reporting, reflection and learning which followed both missions. It is impossible to read the gospels and not conclude that Jesus is consciously preparing the disciples for the ministry which they will undertake both during his lifetime and after his resurrection. Many small instances of detail or seemingly casual remarks are used as the pretext for teaching and preparation for mission and ministry. Those who come to Jesus are continually invited to follow him with a view, sooner or later, of being sent out by him. After the resurrection, the same pattern continues. In many of the resurrection appearances we have *episcope* represented in a renewal of call and a commission, often accompanied by prayer for the empowering of the Holy Spirit (passages which in turn have influenced the shape of ordination services).[14]

Jesus also demonstrates that he is **keeping watch over both himself and others** on different occasions in the gospel narratives. The bulk of the opening chapter of Mark is an attempt to describe a typical 'day in the life' of Jesus' Galilean ministry. Here and elsewhere the gospel writers emphasise that at the heart of the rhythm of life Jesus models and develops is the discipline of solitary prayer away from the busyness of the day and the busyness of the community. Periods of intense activity are punctuated by periods of withdrawal to be refreshed. We see Jesus talking to vast crowds and giving of himself but also spending time in the homes of his friends. We see times when he is concerned for the needs of his disciples, as when the Twelve return from their mission and Jesus says to them: 'Come away by yourselves to a lonely place and rest a while.' It is Jesus who says to all of his followers according to Matthew: 'Come to me, all who labour and are heavy laden, and I will give you rest. Take my yoke upon you, and learn from me; for I am gentle and lowly in heart, and you will find rest for your souls. For my yoke is easy and my burden is light.'[15]

From Jesus to the Apostles

The same patterns of *episcope* observed in Jesus' ministry are continued into the lives and ministries of the apostles. The course of their ministry and mission is not seen to be random or self-determined but purposeful and determined with continual reference to the guidance of the Holy Spirit. Communities are consciously nurtured and built up through the four classical means of the apostles' teaching, the fellowship, the breaking of bread and the prayers.[16] New directions are the result of the interaction between the Holy Spirit and the praying community.[17] We see the apostles and elders together carefully watching over and guarding the unity of the New Testament churches as tensions created through the preaching of the Gospel to the gentiles are negotiated.[18] The Epistles also bear witness to this same ministry of serving and building up unity and common vision among the Christians in a city or region, countering the many pressures which served to discourage or distract the Church from its mission. The letter to the Hebrews is a masterpiece of careful literary and theological construction composed, as it seems, for a small congregation or house church in the city of Rome from an anonymous author watching over their common life and seeking to correct, to guide and to encourage. From their earliest days the fledgling churches had those who were guardians and who watched over their lives with great wisdom and carefulness. Revelation, as we have seen, opens with the vision of Christ tending the lampstands of the churches and giving specific words of guidance and warning to each community: exercising *episcope* from heaven.

As Jesus set apart, commissioned, trained and prayed for the disciples, so we see the pattern continues throughout the remainder of the New Testament. As we have seen, one of the major themes of Acts is the ordering and expansion of ministry within the early Church. The first episode to be described after the ascension is the appointment of Matthias. Luke goes on to tell us about the appointment and commissioning of the Seven; about the diversity of ministries in Antioch; and about the appointment of presbyters in the Pauline churches and particularly in Ephesus. We see the apostles seeking to train others as Jesus trained his own disciples. Paul's concerns in the epistles are the building up of teams who will be trained to continue and develop beyond his own lifetime. The pastorals reflect a situation in which Timothy and Titus are themselves encouraged to train up others who will in turn build up the churches.

A particular feature of the setting apart of others for ministry is that of public prayer with laying on of hands which recurs in Acts and is mentioned in the epistles: prayer which normally centres upon the anointing and empowering of the Holy Spirit for the task of ministry and which draws again on the tradition of Jesus' prayer for his disciples. Prayer for the anointing and filling of the Holy Spirit has become in the Christian tradition a function of *episcope*, focused in the prayers of the bishop for the candidates at confirmation and for those set apart for ministry in the ordination service.

The third feature of watchfulness and care for one another is, again, continued by the apostles and, as we have seen, is a centrepiece of Paul's address to the Ephesian elders.[19] It is nowhere more clearly demonstrated than in the final greetings which conclude many of the epistles which contain a host of practical concerns and practical advice and encouragement, demonstrating that a significant part of the apostles' own ministry was taken up with prayerfully and systematically watching over those among whom they served.[20]

Episcope in the Tradition of the Church

As we have seen, within the New Testament period there is clearly a great deal of overlap between the functions of those who take the title *presbyters* and those called *episcopoi*. The following century sees a gradual pulling apart of these two ministries which begins with the necessary setting aside of particular presbyters as *episkopoi* in the Pastoral Epistles, and results in the prevalence in most churches by the end of the second century of a full threefold order of bishops, priests and deacons. It is impossible to chart this development in great detail, particularly in its early period.[21] There has been a great deal of discussion and controversy within the churches down the centuries about episcopacy: that is the nature, function, necessity and role of bishops. However, there has been very little thinking, partly in consequence, about the exercise of responsible oversight, or *episcope*, by all of the ordained as a necessary dimension of their ministry.

The development of the ministry of *episcope* can be charted in a very broad brush way as follows:

> **Stage One:** Presbyters and *episcopoi* overlap in title and in function (the picture reflected in Acts 20).

Stage Two: *Episcopoi* emerge with a distinct function of watching over presbyters as well as over the whole church. Presbyters begin to lose this dimension of *episcope* from their ministry. Their task becomes more one of hands on engaging in ministry (the picture reflected in the Pastoral Epistles).

Stage Three: This breakdown in function develops further into the threefold order of ministry of bishops, priests and deacons, but with the bishop still exercising the ministry of oversight within a cluster of local congregations assisted by the presbyters (the position until the conversion of Constantine).

Stage Four: The bishop becomes a regional figure with the responsibility of the care of a large diocese. Oversight of the local congregations becomes more and more the responsibility of presbyters. The ministry of presbyters (and of all ministers), over time, becomes focused more and more upon the celebration of the eucharist. The importance of the ministry of others within the body of Christ is diminished. Consequently the ministry of *episcope* as part of the ministry of the priest declines (from the conversion of Constantine until the Reformation).

Stage Five: At the Reformation more varied patterns for the oversight of local congregations begin to develop. The churches recover an emphasis on the ministry of the Word and upon the priesthood of all believers. Lay ministry within the local churches begins to assume a greater importance and to develop in more and different ways (from the Reformation until the mid-twentieth century).

Stage Six: There is a progressively richer understanding of the ministry of all of the people of God and of the vocation to service of all of the baptised. The churches in the West enter an explicit situation of mission which calls for different ways of being church and of building church as community. Episcopacy, exercised in various forms in different churches, remains important. However, *episcope* as a dimension of the ministry of all of the ordained becomes an essential part of their role, particularly for those charged with the leadership of local congregations (from the mid-twentieth century until the present day).

Episcopacy at the End of the Twentieth Century

The Lima document attempts to sum up the functions of bishops as follows:

Bishops preach the Word, preside at the sacraments and administer discipline in such a way as to be representative pastoral ministers of oversight, continuity and unity in the church. They have pastoral oversight of the area to which they are called. They serve the apostolicity and unity of the Church's teaching, worship and sacramental life. They have responsibility for leadership in the Church's mission. They relate the Christian community in their area to the wider Church, and the universal Church to their community. They, in communion with the presbyters, deacons and the whole community, are responsible for the orderly transfer of ministerial authority in the Church.[22]

The charge to bishops in the Alternative Services Book reads:

'A bishop is called to lead in serving and caring for the people of God and to work with them in the oversight of the Church. As a chief pastor he shares with his fellow bishops a special responsibility to maintain and further the unity of the Church, to uphold its discipline and to guard its faith. He is to promote its mission throughout the world. It is his duty to watch over and to pray for all those committed to his charge, and to teach and govern them after the manner of the Apostles, speaking in the name of God and interpreting the gospel of Christ. He is to know his people and be known by them. He is to ordain and send new ministers, guiding those who serve with him and enabling them to fulfil their ministry.

He is to baptize and confirm, to preside at the Holy Communion, and to lead the offering of prayer and praise. He is to be merciful, but with firmness, and to minister discipline, but with mercy. He is to have a special care for the outcast and the needy; and to those who turn to God he is to declare the forgiveness of sins.'[23]

The thanksgiving immediately before the ordination draws heavily on the language of Ephesians, emphasising by implication that the role of the bishop is to equip the people of God for the work of ministry and to build up the body of Christ. Immediately after the ordination the Archbishop prays:

> 'Almighty Father, fill this your servant with the grace and power which you give to your apostles, that he may lead those committed to his charge in proclaiming the gospel of salvation. Through him increase your Church, renew its ministry, and unite its members in a holy fellowship of truth and love. Enable him as a true shepherd to feed and govern your flock; make him wise as a teacher, and steadfast as a guardian of its faith and sacraments. Guide and direct him in presiding at the worship of your people. Give him humility, that he may use his authority to heal, not to hurt; to build up, not to destroy. Defend him from all evil, that as ruler over your household and an ambassador for Christ, he may stand before you blameless and finally, with your servants, enter your eternal joy.'

The charge and the prayer from the Alternative Services Book are beautiful and powerful words. Most Anglican congregations and clergy will never have heard them used in public worship since they are only present at the ordination of a bishop in exceptional circumstances. Many Anglican clergy I have spoken with have never read the service for the ordination of a bishop, either thinking it irrelevant to their ministry or, quite often, presumptuous even to read the text and think it might apply to their own service. However, it seems to me that the prayer in its entirety could be used with great effect at the institution and licensing of a new incumbent to a parish church expressing the dimension of *episcope* which is a necessary part of the exercise of that ministry. Only the sphere in which that ministry is exercised is different. Similarly there are only a few parts of the charge which would need to be omitted or altered before those words also could be applied to someone charged with responsible and collaborative leadership of a congregation or group of congregations.[24] The Church needs those who exercise responsible leadership beyond the local congregation: who guard its unity and who guide its life. However, *episcope* is a necessary part of the ministry of all of the ordained, particularly of those charged with a responsibility of leading the life of local Christian communities in a time of transition and of mission. The following chapters will explore this dimension of *episcope* as it relates to local church leadership.

12

EPISCOPE IN LOCAL CHURCH
LEADERSHIP (1): VISION, UNITY
AND TRANSFORMATION

An essential part of *episcope*, as we have seen, is the guarding of the unity of the local congregation and the development of its common life and mission within the surrounding community. This chapter and the following examine the dimension of *episcope* primarily from the context of the rector, priest, vicar or minister charged with this responsibility within one or more parish churches or local churches in, for example, a Methodist circuit. To concentrate on this form of the ordained ministry in this way is not to deny that there is an element of *episcope* within every sphere of ministry. I have concentrated on parish ministry here partly because this is where the majority of the ordained spend the majority of their time; partly in the hope that the principles worked out in one context will transfer easily to another; and partly because this is where I sense the need is greatest. For much of this century the Church of England has trained curates in its theological colleges and courses, not incumbents. Men and women have been prepared for the different aspects of priestly ministry and have been equipped to lead services, preach sermons, and care, in different ways, for the sick and the vulnerable. Yet we have not been prepared, by and large, in those dimensions of *episcope* which involve understanding and working with groups and communities as well as individuals. We are therefore left naked in a situation of great change in society and in the churches.

Several cautionary words are necessary. First, it will be clear from the shape of the book as a whole that I am not advocating that the vicars[1] should become specialists in *episcope* to the exclusion of their presbyteral and diaconal role, as some have argued. The third dimension of ministry must be complementary to and in harmony with the first and second dimensions but *episcope* is a necessary

154

dimension to local church ministry. Second, I am not wanting to suggest in any way that the necessary exercise of *episcope* by an incumbent somehow negates the ministry of other members of the body of Christ in a particular church or makes it less important. The opposite is likely to be the case. A church in which the vicar makes no attempt to exercise *episcope* but simply does the work of the ministry himself is likely to be one in which the gifts and mission of the whole people of God are neglected. Thirdly, simply because *episcope* is part of the ministry of the ordained does not mean that it is necessarily only the ministry of the ordained or the ministry of an individual within a congregation. Undoubtedly *episcope* is stronger in a local church if it is exercised collaboratively by a vicar and PCC together; or an incumbent with an extended staff meeting including both ordained and lay members. However, until an incumbent has grasped the need for such a ministry and has begun to grow in its use, he or she is unlikely to be able to involve others in the task. Fourthly, the need for an incumbent to exercise *episcope* does not mean that there is no longer any need for an *episcopos*. Accountability, oversight and leadership within a diocese or wider area remain essential.

A local church is never a static community but, ideally, one which is moving forward together towards common goals. Catching, developing, articulating and sharing common vision for that process is a vital part of the exercise of this kind of leadership. What kind of theological priorities should underlie this ministry of guiding and developing the life of a congregation?

Inherited Shape

All communities are shaped to some degree by the beliefs, values and history which underpin their life together. These values may not always be articulated clearly or intentionally but will inform and affect much of what takes place. Different members of a single congregation may well hold different and opposing values which may result in conflict over seemingly trivial as well as more major matters. The group charged with exercising *episcope* and preserving the unity of the Church as well as its forward movement and development must be able to see deeper than the surface issues and to discern the underlying values, sometimes in order to challenge them and sometimes to affirm. A key element in diaconal ministry, as we have seen, is the ability to listen carefully. Exercising *episcope* well depends a great deal on good listening: taking the time and the trouble to hear the story, the core beliefs, the values of a congregation from different perspectives. This is particularly important at the beginning of a new incumbency or period of ministry but remains vital at all times of reflection upon a new direction or phase of a congregation's life.[2]

Ideas which shape the lives of congregations may include the desire simply to survive as a struggling congregation for a few more years, particularly if many churches in the surrounding area have been closed and the parish share assessment keeps rising; the desire to preserve the building as something precious to hand on to the next generation; or the desire to maintain excellence in a particular area of the congregation's life as an example or resource to others in the area (such as the choir or music group or pattern of services). A congregation's life may be shaped by its desire to communicate the Gospel to others and to see them come to faith; its desire to increase numerically; a need to ensure the children of church members grow into adult disciples; or else its longing to serve the local community in sacrificial ways. Other congregations may find their life has simply fallen into a seasonal pattern of repeating what happened twelve months ago at different seasons of the year whilst all rationale for the different activities has long since been forgotten. Other congregations and wider movements are shaped by what they are against rather than what they are for; others by national trends and fashions either of today or of thirty years ago; and still others by the particular passions of previous incumbents.

Increasingly, local churches seek to express their values and their short-and long-term aims and objectives in 'mission statements' of different kinds which sum up what a particular church believes it stands for and represents and where it might be going. Parish profiles drawn up for the purpose of seeking a new vicar or curate often contain a huge variety of this kind of mission statement. Attempting to draw together a common statement of aims and values can of itself be a useful exercise in listening to one another and to the differing views within any one congregation. Yet there are also some drawbacks. Although the language of 'mission' sounds theological enough, the term is actually one which has been imported into the Church from industry rather than from the theological tradition. The context in which a mission statement is used in industry is to define the aims and objectives of a particular organisation over and against its competitors. Different branches, for example, of McDonalds or Center Parcs or Body Shop do not have different 'mission statements'. The common and agreed understanding is what unites different parts of the same company in working towards a common goal. Defining the values and aims of a local church is surely not simply a matter for the local church but is a point at which we must engage again with the whole of the Christian Scriptures and the tradition. What are the key concepts and ideas which need to shape the life of a local congregation? What vision for the local Christian community do those exercising *episcope* within it bring to its nurture and development? Has that vision been tested theologically and in experience? Where do those exercising oversight find our values and our inspiration?[3]

An Emerging Shape . . .

As was outlined in Chapter 1, the whole of the Church in the Western world is having to rethink its basic shape. The era of Christendom has given the primary shape to national and congregational church life in England for many centuries. We assumed that the majority of the population were members of the Church unless they indicated otherwise; teaching the faith was a matter of educating children as they grew up; the parish system needed to cover every part of the community. As Christendom gives way to the post-Christian era, the Church nationally and locally is changing and seeking a new shape appropriate to this new missionary age at national and at local level. Different suggestions have been commended by various writers and movements and we cannot yet see clearly what the emerging pattern will be. Yet some outline of its shape is essential for those charged with *episcope* in local congregations. What kind of Church are we to pray for and seek to see established?

... of Rhythm and Road

The life of the missionary Church needs to be structured around both a rhythm and a road. The rhythm is the heartbeat of its life and is the rhythm of worship and of mission. The congregation comes together for worship which feeds, nurtures and sustains its life and is sent out again in mission and service in the whole of society, building the kingdom of God. Part of that building of the kingdom, certainly, is the building up of the Church, the body of Christ, but much of the building of the kingdom will take place in our wider society and world. Jesus' summary of the law is a state-ment of that rhythm: we are called first and foremost to love God and to love our neighbour as ourselves. The great commission in Matthew 28 and elsewhere is an important and vital command of Jesus to his Church – but the making of disciples is not the whole sum of what Christians are called to do and to work towards. We are not commanded by Jesus to pray, 'Our Father in heaven, hallowed be your name, May your Church increase daily in numbers and in influence.' We are commanded to pray daily for God's kingdom of justice and righteousness to come; for God's will to be done on earth as it is in heaven. That is our mission because that is God's mission.

The great sacrament of rhythm in the Church's life is the eucharist. We are invited to come together in worship of God in his goodness, in thanksgiving for all that we have received; to listen to his word read and proclaimed and in prayer for his world; and we are com-manded to go to serve him and to live out our worship as a living sacrifice in his world.[4] The heartbeat or rhythm of worship and mission will shape much of what takes place in the life of a local congregation both those aspects of its life which enable worship to be offered and sustained week by week and those aspects which enable and support its members in their mission to society.

Yet alongside and leading into and out from the great rhythm or heartbeat of the Church, there will also be the road of discipleship and of learning the Way. Those who are young and those who are adults who are returning to faith or coming to faith for the first time need to be provided with opportunities for guidance, for learning, for growth which are appropriate to their own stage of the journey. The biblical commands to build this road are clear both in the words of Jesus and the example of the apostles. The great sacrament of the road or the journey is the sacrament of baptism marking either the beginning or the midpoint of the journey. Building and providing this road or way into faith will, once again, shape much of the life of the local congregation from its provision of groups for children and young people to its evangelism, nurture and discipling of adults through midweek groups, courses and equipping in ministry, and reflected liturgically through its range of services of initiation.

The challenge for the local church in a context of mission is to weave and shape its life around both rhythm and road. If the life of the church is shaped around the rhythm alone, we may serve the needs of established Christians very well and they, in turn, may be effective in the wider community as teachers, youth leaders, police officers, advice workers and so on. But the saving message of the Gospel will not be passed on to those around; there will be no renewal of the existing congregation. There is no road. Conversely, if the life of the local church is shaped entirely around the building of a road to faith, we may become extremely effective at seeing people come to faith and grow in their discipleship, but we are initiating them and enlisting them simply into the task of seeing others come to faith rather than into the full riches of the Christian life – of worship and of building and proclaiming the kingdom of God. Both rhythm and road are essential.[5]

Dynamic

A clear vision of the priorities and values by which the life of the church is shaped and ordered is essential for the effective exercise of *episcope*. Alongside that clear vision of shape, we need also some understanding of the internal dynamic of local Christian communities, particularly as they relate to the size of the congregation and the role of the ordained minister. Congregations are not, as we have seen, random collections of individuals who simply decide to turn up at a certain place of worship at a set time on a Sunday morning. They are no longer simply a cross-section (or the majority) of a geographical community already linked together by ties of family, work and leisure. In urban areas and, increasingly, in rural settings, congregations are intentionally formed communities of people who would not know each other if they were not part of the same church. Those communities are made up of individuals, families and groups continually spinning a complex and ever changing web or relationships.

Seeking to develop and increase the size of a local church is not, therefore, simply a matter of advertising the service time more widely so as to add to the number of people who turn up on Sunday mornings, but about incorporating new members into an existing and complex community whose members relate to one another in particular ways. The size of a congregation is a particular factor governing the style of those relationships. We all behave differently in a group of ten, a group of 30 and a group of 200 other people. Appendix 2 gives one model for describing the internal dynamic of Christian communities. Others can be found which are equally valid. Some understanding of these issues is vital for those whose calling is to shape the lives of communities.

Articulating and Testing Vision

A vision for the direction and development of the life of a congregation will emerge as time is given to reflection both upon the 'ideal' picture of what the church is called to be and to the reality of congregational life as it is at present. The quality of a vicar's theology and understanding of the church and their capacity to listen, observe and describe the situation will both be tested in the process. Both the 'ideal' and impressions of reality need to be as widely discussed as possible within the church community if any resulting vision is to be widely owned. The situation in which an incumbent articulates what is wrong with the church without also giving a picture of the vision from which she is speaking is a very discouraging and confusing one for church members.[6] Through prayer, through study, through listening, trying out ideas, listening again and learning, a picture emerges both of where the community is now and at least a partial picture of where it is called to go.

Working out how to begin the journey, what route to follow and how to travel are different questions but equally significant. Clergy and churches, on the whole, are not good at planning. Many visions are born in the life of some local congregations but few are realised. It is often at this point that a church will find it helpful to involve an external consultant to guide them through the next steps of a vision for development; through the consequences of change (which are not always obvious); through costing the changes in terms of both energy and finance; and through the careful balancing of priorities in terms of time and personnel. Involving a third party from the diocese, wider denomination or para-church agency can feel to be a risky enterprise. It will be a somewhat dangerous enterprise for the health of the church if you engage the kind of consultant who will simply apply a pre-packaged formula to every situation. But the right kind of accountability and support can be a real blessing and is part of the responsible exercise of *episcope*.[7]

Episcope in Action

The following example gives an illustration of how this aspect of *episcope* might function in the context of a local church at the beginning of the ministry of a new incumbent. The process can be transferred reasonably easily to that of a fresh examination of the unity, mission and direction of a community three, five or fifteen years into the same vicar's ministry.

> Jane has recently taken up her post as Team Vicar in St Saviour's parish where she has responsibility for one parish church set in a parish of 8000 people on the outskirts of a large city.
>
> In her first months in post she has a number of immediate problems to deal with which she has not met as a curate: the death and funeral of someone at the heart of the church's life; an ethical issue relating to the lifestyle of the youth leader; a request to marry someone who is divorced. Nevertheless she seeks to make time in those months to get to know both the parish and the congregation. Drawing together a small team of volunteers, the census and other information held on the area is updated and studied closely and a profile of the area is built up around a large map, which is later displayed in the back of the church.[8] The group also think through and collate some very simple statistics about the congregation and draw a graph of Sunday attendance figures over the last ten years; a graph of Sunday giving; an age/gender profile of the electoral roll members; and a map showing where the congregation live.
>
> Jane supplements this formal gathering of information through many informal conversations with key people in the

local community and as many as possible within the congregation. She gains a sense of the way in which St Saviour's is seen by the local community and sees itself through asking very simple questions and listening with care: Tell me the story of this church and this community. How do you see this church now? Where do you think the church should be going in the future?

A great deal of information comes out of these conversations. It becomes clear that there are a number of different groups in the church, each of whom would like the church to develop and grow in a slightly different direction. Following a PCC Awayday, and with the PCC's agreement, Jane draws together a small group of people who can share with her in the task of piloting a course for the future. The group is set up for a single year only with a view, possibly, of handing on to a different kind of structure in the future.

Six months into Jane's incumbency, the group begin to meet together. They invest time initially into getting to know one another and telling their own story. Each time they meet, Jane leads them in some reflections on the nature and shape of the church and the group follows a simple pattern of liturgical worship: silence to give space to listen to God; and shared intercessory prayer. After the first few meetings they begin to engage with the many questions facing the life of the congregation.

Whilst this is happening, Jane is also setting aside time herself to reflect and to pray: she follows the practice of a regular quiet day every six weeks or so and a prayerful review of this process of discernment forms a central part of the day. She meets regularly with a work consultant suggested by the diocese; discusses the progress of the review within the wider clergy team and meets once with the archdeacon.

Three months after the group began to meet, a clear future direction is beginning to emerge. They decide to recommend to the church that the next year is spent developing the worshipping life of the congregation and affirming the contribution each member is able to make to the life of society: in other words on establishing in a deeper way the rhythm of worship and mission. In the following year they will go on from there to develop and build the road to faith for adults, supplementing their existing ministry to children. Two meetings are called for the whole congregation.[9] At the first meeting the group present their discussions and recommendations and take questions. At the second, a fortnight later, there is a full discussion in small groups and a larger forum and a consensus begins to emerge. A short parish plan, giving areas in which the church will concentrate in the next year and the following year is presented to the PCC and adopted. A copy is also sent to the bishop, who writes a warm and supportive letter. The plan is reviewed at each meeting of the church council as different initiatives begin to unfold. Although there are differences about particular elements of the strategy, a consensus is established on the overall way forward which draws the congregation together and allows them to be committed to a common task.

Change and Conflict

Guiding and guarding the unity of a group of people on a journey will involve helping that community to come to terms with change.[10] Some sense of what is essential and helpful on the part of those leading that congregation and the ways in which people are likely to react when experiencing change is essential for those exercising *episcope* at local church level. Does the responsibility for initiating change rest with an individual or is it more widely shared within a group? Are there proper structures and facilities in place for listening and encouraging voices of dissent as well as those of approval? Are the changes that are proposed consistent with the journey this community is making at this particular time? Has care been taken to ensure that the pace of change is appropriate: neither too fast to lose some people nor too slow to lose others?

One of the consequences of change in local church life is likely to be at least some conflict. Those charged with *episcope*, once again, need to have some understanding of how to handle themselves in situations of potential conflict, how to deal with the difficult emotions conflict is likely to arouse, and how to remain ministers of reconciliation for the whole congregation during a period of turmoil for some parts of it.[11]

Working with Communities

Traditionally, ordained ministry has been seen as a call to work with individuals: to encourage them, accompany them on their journey of faith, stand beside them in moments of crisis. As we enter a period of mission, the ordained need to learn how to understand, read, work with and build communities as well as individuals. A similar degree of attention needs to be paid to this dimension of ministry as well as to that of working with individuals if local churches are to reach their full potential for development in the next decades.

13

EPISCOPE IN LOCAL CHURCH LEADERSHIP (2): ENABLING THE MINISTRY OF OTHERS

Foundations

The witness of Scripture is that God works collaboratively: recognising, enabling and developing the gifts of women and men even as seemingly greater purposes are worked out in history. In the deepest possible sense, God works collaboratively as Trinity: the Father in partnership with the Son and with the Holy Spirit in the great dramas of creation and redemption. The deepest expression of the nature of God is that of an open community of persons and a vital part of that community is expressed through a common labour of love in which others are invited to participate. The Father, the Son and the Holy Spirit, separately and in concert, are both senders and enablers of others in the great mission of God in his world. Those who are called and sent by God are themselves to be senders and enablers as that mission is extended in each generation.

There are many examples in the Bible of collaborative working and collaborative wisdom. The Pentateuch in two different places recounts the story of Moses' struggle to adequately fulfil the range of his responsibilities in leading and settling disputes among the people.[1] The consequences of that struggle are serious both for leader and people: there is great discontent among the one despite exhaustion in the other. The answer to the problem is the sharing of that responsibility in different ways with those nominated and appointed by the people of God.

In the later parts of the Old Testament, both kings and prophets work closely with others in the particular work they have been given. Elijah at his most isolated, dejected and alone is taught valuable lessons about the resources available to him among the people of God and is sent back to commission others to the task to which they and he are called together.[2] Nehemiah and Ezra are masters at deploying the gifts of different groups among the returning exiles in different ways in order to accomplish a common task.

Jesus himself is continually calling people to him in order to enable them in ministry, generally alongside others and not in isolation. The Twelve and the Seventy are sent out two by two and not individually. As we have seen, the apostles continue the pattern seen not only in the appointing of the Seven (a passage with deliberate echoes of the visit to Moses by Jethro), but also in the emergence of the mission teams of Paul's journeys and in the ethos of ministry reflected in the New Testament epistles.

The calling and enabling of others to share in the work of ministry should therefore not be seen as some minor part or add-on optional extra to the vocation of the ordained Christian minister and leader. This aspect of ministry is an essential part of their work to which they should expect to devote a significant amount of their time and energy and seek to develop appropriate skills.

As we have seen, the Church has recovered in the second half of this century a strong emphasis on the vocation of the whole people of God to service, using different gifts in different ways. Ministry is first and foremost the calling of all those who are baptised Christians – not simply of those who are ordained. The ministry of the ordained derives from and is secondary to the call of the whole Church to service. Often, this renewed emphasis on the priesthood of all believers is seen, by implication, as leading to a decrease in the significance of the ministry of the ordained. The reverse is, in fact, the case. The more we believe in the ministry of the whole people of God, the more vital the ministry of the ordained becomes, particularly in this third dimension of *episcope*. Like most things in the kingdom of God, a congregation of Christian people do not begin to use their gifts in ministry simply by accident or through the spontaneous promptings of the Holy Spirit. Clear oversight is needed by those in whom proper authority is invested in order to bring out and develop the gifts of each Christian for the benefit not only of the Church but of our wider society.

When the Church's concept of ordained ministry has been one-dimensional only (focused around the ministry or the Word, or of the sacraments, or even around both) then there has been a corresponding negating and de-grading of the ministry of the whole people of God. In order for the ministry and gifts of the whole people of God to be developed and recognised, we need a concept of ordained ministry which is truly three-dimensional: grounded in service to others; focused in the enabling and sustaining ministries of Word and sacrament; and giving due priority through *episcope* to the support, nurture and sustaining of others in ministry.

Resourcing Ministry to the Whole of Life

There is a loss and a danger if this enabling and resourcing of ministry is seen as simply the supporting of ministry within the local congregation. There is a tendency for growing churches to become centrifugal in respect of the energy of their lay members as well as of their clergy, and for the horizons of effort and of personal development to shrink to that which benefits the life of a single church. Part of the task of *episcope* is to ensure that a congregation's horizon in respect of their vision is clearly set upon the building of the kingdom of God throughout the world, not simply the development of a single congregation in a single place. In part this happens through the example and model provided by the clergy as we noted in Chapter 6; in part through preaching; in part through the concerns supported in public and private prayer and financially by a congregation; in part through a careful oversight of where the energies of church members are directed and taking care to support and affirm those whose main call to ministry lies beyond the local congregation.

Many of the ordained need to recover confidence and do some fresh thinking in this area. Those whose main vocation can be expressed through their daily work will often need affirmation and support; help in discerning where God is at work (in both senses of the phrase); help in balancing time and priorities; a listening and confidential ear in areas of ethical difficulty or in puzzling through the challenges of giving a consistent Christian witness. Not all of this support can be given through one to one contact between church member and vicar – unless we are to stay permanently with the pastoral way of being Church, described in Appendix 2. Much will be provided through supportive and creative small groups or courses.[3] Yet those responsible for oversight of the local church will set the tone and the direction and the horizons in which this kind of discussion, affirmation and support can take place. Again this is done through reflection on the themes of our preaching; through spending time with people in the workplace as well as in the church or home; through listening and learning about the pressures on the lives of others; through remembering to pray for the working lives of others; through affirmation and concern.

Similarly, care will need to be taken by the church and those who watch over its life to affirm and guide every Christian through their different vocations and responsibilities in the area of family life. We live in a society in which there is an astonishing diversity in patterns of living and where many individuals navigate their ways through very complex demands. For those who are married there will need to be continued reflection on the call to faithfulness; to lifelong commitment; to the priority of the marriage relationship; to working through the changes which life brings within that relationship. Particular care will need to be taken, especially when working with new converts, that Christian faith and Christian ministry do not themselves become disruptive of marriage and family life in unhealthy ways.

Those who are parents need opportunities for reflection and guidance on this part of their God-given calling and responsibilities not only at the beginning of that responsibility but as their children grow and change. For the many who find themselves in complex step-families, particularly where one or both partners have been married before, there may be a need for continual encouragement and support, especially in times of change and adjustment. Many in our congregations will value support and creative thinking in terms of their responsibilities towards their own parents in the light of their Christian faith. There will be some who are deeply disappointed in the ways in which their lives have not (as it seems) been fulfilled either through their not marrying or through being able to become parents or both. Others will find themselves wrestling with questions about their own sexuality in the context of a Church which is itself wrestling deeply with these issues.

One of the great temptations of the industrial age has been to divide life into different compartments: the public world of work; the private and domestic world of home; the semi-public world of leisure activities and hobbies – with the three areas seldom meeting or interacting.[4] It is possible for the character, values and personality of the same individual to be very different in each of these spheres of life. A former chairman of an international fast food chain is famously quoted as saying: 'My priorities in life are God, my family and McDonald's Hamburgers – and when I get to work I reverse the order.' This dis-integration of individuals and communities is not a good way to live and there are continual signs of a deep hunger within society for the re-integration of the different dimensions of living, part of a deeper hunger for God.

Often, where people have a Christian commitment, church will simply fit into the semi-public world of hobbies and leisure activities. Christian faith will only seep very slowly into work-world or home-world. In other situations, church-world becomes a fourth, separate and self-contained sphere of life: somewhere where we are a different person again from the other three places. Yet the capacity at least is there for Christian faith to become the part of our lives which allows for the integration of separate existences and personalities as we seek to live out our lives in the context of God's love and grace and our particular vocation. For that integration to begin to happen the worlds of work, home and leisure must all be acknowledged and affirmed within the life of the local congregation. This means in turn that those responsible for *episcope* within that local church need to consciously order its life to keep pushing back the horizons of its vision. It is a paradox that the more directly clergy take on the responsibility of leadership and the development of a local congregation as part of their vocation, the more the danger multiplies of the vision of that church shrinking to encompass only its own development or that of like-minded churches. The very use of the term 'leader' as the primary description of the ordained minister immediately highlights the importance of what happens to build up and extend the ministry of a local congregation as opposed to the building and establishing of the kingdom of God.

Resourcing Ministry Specific to the Churches

There are clear limits to a minister's role in resourcing ministry to the whole of life. It will be important, as we have seen, to keep horizons wide and broad and to maintain a vision of the kingdom; to encourage, sometimes to encourage and counsel people individually; to facilitate conversation and reflection about the whole of life through sermons, courses and small groups; to network those who may be doing similar jobs or be in similar family situations. However, the exercise of *episcope* here does not involve taking on responsibility for the way in which people do their jobs or carry out their family responsibilities. *Episcope* means drawing alongside, watching, prayerfully supporting and encouraging and, occasionally, perhaps, offering a word of correction.

The minister's role in resourcing ministry specific to the churches is very different and new skills are involved. The minister has a share, possibly the major share, in identifying a need; in seeking those with the gifts and time available to meet that need; inviting them to take part; supporting and sustaining them in ministry; and dealing with any problems or difficulties which may arise. In most cases, those who offer for volunteer lay ministry will be very highly motivated and will invest a great deal of themselves in what they are doing. In terms of their own lives and faith and understanding of God, a very great deal is at stake. In a medium-sized congregation the minister may find herself exercising *episcope* over 60 or more people who are involved in some aspect of Christian service within the congregation in choirs, music group, childrens' groups and uniformed organisations, Church Council and committees, home groups and visiting schemes. The tasks themselves need to be done well for the sake of the whole body of Christ in that place but also for the volunteers who give their time and energy for the sake of their commitment to Christ. The following principles attempt to describe good practice for this aspect of *episcope* in local church leadership.

1. Episcope as a Shared Responsibility

It would be tragic if the Church as a whole were to move away from a concept of ministry in which the ordained minister *does* everything, only to take on a concept of ministry in which the ordained *decide* everything. To say that *episcope* is a part of the responsibility of the ordained within a local church does not mean that this aspect of ministry should be exclusively the preserve of the clergy. Churchwardens in an Anglican parish and Stewards in a Methodist Circuit are called to exercise *episcope* as part of their office. A Parochial Church Council has legal and theological responsibilities for oversight of the life of a congregation in partnership with the incumbent. The wise incumbent will take care to set up a small body of people who will share in the oversight either of the whole church or different areas of ministry, and particularly the oversight and development of lay volunteer ministry within the congregation. This small group might go by a number of different names: standing committee; extended staff meeting; leadership team; or even elders meeting. It will develop in different ways according to the tradition of the church. However, one of its key functions, in addition to handling questions of overall vision and direction, will be shared oversight of ministry, both policies and personnel.

2. Differentiation of Tasks and Responsibilities

Although each person's contribution to the life of a local church is equally important, it is common sense to make some kind of differentiation between the very different range of responsibilities carried by different individuals. The co-ordinator of children's groups working with five other volunteers and over 20 children has a different kind of task entirely from the person on the rota for dusting the buildings once a month. It is not that one task is more important than the other. Each is vital. But the different kinds of training, ongoing support, entry into the task, and induction, will be very different.

Rota ministries

Many simple, diaconal acts of service within a local church will be most efficiently and fairly organised through a rota. These will mainly be tasks which just about anyone can do: clean the church; organise refreshments after services or social events; steward and welcome at services; cut the grass; tidy the grounds and undertake routine maintenance on the building. Ideally those who have gifts in and concern for a particular area of church life will organise and head up the rota but sharing in these kinds of tasks would normally be open to everyone in the congregation. In practice, the best way of recruitment will normally be through personal approach rather than by asking for volunteers. Drawing people in to this kind of Christian service is often an ideal way to begin to welcome and affirm those who are new in the congregation. However, if the principles of diaconal ministry above are to be taken seriously, those who exercise more directly spiritual 'leadership' will also want to take their place.

Fostering a sense of common ownership of the task is important. A regular letter when the rota arrives, thanking people for their continued service and reminding them of the importance of the task, is very worthwhile. Good, simple induction into what the task requires and training or instruction into any safety rules or pieces of equipment is vital. Those who organise a rota where people's turns come round very infrequently (monthly or more) will find they need to ring people up week by week to remind them they are on duty. Giving people permission to withdraw from this ministry when they need to will be important, as is saying thank-you in appropriate ways both public and private when that time comes.

Team ministries

Many other common tasks within a congregation will require some degree of Christian or personal maturity, particular gifts, and sometimes training or experience. Rather than being seen as the preserve of particular individuals, these tasks are best undertaken by teams of people, working together towards a common goal and meeting together with greater or lesser frequency depending upon the different tasks. Examples of teams in local churches might include those leading the parent and toddler groups; those who lead different groups for children on Sundays or during the week; those who read in church or lead intercessions; those who share in the preaching ministry; the music group and/or choir; those who co-ordinate the church's work with different sections of the community or who support the local primary school.

Because of the particular gifts and maturity needed, membership of these teams would not generally be open to all and recruitment will not be through asking for volunteers but through seeking to discern people's gifts and vocation within the ministry of the whole body of Christ (see below). Much more thorough induction will be needed than for someone who agrees to be a member of a rota and, in some circumstances, a trial period might be helpful both for the prospective team member and for the team itself. Again, the tasks and expectations will need to be clearly defined by the team leader and some written documentation is helpful.

Good team meetings will seek to build relationships and fellowship between the different members (through people telling their stories, ice-breaker questions, study together, and social events); to continually refresh the vision for the particular task; to provide a small amount of 'in-service' training (supplemented by other one-off events); as well as focus on the task in hand. A group of children's group leaders which gathers simply to work through a committee-style agenda, and plan next term's programme and the Christmas party, will not grow and flourish as much as the team which meets to share something of themselves, of their common vision for the task, which deliberately encourages one another and gives a part of each meeting to thinking together about the broader issues involved in teaching the Christian faith to children.

Those working as part of a ministry team within a congregation will value the occasional opportunity to review their ministry in an informal way and also to indicate for how long they may be able to sustain their involvement. Within a team which is working well there is scope for correction and development of individuals in any area of ministry. People may also be helped by being pointed towards good books, resources or training courses. Whatever we do, we all appreciate being thanked and encouraged on a regular basis!

Leaders of teams and groups

Some of the teams within the church may well be led by the clergy themselves. However, the majority in a developing congregation will be the responsibility of lay leaders. Team leaders and those who lead small groups of Christians within the church will need different skills and gifts again and often a more developed sense of vocation to the particular ministry. Appointment to a position of significant responsibility will only be after reasonably wide consultation and the appointment will need to be owned and approved by the whole church through its elected council. It may be appropriate in many instances for team and group leaders to be commissioned publicly during worship, perhaps setting aside a particular service each year for this purpose. Additional policy guidelines may be sensible: limiting each person normally to one leadership responsibility is an excellent guideline as is a notional time limit/review of post every three years. The ideal form of training and preparation will be the apprentice-style model where the new leader has the opportunity to work within the team or work with an established home group leader before taking on responsibility themselves. This in turn will mean that part of being a leader of a team or small group implies seeking out and giving initial training to those who are growing into leadership in an apprentice-type system. Because tasks are harder to define, describing them on paper is more demanding but well worth the effort involved.

Like team members, team and small group leaders need support. This in part is provided through relationship with one another and those responsible for their support, in part through further ongoing training, and in part through the continual refreshing and re-visioning which can come through the best kind of leaders' meetings: more on this below.

Leaders who take care of leaders

In a smaller congregation the vicar may be the most natural person to exercise oversight over all those who lead teams and small groups in the parish. As the life of the congregation develops, however, the incumbent will need to take careful note of the number of people he or she is expected to support personally in their ministry. Once this number exceeds ten or a dozen people, it is highly likely that 'support' will come to mean 'come to a meeting every couple of months and ring me if you have any problems'. The pattern of lay ministry and leadership by this point has become 'sink or swim'. The chances are that lay leaders will be under strain and pressure and beginning to drop out of their tasks and responsibilities and, what is more, it is becoming harder to find new leaders to take their place.

At this point in the church's development it becomes essential to develop the ministry of those who can share *episcope* in a much more direct way: leaders who themselves take care of leaders. A church with a developed network of under-fives groups needs a recognised co-ordinator who can nurture the teams for each session and the session leaders. Someone in this position can find themselves leading a team of upwards of 20 volunteers. A series of groups for children and young people likewise needs an overall co-ordinator who is able to give shape to the work, oversee the different teams as well as take care of the members. House group leaders in particular need pro-active, regular support. Carl George advocates the appointment of leader-coaches on a ratio of no more than one coach to five leaders.[5] Those who exercise this kind of ministry in a local congregation clearly need the right gifts, experience, training and recognition by the congregation. The training in particular may require financial provision by the church as a whole. Diocesan resources may be available help. In some instances they will be paid members of staff. However, in other circumstances they will remain volunteers, perhaps giving a substantial amount of their working week to this kind of ministry and supporting themselves through other means. To the clergy, the small group of people able and equipped to serve in this way will be close colleagues. Relationships will need to be built up and developed within this group, lay and ordained, who share a common calling to the ministry of oversight of others' ministries within the same congregation.

Does this distinction between different kinds of ministries mean the development of a hierarchy within the congregation? Certainly it can do exactly that, particularly if the minister's role and job description involves them in continually moving up the hierarchy so that, in the end, their only responsibility becomes caring for those who lead the leaders. As I have consistently argued in the preceding chapters, the minister must continue to be *diakonos* and *presbyteros* as well as exercising *episcope*. This means in practice that the vicar will combine significant elements of 'hands on' service of others with the enabling and oversight of others' ministry: a slice of the total 'pie' of ministry is a much better model than moving up a pyramid (or down a plantpot[6]). Most congregations feel alienated by organisational diagrams of churches which portray them as humble members of the flock, giving prominence and power to those in different grades of leadership. Great care needs to be taken in developing appropriate structures for *episcope* to continually ensure that they are genuinely enabling and affirming of the ministry of the whole people of God.

3. Gifts and Vocation

In order for lay ministry to flourish and develop within a local congregation in a healthy and life-giving way, a number of key Christian concepts need to become part of the way a church intuitively thinks and responds. Attempting to develop the structures for lay ministry without first teaching the principles that underly that ministry will lead to continual frustration. Foundational is the belief that *all of God's people are called to service* in one way or another, described above. Paul's teaching upon the church as the *Body of Christ* and *different and complementary gifts* given to different members of the body is also of first importance.[7] Members of the congregation will need to be helped both to understand the range of gifts people might offer the church, and to discern their own particular charism(s).[8]

Many churches will need help in moving from an *ethos of volunteers* to an *ethos of vocation*. Often as a visitor to a congregation I see in the notice sheet or hear in the notices fervent appeals for people to offer their services in this or that area of church life. To ask for volunteers for many ministries is often to diminish their importance and the gifts of the people who may be called to do them. We are actually saying that 'anyone can do this'. It is better to identify a shortlist of people who have the necessary qualities and then approach them directly, explaining the need, the time involved and inviting them to consider prayerfully whether this might be something they could offer. The people approached are all affirmed by this kind of invitation (even if they decline). They are convinced that this must be an important ministry and worth giving time to. The congregation – including visitors – are safeguarded from continual appeals for help which often appeal to their sense of guilt as a motivator (the Sunday School will collapse unless . . .) and which combine to give the impression that the congregation is run by a handful of hard-pressed volunteers perpetually on the brink of exhaustion.

4. Legal Requirements and Pastoral Safeguards

Areas of ministry that involve children are now covered by legislation and every church is duty bound to follow the letter of the law and morally bound to promote best practice. The Children Act 1989 and Home Office Codes of Practice, Working Together (1991) and Safe from Harm (1993) are the principal documents, but reform still continues and new codes of practice are promised. The legislation itself can be complex. Denominations and Anglican dioceses have produced their own guidelines (which vary in quality and clarity).[9] The area of oversight of those working with children is one of great responsibility and pastoral sensitivity and must be given priority both by the ordained and by Church councils and lay leaders.

Several dioceses have also given attention in recent years to sensible guidelines and pastoral safeguards for those working with adults as well as with children and young people. Although these apply in the first instance to clergy for whom they are written, many sections can be used as helpful guidelines for those involved in shared pastoral care, pastoral counselling and prayer ministries and the leadership of small groups.[10] Any church which develops lay ministry to a significant degree in these areas will need to develop, borrow or adapt policies for the oversight of these ministries and, again, invest in the right kind of training and preparation for each form of ministry.[11]

5. Manageable, Defined Tasks

The popular secular management handbook, *The One-Minute Manager* has been a best-seller for so many years because it succinctly sums up very concisely and memorably three essential skills involved in *episcope*: the oversight of people.[12] The first, and probably the most vital, is the ability to sum up and define a task and objectives clearly enough for someone else to understand them. The ability to do this is a skill rather than a gift conferred at ordination and it is acquired, like most skills, through a mixture of some training and lots of practice. Upon the minister's ability to clearly break down and define what is involved in taking on a particular role within the church will depend a great deal of a church's effectiveness in lay ministry. What exactly are you asking me to do, vicar?

Recognising that clergy also have a tendency to pass on unmanageable tasks to others is also very important. Most schemes for shared pastoral care in parishes break down because the span of care envisaged is simply too large. Lay pastoral workers who have families and full-time jobs are asked to visit regularly long lists of people who are on the edge of church life.[13] The results of this delegation of unmanageable tasks are frustration all round: most of the people remain unvisited; the pastoral team member never comes to the end of the task and feels perpetually guilty and unmotivated; the minister resolves never to delegate again.[14]

Once the task has been defined, it needs to be communicated.

Written communication is an essential support to the spoken word. Writing things down focuses the mind and allows us to pass on quite complex ideas efficiently and in a way which can be permanently remembered. Written job descriptions are standard in the world of work not only because they are in some sense contractual documents but because the task which is being described and defined is seen as important enough to want to do well. Need we say more?[15]

6. Low Initial Training – High Ongoing Support[16]

The model of training and deployment for lay ministry in many congregations is high initial training (especially if provided by a deanery or diocese) followed by low or non-existent ongoing support – the 'sink or swim' model. Many clergy pass that model of ministry onto lay people in their congregations because that is exactly what they have experienced themselves: three years of college training followed by a closely supervised curacy followed by an incumbency in which the vicar rings for help if there is a crisis. Reversing the traditional patterns is a much better way. There are not many ministries within the local church which need a vast amount of advanced training and preparations. Most ministerial skills are best learned through continual but supervised practice in which there can be time for reflection and learning afterwards. In these situations the motivation to learn is much higher; what is learned can immediately be applied; there is an incentive to study insofar as it is relevant to the existing situation. But most ministerial situations also create the need for regular feedback and support and the provision of that support is a necessary function of *episcope*.

In describing and analysing the support needed by small group leaders, Carl George identifies three important felt needs, which transfer well to other ministries as well: the need for continued envisioning about the purpose of this ministry and the role it plays in the wider kingdom of God; the need for peer interaction and support – to talk with others who are engaged in a similar kind of task; and the need for continuous retraining and learning relevant to their situation. Putting these three elements together, George has constructed a pattern for a leaders' meeting around the acronym VHS: a two-hour meeting for the leadership community constructed around Vision – Huddle – Skill.[17] The meeting is as far from a traditional housegroup-leaders' meeting (focused around feedback and planning, in a single large group) as it is possible to go. Vision is a combination of quality worship, prepared stories about what is happening around the groups, biblical input and looking ahead by those responsible for leading the church. Huddle is time in small groups of leaders, with leader-coaches, talking in detail about what is going well and not so well and how you feel about it. Leader-coaches will also have been in contact with their leaders in between the VHS meetings to offer debriefing, support and encouragement and will occasionally visit the group meetings themselves. Skill is 40 minutes of training in the different component parts of being a small group leader. Apprentice leaders have the opportunity for 'basic training' during the Huddle time. The jargon and titles may not appeal to everyone but the need for support is a prerequisite of ministry.

7. Review, Rest and Renewal

Regular supervision and support will be a feature then of most lay ministry for those who are part of teams or leading teams. Regular review of what is happening in a church with a great deal of active lay ministry is also important. Those exercising *episcope* will need to teach and model good principles of rest and renewal but also take time at regular intervals to see how people are doing; to suggest they think about a change of direction or a sabbatical every few years; or think about handing the ministry on to others who are emerging within the congregation.

Resourcing Ministry Beyond the Local Church

Finally, part of exercising oversight over the ministry of others within the local church is having an eye on the need for ministry beyond the local church not only in the local community but in the wider Church. The principle of the Vineyard churches, that a congregation should seek always to give its best people away through church-planting or in other means, is a valuable one for a congregation to take to heart. Para-church mission agencies (such as the Mothers' Union[18] or Youth for Christ) need the service of able leaders who bring the experience of many years of ministry in the local church to their wider concerns. A church rich in musicians may well find it is able to export at least some of its wealth to a neighbouring congregation.[19] There is still a great need to pray and to encourage those who may want to explore a vocation to the ordained ministry, which will normally involve being prepared to serve the wider Church, in order to continue in time this ministry of *episcope* which is so sorely needed.

14

EPISCOPE IN LOCAL CHURCH LEADERSHIP (3): WATCHING OVER YOURSELF AND OTHERS – BALANCING MINISTRY IN THREE DIMENSIONS

Instructions to ministers of the local church to 'Watch over yourselves' go back at least as far as Paul's address to the Ephesian presbyters.[1] The apostle, we presume, has in mind both mutual oversight in which people watched over one another but also each person taking care of themselves as a responsible servant of Christ. This care is within the general context of the love of God for each person he has created including those called to serve him through ordained ministry.

Never has this need for mutual oversight and watching over oneself been more important than when the Church is called to make a transition of cultures to become once again a missionary Church in a post-Christian era. If one of the keys to the healthy life and development of a local congregation is the ministry of the incumbent then it is in the highest interest of the congregation, the diocese and the vicar to stay in the best possible shape. For most people that will mean a high level of support is needed.

In all the ways outlined in the opening chapters, clergy are committed to a high stress job in a changing Church and society. Day by day parish clergy are coming into contact with people in distress of varying kinds in communities in which there are fewer resources of faith to help in times of great crisis. There is a great deal to be done and a sense that resources are scarce. Uncertainty about their role and ministry is combined, even where that role is clear, with a vocation to bring about change in the congregations among whom they are called to serve. Becoming an agent of change itself generates a high degree of personal stress. The clerical role can often lead the clergy to become isolated in their patterns of living and in their relationships.[2]

Clergy therefore need support in significant measure and ought to expect and be expected to invest a significant amount of time in the sustaining of the different dimensions of their lives. At a very basic and mechanical level, if a simple machine such as a car or a lawn mower is not serviced regularly then it will certainly break down. If any person's lifestyle is such that they themselves are not being nurtured and cared for then eventually their capacity to give out, do their work well and even sustain their closest relationships will be diminished.[3]

Diocesan and Denominational Responsibility

Who takes responsibility for caring for the clergy? The answer to the question is not as simple as it seems. At one level, certainly, that responsibility rests with the diocesan bishop (or denominational equivalent) and those who share with him in the task of *episcope* over clergy and churches in what is normally a wide geographical area. In most dioceses the role will be shared by suffragan bishops, archdeacons, directors of training and, to some degree, rural deans. Most clergy value the time and support that bishops and arch-deacons are able to give but recognise that the span of care a diocesan bishop works with may be 1:200 or higher. Even an arch-deacon will commonly be called to relate to up to 100 clergy.[4] Care and support which is given from a diocese and from most denominational structures will of necessity be limited to very occasional and somewhat formal contacts, particularly with the diocesan bishop. These may not in themselves be sufficient to allow the natural barriers which are there to be broken down and real trust to begin to grow.[5]

A diocese is able to provide greater care in times of great crisis but will be as concerned also for the interests of the congregation and the wider Church as for the individual, particularly if there is a risk of scandal. Each diocese forms its own policy on ministry and ministerial support, appraisal and pastoral conversations, and in general terms much progress has been made here in recent years. In some dioceses these conversations are voluntary, in others mandatory. At their best, formal pastoral conversations can be extremely helpful and provide a means to review ministry over a one- or two-year period and set major directions for the future in terms of training or development within a framework of accountability and a good working relationship. Less commonly, they can be unsatisfactory encounters with someone one may not know particularly well and who does not seem to be properly prepared, with no obvious positive benefits.[6]

Peer Support

Whether or not a pastoral conversation or appraisal exists at all or is helpful probably lies beyond the power of the individual incumbent. Even where the care and contact provided by the diocese is entirely good, positive and helpful (as it often is), it cannot be enough. Much more is needed to sustain ministry. Peer support can be invaluable at a number of levels but has the potential to be a cause of stress in others. Clergy in a deanery, an ecumenical fraternal or even a single parish often function as competitors, increasing one another's stress levels rather than offering support.[7] However, where this kind of dynamic can be broken down through the building of relationship, community and common goals there can be a great deal of mutual support.

A particular responsibility rests with those who lead the meetings where there is a potential for support to ensure that this kind of care is facilitated, not inhibited. Peer support is also a possible (although not inevitable) consequence of clergy clusters, groups and formal teams. There is also the potential for very real peer support and fellowship in the kinds of mixed clergy and lay groups within a particular congregation described in the previous chapters.

What are the elements which can transform a rather dry business meeting of peers in ministry into a community where there is mutual support and care for one another? Six elements stand out particularly.

First and foremost, **time** must be given within the formal meeting structure to build relationship and community. These things do not happen by themselves. Clergy normally have well-honed social skills which enable them to conduct superficial conversations with a variety of different people with great ease. This ability, combined with well constructed personal defences and a desire to help others rather than be helped themselves, means that it is possible to navigate through chapter, fraternal and parish staff meetings without disclosing personal need at any level, and simply projecting confidence to all.

Building community to the point where mutual support becomes a reality amongst clergy therefore involves building trust within relationships to the point where those defences can be relaxed a little and some help can be received. This will mean spending time within a meeting telling one's own story and listening to that of others. It will mean being prepared to think about questions together which enable mutual sharing and support.[8] It will mean developing shared traditions and memories (cream cakes at meetings; parties when people arrive or leave). It may mean taking time outside meetings to meet socially and giving priority to those social events. An annual residential for members of a chapter or fraternal can move the group on more than in 18 months of occasional meetings.

Second, it will mean **study** together around common themes. Study is itself renewing and stimulating, as we have seen. Study together is a way of developing a set of common concepts and vocabulary among people who have very diverse views. For that reason it may be best to study together something which is not too close to anyone's perspective or point of view. Reading a book together; doing some bible study; looking at journal articles around a common theme; seeing a film or play and discussing its implications together – all build a sense of community which leads to mutual support. About half the time allocated for clergy staff meetings, chapter meetings and fraternals should be given to this kind of sharing together and study. The business of the meeting (including listening to visiting speakers who will not in general contribute to this support dynamic in the group) should be kept for the other half of the meeting: one of the main purposes is to build the network of mutual support.

Thirdly, the level of **disclosure** in the group and certainly in the quiet conversations that happen around it needs to go beyond that of polite, surface conversation. The kind of community building and sharing will go some way towards that end. However, the level of disclosure set by those responsible for leading any particular group will have a huge influence on the tone and the worth of the meeting.

Fourthly, there must be an element of common **worship** which is meaningful and connects in some way with each member of the group. With a scattered deanery chapter or clergy fraternal which is meeting infrequently, it will help if the shared worship connects in some way through the daily prayer and worship of each member, perhaps through common prayers or a shared cycle of prayer.

Fifthly, where the group has formal **leadership** (as in a parish staff meeting or a clergy team headed by a team rector), the person leading the team will need to spend time with individuals in formal and informal ways. This will need to be, in part, proactive time (that is, arranged by the team leader) with a view to coming to understand in depth the job, pressures, rhythms, strengths and weaknesses of the team member. Where the team includes lay people or non-stipendiary ministers, this will mean understanding their world of work as well as their ministry in and through the church. In part, it will also mean ensuring good and easy access for each member of the team to the team leader, ensuring both the physical and psychological barriers to this are overcome. Worth, appreciation and respect need to be articulated.

Sixth and finally, mutual **support** will emerge gradually at different levels in a team or community where all of these things are taking place. Yet that support will also develop by being explicitly encouraged and modelled both by the leader of the group and by its members.

Not every ordained person has access to a group of peers which is or which has the capacity to become a source of peer support. Where this is the case, the formation of a group of like-minded individuals, lay or ordained, becomes very important. Irvine sees the formation of such groups as one of the important solutions to the problems of clergy stress and his book contains excellent guidelines for the purpose, formation and setting up of such support groups.[9]

Personal Responsibility

Both diocesan support and peer support are likely to be available to different degrees in different contexts but are unlikely, even where they work at their best, to supply all that is needed. The nature of the Church as an institution and of Christian ministry are such that the final responsibility for ensuring adequate means of support are in place needs to rest in the last analysis with the individual concerned. The more the Church develops a culture in which support, supervision and help are seen as normative rather than exceptional and in some sense a sign of weakness, the better it will be for the health of all ministers.

The kinds of support an individual might seek to initiate will vary from person to person and at different stages of life and experience. It is unlikely that all the support needed will come from a single individual. A matrix of different kinds of support is a more helpful model. For the majority of clergy much of the time some kind of relationship with a spiritual director will be important. The development of a person's spiritual life lies at the heart of ministry. It is too great a responsibility to be carried alone. Doctors are not allowed to treat either themselves or members of their families for physical or psychological illness for the very good reason that it will be hard to be objective. It is many times more difficult for a minister to be objective about his or her spirituality and its relationship to ministry than it is for a doctor to be objective about physical symptoms.

Many will be helped also by an ongoing relationship with someone who acts as a mentor, senior friend or work consultant where open discussions about the pattern and detail of the job one is called to do can take place within the context of a supportive relationship, with a measure of accountability, but outside of the formal structures of the church. This kind of relationship is particularly important at the beginning of ordained ministry and in times of transition, especially to a first incumbency. Others who engage in a great deal of one-to-one conversations will want to consider and put in place some form of pastoral supervision of those relationships. The net of support which is constructed from diocesan frameworks, peer groups, informal structures and individual relationships initiated by the minister will in turn create opportunities for continued personal development and retraining which will be a creative part of a lifetime of ministry.

Self-Awareness

Stress comes in two forms in parish ministry. The first kind is the stress of the normal everyday experience. Day by day and week by week ordained ministry brings its sorrows, joys and pressures. Sensible rhythms of time off, re-creation, networking and support need to be established, sustained and adjusted through life so that strength, vitality and vision are maintained from year to year. The second type of stress is the kind which results from a particularly demanding period of life or ministry which could not perhaps be predicted or expected: a personal bereavement combined with financial problems in the parish; a series of unconnected but extremely demanding funerals; a breakdown in relationships with or between leading members of the church; one or two hugely demanding pastoral situations.

It is very important in exercising oversight over oneself that care is taken to build self-awareness about demanding periods of ministry whether these are part of the rhythm of the year or unplanned. To some extent the diary and the timetable can be adjusted to take account of particularly heavy periods of the year. Additional time off can be planned after a busy festival or towards the end of a demanding building project. Recognising the physical, emotional and spiritual signs of stress within oneself means that you begin to learn and listen for early warning signals which suggest you either need to ease up or plan some space when the immediate crisis is past. When we keep going through these early warnings we quickly find ourselves in the wastelands of stress: exhaustion, bad temper, depression, addictive and dependent cycles of behaviour, vulnerability to temptation, ill-health and damaged relationships.

Developing self-awareness is a vital part of formation for ministry. It happens through intentional dialogue both with others and, most importantly, with ourselves. There are important ways to facilitate that dialogue. One is the keeping of an honest journal particularly in demanding periods of life. The second is to build into life regular periods for reflection and review, hopefully with a supportive guide in which the journal provides some of the raw material for analysis.

Balancing Ministry in Three Dimensions

As we have seen, the task and nature of ordained ministry cannot be adequately embraced by any of the single concepts normally used as a shorthand. Neither 'minister' nor 'deacon', 'priest' nor 'presbyter' adequately catches all that needs to be caught. 'Leader' carries with it too many overtones from the secular world and too few from the Scriptures and the tradition. A much richer, three-dimensional picture of ministry is needed for all of the ordained which embraces *diakonia*, the presbyteral ministries of Word and sacrament, and *episcope*.

Each person who is ordained will balance these three elements of their ministry in different measure according to the job they are called to do and, to some degree, the balance of their own gifts and abilities. Titles may reflect that balance or may not. The title 'Bishop' will normally be accurate in that those called to that office by God and the Church will find that the majority of their ministry will be in the dimension of *episcope*. They are also likely to find that *diakonia* and presbyteral ministries should not be left behind completely if that calling is to be fulfilled after the pattern of Christ. Those called to be ordained and to remain deacons should find that the main weight of their ministry is in the area of *diakonia*. However, they will find that they cannot avoid *episcope*, oversight at least of themselves and probably of others if they are encouraging others to serve at all. They will also function to some degree at least in the presbyteral dimension: in the ministry of the Word and of prayer if not in the full range of the sacraments.

Those who are ordained priest or presbyter but not in full-time parish ministry will similarly find a three dimensional picture more helpful than a single concept in ordering and reflecting on their own ministry. The minister in secular employment, the hospital or prison chaplain, the theological college lecturer will find they are called to operate in different measure across the three dimensions. In parish ministry the mix will change from appointment to appointment and, as the church develops and grows, the mix of ministry should also be under continual review.

A Portfolio Approach

Balancing these different dimensions of ministry may seem, at first sight, to be impossibly complex. We naturally tend to want things to be simple: easy to understand and to put into practice. Therefore we search for simple ways of describing the task and nature of ordained ministry only to discover that much of what we find ourselves doing does not fit easily within that simple understanding.

The working lives of many people are complex and have several different dimensions. A ward sister is involved in the basics of nursing care, in managing the working lives of a team of colleagues and in representing the interests of her department within the wider arena of the hospital. A head of department in a comprehensive school, a police inspector, a section head in a factory, a tax inspector, a farmer or a mechanic with his own business have similar demands within their working life and, if they are Christians, may well be balancing these demands against those of a vocation to lay or perhaps ordained ministry. The clergy should not, therefore, shrink from a more complex way of seeing and describing their role simply because it is more complex. The test, in the longer term, is if the description is more helpful in enabling them to fulfil the ministry to which they have been called.

Charles Handy and others have described one of the features of modern working life as that of having not a single role but a portfolio of different kinds of work. The mix of the portfolio will change during different periods of a person's life according to the kind of job they are doing and the different responsibilities they have. Not every aspect of work within the portfolio will be paid: some may well be voluntary service. The balance between paid work and voluntary service, again, will shift in different periods of living.

The portfolio approach is a good way to balance the three dimensions of ministry (and for the ordained minister in full-time employment, to balance the whole of their living). At present, too many clergy have only one file in their mental portfolio of work: the file of 'ministry' or 'priesthood'. (See illustration on p. 190.) A great deal is crammed into that one file so that priorities are often confused rather than being well ordered. Other activity will not fit into the file at all and spills over onto the floor, increasing the inner and outer chaos of ministerial life.

Approaching ministry as three dimensional opens out two other major file divisions within the portfolio. The tasks and characteristics of ministry can be distributed and weighted then more evenly between these three dimensions of ministry. (See illustration on p. 191.) Each is acknowledged as a genuine aspect of ministerial vocation: files which are on the floor can be found a legitimate home within the portfolio. The balance between the different files will change according the exact make-up of a person's ministry, gifts, calling and stage of life. That balance will need to be reviewed regularly both by the person themselves, by those they serve and those who exercise oversight over them. However each dimension will need to be present at each different phase of life and ministry to some degree, and skills and character in each area will need to be developed continuously.

The Keys to *Episcope*: Discernment and Responsible Initiative

For each of the three dimensions of ministry, I have tried to define something of the spirituality of ministry in this dimension and a single quality or characteristic which is both a requirement and a consequence of this aspect of ministry. The spirituality of **diakonia** is that of **learning to listen** to God. The defining characteristic of this first dimension of ministry is **integrity** of life resulting from both the attitude and actions of a servant. The spirituality of the second dimension of ministry is that of **intercession**: prayer on behalf of others; and the defining characteristic is **holiness**.

The spirituality of **episcope** is perhaps harder to catch or to define. **Discernment** perhaps sums it up best of all: the ability to watch over other people and situations for their own good, health and protection and to keep watch in prayer; the ability to weigh situations before God and to form right and careful judgements which

191

affect the lives of others as well as one's own life. The quality of discernment is, in part, a gift of the Holy Spirit. In part it is developed and cultivated through the disciplines of a godly life; through continual exposure to that which is true, honourable, just, pure, pleasing, commendable, excellent and worthy of praise.[10] The exercise of *episcope* more than any other dimension of ministry calls for the making of good and godly decisions about situations and people, in which the guidance of the Holy Spirit is sorely needed.[11]

The quality at the heart of *episcope* is perhaps best described as **responsible initiative**. *Episcope* is an active not a passive dimension of ministry. Those who are called to this dimension of ministry will not be hasty in the making of decisions and in taking action; but nor will they leave situations as they are where things need to be changed and to be transformed, however costly those decisions might be. Ordained ministers in the Church of Jesus Christ need the capacity to make good decisions prayerfully and the initiative to carry those decisions through into action and transformation.

APPENDIX 1:

A CHART OF MINISTRY IN THREE DIMENSIONS

📁 **DIAKONIA**

- 📁 Simple, Hidden, Practical Acts of Service
- 📁 Service to the Community
- 📁 Competent and Careful Administration
- 📁 Listening to others
- 📁 Attitude
- 📁 Spirituality
- 📁 Serving and Being Served

> *Spirituality: Listening*
> *Characteristic: Integrity*

📁 **PRESBYTERAL MINISTRY**

- 📁 The Ministry of the Word
  - 📁 Study
  - 📁 Preaching
  - 📁 Catechesis
- 📁 The Ministry of the Sacraments
  - 📁 Baptism
  - 📁 Holy Communion

> *Spirituality: Intercession*
> *Characteristic: Holiness*

📁 **EPISCOPE**

- 📁 Vision, unity and transformation
- 📁 Enabling the Ministry of Others
- 📁 Watching over Yourself and Others

> *Spirituality: Discernment*
> *Characteristic: Responsible Initiative*

APPENDIX 2:

A MODEL OF CHURCHES ACCORDING TO THE DYNAMIC OF COMMUNITY

The following model attempts to describe a number of different dynamics which operate within local congregations according to size. The model was taken originally from a pamphlet produced in New York by Arlin Rothauge but has been substantially revised over a six-year period.[1]

The largest number of churches in the United Kingdom fall into the first category of church, called by Rothauge the *Family Church*. A family church consists of a congregation of up to 60 people,[2] although often the number involved will be less. In a family church, everyone in the congregation (more or less) knows everyone else. The feel of the church is that of an extended family. Often the key offices in the church are held by representatives of two or three human families or dynasties who pass on these roles among their own number. The family church is a durable structure, able to sustain itself through the ministries of different incumbents, who act (more or less) as

The Family Church

- 1–50 members
- Dominated by a few human dynasties
- 'Gatekeepers'
- Minister as chaplain to the family

The Pastoral Church

- 50–150 members (100 adults)
- Minister is pastor to everyone
- High expectations of personal care
- Pastoral Care ceiling

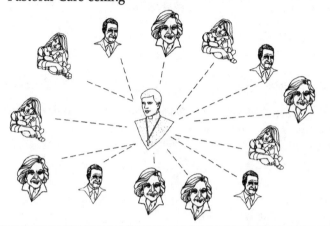

chaplain to the family, being there at times of crisis to offer care and support but not entrusted with the leadership and direction of the group. Surprisingly often in the common memory of a family church is an instance where the trust placed in an ordained minister has been betrayed. However, despite their durability, family churches can be hard to join. This is partly because it takes a long time to feel that you belong: you need to know and to be known by the majority of the congregation. It is partly also because family churches need to guard their boundaries informally but carefully. Only those who meet with the approval of those who act as gatekeepers to the community will be welcomed to be permanent members.

Where a church grows and develops beyond this size and stage it is normally through making the transition to a *Pastoral Church* dynamic. For this to happen there needs to be an entrusting of some degree of power and responsibility to the minister by the key lay people in the congregation and a letting go by the congregation of the need to know everyone else. In the pastoral church, the key relationship is between each member of the congregation and the ordained minister. There is a high expectation on the minister of personal attention and care, particularly during times of crisis. The pastoral church is the easiest of all of these models of church to join: all that is needed to belong is a relationship with the pastor. My sense is that most small to medium-sized churches which are seeing growth in their congregations are growing into this kind of a church. However, pastoral churches are exceedingly vulnerable to changes in the minister. Each time there is a change, a substantial proportion of the congregation will not make the transition to the new incumbent. Also, pastoral churches will continue to grow only until they reach their pastoral care ceiling. This is fixed at the

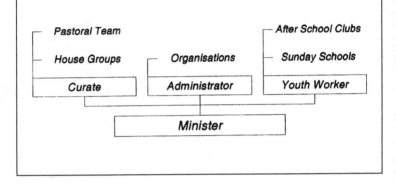

> ## *The Programme Church*
> - 150–400 members (100–300 adults)
> - Lay-led programmes
> - Extended pastoral care net
> - Minister resources programmes

incumbent's capacity to maintain relationships with every member of his or her congregation. Once that ceiling has been reached, new people may join the congregation but others will be leaving at an equal and balancing rate.

The level of this pastoral care ceiling will vary according to a number of variables but 100 adults is a good guide figure. It may be a little lower or higher depending on the energy and vitality of the vicar; on the levels of need and deprivation in the area; and on the proportion of new Christians within the congregation. The addition of another ordained member of staff, such as a curate in a title post, will raise the ceiling typically by about 30 people. However, the numbers attending church will fall again once that particular curate moves on. Once a church has reached its pastoral care ceiling, the minister in particular will tend to work at slightly more than his or her capacity, particularly if they are also working and praying for the church to grow. It is at this point that clergy are most vulnerable to developing addictive patterns of behaviour in relation to their pastoral work. It is a heady thing indeed to be continually needed by a large congregation of different people and the temptation is to work long hours – and yet still find that all of the work cannot be done.[3]

An increasingly common pattern for ordained ministry, as we have seen, is that of *Multiple Church Ministry* where the ordained minister(s) may serve a team, cluster or group of between two and seven or more congregations, often commuting some distance between the different communities by car on Sundays. These congregations themselves may be family or pastoral churches. As will be obvious, family churches are likely to be more resilient in these situations than pastoral churches, particularly if the same minister cannot be in the same place at the same time each Sunday

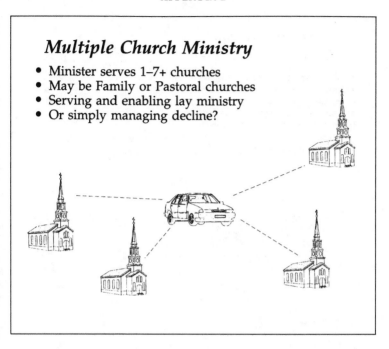

Multiple Church Ministry

- Minister serves 1–7+ churches
- May be Family or Pastoral churches
- Serving and enabling lay ministry
- Or simply managing decline?

morning. Where the pastoral church model is the only model for the growth of a congregation, however, the danger and the reality is that there is very little creative development in a multiple church ministry. The strategy is simply one of managing decline unless other ways forward can be found.

A better way forward for each of these kinds of churches is to attempt to develop into what we might call a *'Nurturing Communities' Church*.[4] This kind of church begins to develop when those responsible for oversight in a pastoral church begin to intentionally and deliberately build community between the different members of a congregation, and that community begins to be the primary expression of belonging and of mutual care and support within the church. The earlier this process begins, of course, the better and it would not be impossible to see a family church develop into a nurturing communities church if that was thought to be desirable. The growth of community structures will be both informal and formal. Informal structures begin to be nurtured and encouraged through social gatherings and projects outside of church services where real relationships can grow. Formal structures begin to evolve as the church forms small groups for mutual support and care.

The pastoral role of the minister shifts from that of being the primary carer to being the person who ensures that care is provided, whilst still exercising something of a caring role themselves. The minister needs to let go of the need to know and to care for every person within the congregation. The congregation need to let go of their need to know and to be cared for by the minister. Clearly, on this model, the minister needs very developed skills in the dimension of *episcope*: the ability to discern and develop the gifts of others; the ability to devolve the responsibility of care from the

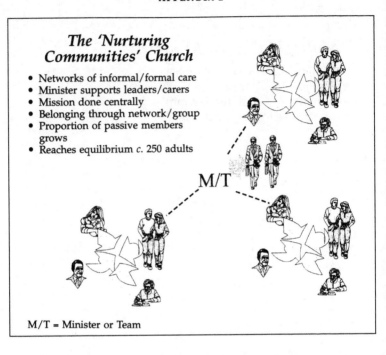

The 'Nurturing Communities' Church

- Networks of informal/formal care
- Minister supports leaders/carers
- Mission done centrally
- Belonging through network/group
- Proportion of passive members grows
- Reaches equilibrium *c.* 250 adults

M/T

M/T = Minister or Team

clergy to the whole body of Christ; the ability to guide and nurture the life of formal and informal communities as well as the life of individuals. Most commonly on this model, the responsibility for mission in the church remains with the church centrally and often with the clergy.

Churches which are able to develop along these lines will often evolve parallel structures of providing pastoral care and support to their congregations through both an expanding network of small groups and a lay team who share in the visiting of and contact with those who are not part of small groups. The principles involved in developing the ministries of these groups and teams are outlined in chapter 13. Through the building of a strong network of nurturing communities, a much larger congregation can be sustained and will grow. This has obvious benefits not only in the larger number of people who are able to be part of a vibrant and growing church but also for the different areas of ministry which a congregation of this size might be able to develop and support.

However, observation of churches in the UK which have grown to this kind of size in this dynamic suggest that these congregations also reach not a ceiling but an equilibrium. As the church grows in number, more and more of its energies are drawn into extending care and support to more and more people. Because only a limited number within the church are able to be actively involved in Christian ministry, the proportion of passive members within the congregation steadily increases until there is very little energy remaining for mission and for growth centrally or anywhere else within the congregation. At that point, development will again stand still until a different dynamic is found to take the situation forward.[5]

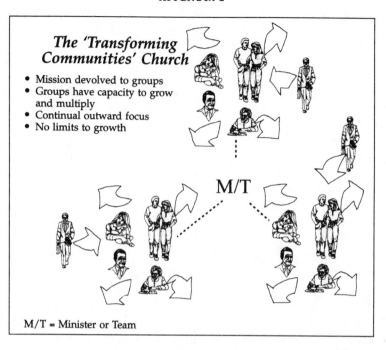

The 'Transforming
Communities' Church

- Mission devolved to groups
- Groups have capacity to grow
  and multiply
- Continual outward focus
- No limits to growth

M/T

M/T = Minister or Team

The theological difficulty which lies behind this inbuilt limitation to the nurturing communities model is that within it only a part of ministry is devolved from the ordained to the whole people of God: the pastoral care of those already within the congregation. A much better dynamic both theologically and in practice is also to seek to devolve mission from the 'centre' of the church to the whole body of Christ. The result is the dynamic of the 'Transforming Communities' Church. Here the small groups and communities are not only centres for nurture and pastoral care but are also becoming centres for mission and growth in different ways. The ways the groups express mission in their life will, hopefully, vary a great deal within one parish church. However, that mission will certainly include evangelism, nurture and discipleship. Therefore the groups will need the freedom and the capacity to continue to grow and to multiply. Each member of the church who participates in one of the small communities is fully involved in living out the mission of God according to their gifts and vocation with the support and encouragement of a committed group of Christians. The model is appropriate to both smaller churches and to larger ones. The groups come together on Sundays to worship and to celebrate but meet in homes during the week to encourage and enable one another in mission. The experience of the world church suggests that there are almost no limits to the growth of a congregation which seeks to express and develop its life in these ways.[6]

NOTES

CHAPTER 1

1. See, most clearly, Robert Warren in *Building Missionary Congregations* (CHP, 1995); and *Being Human, Being Church* (Marshall Pickering, 1995).
2. The figure quoted by the Church of England report *All God's Children* (National Society/CHP, 1991) is that only 14 per cent of children were in contact with the churches in 1991.
3. The most notable feature of this learning has been the rise in the use of resources such as Emmaus and the Alpha Course in the second half of the Decade of Evangelism. In September 1998 it was estimated that around several thousand churches in the UK are running Alpha Groups and engaging with Emmaus.
4. The recent research by Philip Richter and Leslie Francis highlights the different reasons why people leave congregations they have once been part of (*Gone but not Forgotten*, DLT, 1998).
5. See Steve Croft, *Growing New Christians* (CPAS/Marshall Pickering, 1993) and *Making New Disciples* (Marshall Pickering, 1994) for a description of this.
6. Clearly established at the beginning of the Decade of Evangelism by John Finney's research in *Finding Faith Today*, Bible Society, 1992.
7. See John Finney, *Finding Faith Today*, Chapter 5, pp. 51–59: '7 per cent said a minister was the main factor for them becoming a Christian and no less than 43 per cent said he or she was an important supporting factor.' The proportions would, it seems to me, be even higher if questions were being asked about finding your place within the Church rather than simply finding faith.
8. A full description of the Family-Pastoral-Programme way of seeing church communities is given in Chapter 10.
9. Think, for example, of class sizes in primary schools, or hospital waiting lists, or the number of young children at a Parent and Toddler Group.
10. From 1993–96 in the Diocese of Wakefield, which I served as Mission Consultant, only 0.5 per cent of churches was able to grow significantly beyond a congregation of 120 adults despite a great deal of effort going into evangelism and nurture among adults. A much larger proportion of smaller churches had the capacity for growth. Source: unpublished statistics from the Diocese of Wakefield annual count of congregations on seven Sundays in May and November.
11. For good analysis of the change in society affecting the Church, see Thomas R. Hawkins, *The Learning Congregation*, Westminster, John Knox Press, 1997, Chapter 1; Alan E. Nelson, *Leading Your Ministry*, Abingdon Press, Nashville, 1996, Chapter 1; Philip Richter and Leslie Francis, *Gone but not Forgotten*, DLT, 1998, Chapter 1;

Paul Goodliff, *Care in a Confused Climate – Pastoral Care in a Post Modern Culture*, DLT, 1998, Chapters 1 to 6.

12. These ideas are developed more fully by Eddie Gibbs in *Winning them Back*, especially Chapter 6: 'The Protestant Mindset and Urban Reality', Monarch, 1993.

13. See, for example, the Church of England Report, *All Are Called* (CHP, 1985) and Ruth Etchells, *Set My People Free – a lay challenge to the churches*, Fount, 1995.

14. My colleague Dr Mark Bonnington argues that the Free Churches which have retained the principle of one stipendiary minister within each congregation (such as Baptist, Pentecostal and FIEC churches) have seen greater growth than those which have abandoned this pattern. This would be a fruitful subject for ecumenical research. Much more thinking is needed on the changing dynamic from a single pastor pattern to that of multiple congregations.

15. *Emmaus: The Way of Faith*, eight volumes, by Stephen Cottrell, Steve Croft, John Finney, Felicity Lawson and Robert Warren, Bible Society and Church House Publishing. The Alpha Course and related publications by Nicky Gumbel and others, Kingsway.

16. Robert Warren, *Building Missionary Congregations*, Church House Publishing, 1995. The booklet had to be reprinted several times in its first year of issue. The material was subsequently developed by CPAS in a workbook and national training tour. The project continues under the auspices of Springboard.

17. See, for example, *On the Way – Towards an Integrated Approach to Christian Initiation*, Church House Publishing, 1995; Peter Ball, *Adult Way to Faith*, Mowbray, 1992; and Malcolm Grundy, *Evangelisation through the Adult Catechumenate*, Grove Booklets, 1991.

18. The story is well told in *Rediscovering Church* by Lynne and Bill Hybels, HarperCollins, 1996. Again, CPAS have done much to draw the lessons of this movement to the attention of the Churches and maintain a national network in the UK.

19. The standard texts are *Where Do We Go From Here?* by Ralph Neighbour, Houston, Touch Publications, 1991; and William Beckham, *The Second Reformation*, Touch Publications, 1995; for an account of one Anglican church's engagement with the movement, see Howard Astin, *Body and Cell*, CPAS/Monarch, 1998. For the related Metachurch concept of Church-as-Small-Group, see Carl George, *Prepare Your Church for the Future*, Revell, 1991. World Youth With a Mission arrange conferences and networking nationally for those exploring cell-church concepts. Anglican Church Planting Initiatives maintain an Anglican network.

20. The United Society for the Propagation of the Gospel have done a great deal to make this aspect of the World Church better known in the UK through the Root Groups network, courses on a New Way of Being Church and some publications. For an introduction, see Margaret Hebblethwaite, *Base Communities*, Geoffrey Chapman, 1993.

21. Anglican Church Planting Initiatives and the Church Army Institute for Evangelism and Church Planting both serve the church nationally in networking and training and arrange a major conference every two years. See the report *Breaking New Ground, Church Planting in the Church of England*, CHP, 1994.

22. The national report *Youth A Part*, National Society/Church House Publishing, 1996 describes some of these developments.

23. Christian Schwartz, *Natural Church Development*, British Church Growth Association, 1997, and related publications.

24. *The Report of a Working Party on Criteria for Selection for Ministry in the Church of England*, ABM Policy Paper No. 3A, October, 1993, p. 102.

25. ABM Policy Paper No. 3A, p. 96.

26. These advertisements were all taken from a single issue of the *Church Times* in October 1997. I have continued to make random checks on the kind of language used since that date and find that, if anything, leadership language is becoming even more predominant across the traditions.

CHAPTER 2

1. *Leaders Under Pressure*, Colin Buckland and John Earwicker, Evangelical Alliance, 1996.

2. In response to clergy stress surfacing in a number of highly publicised scandals, many Anglican dioceses have published helpful guidelines on clergy conduct in pastoral relationships. See Chapter 14 for details.

3. The two most useful here, from very different traditions, are Gordon MacDonald's modern classic *Ordering Your Private World*, Highland, 1984 and the principles contained in the rule of St. Benedict, published with a very helpful commentary by Esther de Waal in *A Life Giving Way*, SPCK, 1995. The Oak Hill learning centre have produced an extremely helpful workbook by Colin Buckland for leaders entitled *Liberating the Leadership* which examines all of these issues in some depth, with helpful case studies. The course is suitable either for individuals to work through on their own or, better, for a small group with a tutor.

4. The work of Carl George, referred to above, is particularly powerful in analysing the tendency of many clergy to become addicted to caring and being needed, with their congregations functioning as co-dependents in that addiction. George has also developed excellent strategies for devolving pastoral care from the ordained to the whole community of the people of God: Carl George, *Prepare Your Church for the Future*, Revell, 1991 and subsequent publications.

5. See, for example, Mary Ann Coates, *Clergy Stress*, SPCK; also the articles in Section 4 of *Psychological Perspectives on Christian Ministry*, edited by Leslie Francis and Susan H. Jones, Gracewing Fowler Wright, 1996.

6. Andrew Irvine, *Between Two Worlds: Understanding and Managing Clergy Stress* Mowbray, 1997.

7. A much more sinister and serious element has been introduced into media portrayals of the clergy in the last few years: compare the harmless, bumbling vicar of *Dad's Army* with the much sharper gin-swigging, idiotic characters in *Father Ted*; and the powerful character of the priest in *The Lakes*: an all too real figure racked by doubt and temptation. *The Vicar of Dibley* runs against these trends in presenting the priest as one of the few normal, but real, people in the community struggling to make headway amidst a group of loveable eccentrics. However, Geraldine's portrayals of stress and comfort eating are an all too real reflection of the experience of many clergy.

8. This powerful and helpful shift has been articulated and encouraged by Robin Greenwood in *Transforming Priesthood*, SPCK, 1994.

9. Irvine, *Between Two Worlds*, p. 10. Different sections of the Church have, historically,

asserted the priority of Scripture over the tradition as I would certainly wish to do. However these four elements are prioritised, our understanding of ordained ministry must be worked through all four sections of the quadrilateral.

10. Mark Noll in his perceptive book *The Scandal of the Evangelical Mind*, Eerdmans, 1994 traces the tendency of the evangelical movement to be pragmatic rather than reflective; to be led in everything by what 'works' rather than by what is right or true.

11. Robert Warren's picture of the ordained ministry being similar to running up a down escalator strikes a chord with many clergy.

12. George Carey, while still Bishop of Bath and Wells, writes in the foreword to John Finney's *Understanding Leadership*: 'You show me a growing church, where people are being added to the faith and growing in it, and you will be showing me effective leadership because such things do not simply happen on their own. Churches and fellowships grow because of visionary leadership. Conversely, when churches lose heart and fade away, often, though not always, it is connected with "leaders" who cannot lead.'

13. The development of this tradition of Christian youth work is charted by Pete Ward, *Growing up Evangelical*, SPCK, 1996, pp. 45–63.

14. It is no coincidence that a succession of Archbishops of Canterbury in the middle years of this century were former public school headmasters (William Temple, 1942–45 and, supremely, Geoffrey Fisher, 1945–61). An essential element in public school education has been and still is the instilling of 'leadership qualities'. Public school education followed by military or national service and then university were the models of leadership offered to clergy coming forward for ordination and in training until the early 1960s. Thereafter the pendulum took a much needed swing in the opposite direction with Michael Ramsey's preferment to Canterbury. The scholarly priest with little overt concept of 'leadership' became the model for the next generation. The archbishops who have followed Ramsey have been trying to achieve, in different ways, a synthesis between these two approaches.

15. David Watson's journey in terms of his leadership style can be seen as a model of the old public school and varsity model engaging with the needs of the modern Church with great integrity and at great cost. David Watson, *You are my God*, Hodder and Stoughton, 1983 and Teddy Saunders and Hugh Sansom, *David Watson, A Biography*, Hodder and Stoughton, 1992.

16. Expounded, for example, in his *Power Evangelism*, Hodder and Stoughton, 1984.

17. For example, P. F. Drucker, *Management: Tasks, Responsibilities, Practices*, Heinemann, 1974.

18. This is Carl George's language (reference); others would advocate a more organic, living metaphor, such as the body (so Christian Schwartz in *Natural Church Development*). The Revd Ross Maughen in a presentation at Cranmer Hall this year put forward a fascinating 'chaos theory' of local church life: every part is certainly connected to every other but the relationships are so complex that we cannot predict the consequences of our actions.

19. *I Believe in Church Growth*, pp. 380ff.

20. David Pytches, *Leadership for New Life*, Hodder, 1998.

21. *Understanding Leadership*, p. 59

22. John Nelson (ed.), *Management and Ministry*, Norwich: The Canterbury Press, 1996.

23. Other recent books on similar themes include Robin Gill and David Burke, *Strategic Church Leadership*, London: SPCK, 1996; Richard Higginson, *Transforming Leadership*, London: SPCK, 1996.

24. Stephen Pattison, 'An essay on management to its religious admirers', a coda to his book *The Faith of the Managers*, London: Cassell, 1997.

25. So, for example, the excellent ABM report *Beginning Public Ministry* with the significant changes proposed for post-ordination training, the changing relationship between curates and training incumbents and a move towards a portfolio of accredited competencies.

26. Luke 22:24–27.

27. Pattison, op. cit. p. 163.

28. In her book *Guide to the Management Gurus*, Carol Kennedy gives introductions to forty of the most prominent thinkers on leadership and management issues. Almost all of them are men. Carol Kennedy, *Guide to the Management Gurus*, Century Business Books, 1998.

CHAPTER 3

1. Exodus 3, 4 and Exodus 6:2–9. Both accounts emphasise that the God who calls is the God of Abraham, Isaac and Jacob.

2. Exodus 18 and Deuteronomy 1:9–18. Carl George in particular makes a great deal of Jethro's visit and the structure of care which is developed here (*Prepare Your Church for the Future*, pp. 121–27).

3. Judges 21:25.

4. So, for example, Luke 6:12–16; Luke 9:1–6; Luke 10:1–20.

5. So, for example, the book begins with the appointment of Matthias to succeed Judas (Acts 1:15–26); the ministry has to be expanded from the twelve to the seventy as the church grows (Acts 6:1–7); Paul revisits the churches on his first missionary journey, appointing elders (Acts 14:23); we are invited to listen to Paul's charge to the Ephesian elders (Acts 20:17–38).

6. So, for example, Romans 12:1–8; I Corinthians 12, 13 and 14; Ephesians 4:1–16.

7. James 5:14–15; 1 Peter 5:1–5; 1 Timothy 3:1–13; 5:17–22; Titus 1:5–16. See below for a discussion of each of these passages and also a consideration of the question of whether the Pastoral Epistles should be seen to be by Paul himself or by an imitator.

8. Alan Nelson highlights simplistic use of the Bible in Christian books on leadership in a similar way, focusing either on character studies of 'leaders' in the Old Testament or on the brief characteristics required of early Church elders in the New Testament and ignoring cultural and historical differences in both contexts. However, the implicit conclusion from his book is that the Bible is not a leadership manual, therefore we must turn to what the secular world teaches us about leadership for a new paradigm. As with many other recent writers on church leadership, he is accurate in his diagnosis of the need to rethink models of Christian ministry but struggling for Christian language to articulate a way forward. Alan E. Nelson, *Leading Your Ministry*, Abingdon Press, 1996, pp. 46–80.

9. See 1 Samuel 8:10–18 for the clearest expression of the cost of kingship in terms of national security and justice in the nation: a hard bargain, even when the king kept to his part of the contract.

10. Psalms 47, 48, 93, 94, 95, 96, 97, 99. All of these psalms were, in all probability, used regularly at the great annual festivals in Israel and Judah when God's kingship over the nation was celebrated as the central theme of the liturgy. Read these psalms through and see the recurring themes of God as creator, warrior-saviour and righteous judge.

11. Exodus 15, especially verse 3; Judges 5:4–5.

12. To follow these themes further, see Sigmund Mowinckel, *He that Cometh*, Basil Blackwell, 1996; T. N. D. Mettinger, *King and Messiah*, Lund, CWD Gleerup, 1976; B. Halpern, *The Constitution of the Monarchy in Ancient Israel*, Chicago, Scholars Press, 1981 and my own *The Identity of the Individual in the Psalms*, Sheffield Academic Press, 1987.

13. So, for example, Psalm 72, which is a prayer for the king, prays first that he may be given justice and righteousness (vv. 1–7), and second that he might have victory over his enemies (vv. 8–14).

14. So in Psalm 95 God is portrayed as the shepherd who leads his people, through the wilderness, feeding them and nurturing them. Ezekiel's tirade against the shepherds of Israel in Ezekiel 34 is about the rulers of the people, not simply their spiritual guides or counsellors. Psalm 23 was probably originally meant to be used by the king of Israel in worship ('You have anointed my head with oil'). The king, who is 'shepherd-ruler' of the people, declares in the context of public worship that the Lord is his own 'shepherd-ruler'. The shepherd imagery is, of course, picked up and applied in the New Testament to Christian ministers.

15. This is particularly evident in the writings of the prophet of Isaiah 40–55, an unknown 'voice' crying in the wilderness in the later years of the exile whose preaching has been incorporated into the Book of Isaiah. This prophet sees Israel's role in the purposes of God as that of a servant whose suffering is in some way redemptive and healing for the nations of the world; Israel's leaders similarly, must have that servant quality.

16. Luke 1:32–34.

17. Mark 1:14 and elsewhere.

18. Matthew 1:2.1

19. John 18:36.

20. Matthew 5:3.

21. Matthew 13:10–16 and parallels.

22. Matthew 13:31–32.

23. Matthew 7:29.

24. The letter to the Hebrews gives an extensive interpretation of Jesus' ministry as a fulfilment of the Old Testament priesthood: Hebrews 2:15, 4:14 and elsewhere.

25. Matthew 23:1–36.

26. Matthew 5:5.

27. Mark 9:33.

28. See Chapter 10 for a development of this 'Rhythm and Road' way of being Church.

29. Colossians 1:18, 2:19; Ephesians 1:22, 4:15; 5:23.

30. 1 Corinthians 12:7 and elsewhere.

31. Romans 12:3–8; 1 Corinthians 12:27–30; Ephesians 4:1–16. In each case the list of spiritual gifts is specifically linked with the doctrine of the Body of Christ.

32. A good and salutary exercise for those who are convinced of the need for 'strong

leadership' in the Church in a management or church growth sense is to look up the term 'leadership' in a concordance. There is no rich vein of references to follow despite, as we have seen, the high priority Scripture gives as a whole to the right ordering of the people of God. The Christians addressed by the Epistle to the Hebrews are to remember and be obedient to their leaders (Hebrews 13:7, 17), using the Greek word 'hegomenoi', or 'guides', a term not taken up elsewhere in the New Testament. Romans 12:1 contains an exhortation translated 'the leader, in diligence' (NRSV); or 'if it is leadership, let him govern diligently' (NIV). The Greek word means, literally, 'the one who stands in front': something akin to leadership is clearly intended, but the theme is not a strong one. We need to mine a richer theological tradition in our search for ways in which leadership and ordained ministry can connect today.

33. For a short review of the tradition of these three dimensions of ministry, see the WCC report *Baptism, Eucharist and Ministry,* World Council of Churches, Geneva, 1982, Faith and Order Paper 111.

34. The metaphor is from Jeremiah 2:13.

Chapter 4

1. So, for example, Robin Greenwood's fine book *Transforming Priesthood* which pays no attention at all to the diaconal dimension of the ministry of ordained, although he goes some way towards linking the notions of presbyteral and episcopal ministry; the very good Derby Diocesan strategy paper *A Better Way* again links 'priestly' and 'episcopal' ministry (paragraph 6.3) but omits the diaconal dimension; the recent, and generally helpful, ABM discussion paper *Beginning Public Ministry* contains no discussion of the nature of diaconal ministry.

2. The need for a visual aid of this dimension of ministry for the whole Church remains, in my view, one of the most powerful arguments for restoring and developing the diaconal order in its own right within the Church of England. I would not, myself, argue for two diverging paths of ministry, where some are ordained deacon and others presbyter, the route the Methodist Church has taken. All presbyters should also be 'permanent' deacons. However, Anglican orders need to restore the opportunity for those called primarily to diaconal ministry not to be ordained priests and so be living signs of this aspect of the ministry of Christ to the world. All our priests must be deacons but not all our deacons must be priests.

3. Available articles and studies on *Diakonos* are fairly few and far between. The following study draws on the article 'Deacon' in the *Oxford Dictionary of the Church,* ed. F. L. Cross and E. A. Livingstone, 1997; *Diakoneo* and related words by F. Beyer in *TDNT* Vol. 2 pp. 81–93; B. H. Streeter, *The Primitive Church,* studied with special reference to the origins; J. M. Barrett, *The Diaconate* – a full and equal order, Seabury, New York, 1979 and 1981, Chapters 2 and 3; *The Deacon's Ministry,* edited by Christine Hall, Gracewing, 1992; the report *Deacons in the Ministry of the Church,* General Synod of the Church of England, 1988. John Finney has a section on the leader as servant in *Understanding Leadership,* pp.45–49.

4. I and II Timothy and Titus are commonly called the Pastoral Epistles, because of the ordering of ministry in the local church is one of their primary concerns. The authorship of the Pastoral Epistles is one of the unsolved (and probably unsolvable)

problems of New Testament scholarship. They are written in the name of the apostle Paul and whilst some of the text is similar to the other Pauline letters, other parts of the Pastoral Epistles are very different from Paul in their vocabulary and language used and in some of the concepts and arguments used. The arguments are well summarised in the introductions to two recent commentators: Gordon Fee, who takes a position of Pauline authorship; and Jouette Bassler who takes the opposite view. The dilemma is an impossible one to solve conclusively: either these letters were written by Paul or someone pretending to be Paul and writing in his style. My basic assumption is that the letters are from Paul or the Pauline circle, but that in any event they represent ministry as practised and advocated in Pauline Churches in a period slightly later than that of the other epistles. Whatever their original authorship, they were ascribed an authority by the early church alongside the other New Testament letters and found a place within the canon (Gordon D. Fee, *1 and 2 Timothy, Titus, New International Bible Commentary*, Paternoster, 1995; and Jouette M. Basser, *1 Timothy, 2 Timothy, Titus, Abingdon New Testament Commentaries*, Abingdon Press, 1996).

5. Philippians is conventionally dated to the years AD 60–62 (see G.D. Fee, *Paul's Letter to the Philippians*, Eerdmans, 1995; and Peter O'Brien, *The Epistle to the Philippians*, Eerdmans, 1991).

6. The commentators make various suggestions as to why these two groups are singled out at the beginning of Philippians in this unique way. The most convincing is that made by Lightfoot that the gift which the letter acknowledges has been sent by the recognised ministers on behalf of the whole congregation. In mentioning them explicitly at the beginning of the letter, Paul attempts to bolster their authority in the context of his plea for unity through the epistle. J. B. Lightfoot, *Saint Paul's Letter to the Philippians*, MacMillan, 1927, p. 82.

7. The term *diakonos* here is not used as an adjective but as a noun with an accompanying participle: the effect is a rather grand description of Phoebe: '*ousan diakonian*'. James Dunn writes: 'The fact remains that Phoebe is the first recorded "deacon" in the history of Christianity. At the same time it would be premature to speak of an established order of deacon, as though a role of responsibility and authority had already been agreed upon in the Pauline churches. We are still at the stage of ministry beginning to take regular and fomal shape (Barrett, Kasemann), and the form in each case would depend very much on the context and needs of particular congregations.' (J. G. D. Dunn, *Romans 9–16, Word Biblical Commentary*, Word, 1988. C. Cranfield has similar comments in the *ICC Commentary*, Volume II, T. and T. Clark, 1979, p. 781.

8. Ephesians 6:21–22. There are critical questions surrounding the Pauline authorship of Colossians and Ephesians. This passage and the next are close parallels and feature in that debate. For a thorough discussion of the issues, see the commentary of Ernest Best, *ICC*, T. and T. Clark, 1998.

9. Colossians 4:7–9.

10. Colossians 1:7.

11. Here the commentators and the history of interpretation are against me. Most would see the term *diakonos* here as a general honorific.

12. Acts 1:17; 11:29; 12:25; 19:22; 20:24; 21:19

13. Significantly, *diakonia* is also used in Acts 1:17 as the description of the ministry of the Apostles.
14. Luke 22:26 and the parallels in Matthew 23:11 and Mark 9:35.
15. Acts 19:22.
16. Acts 11:29 (translated 'relief' by NRSV) and 12:25 (translated 'mission'); 2 Corinthians 8:4; 9:1; 9:12; and, possibly, Romans 15:31 (all rendered 'ministry'). All of these references to financial giving refer to the practical relief of poverty among the saints. They do not refer directly to the giving of money to support the ministry and work of a local congregation nor charitable giving to those outside the family of faith.
17. 1 Corinthians 3:5; 2 Corinthians 3:6; 6:4; 11:23 (contrasting 11:15); Ephesians 3:7; Colossians 1:23, 25; 1 Thessalonians 3:2; 1 Timothy 4:6. On seven occasions the letters seem to refer to a recognised 'deacon' (see above); in Romans 13:4 the secular authorities are described as '*diakonoi*' and in Romans 15:8 and Galatians 2:17 the reference is to Christ as *diakonos*.
18. 1 Corinthians 3:5.
19. 1 Corinthians 4:1. The Greek words used here are those for domestic servants (*hyperatos*) and household steward (*oikonomos*). Both occur frequently in the New Testament as descriptions of Christian ministers. *Hyperatos* originally meant 'galley slave' – someone who toiled at the oars of a ship. The two words come from the bottom and the top of the domestic spectrum. As a pair they can be taken to reflect the diaconal and episcopal dimensions of ministry respectively. *Oikonomos* is used to describe the ministry of the *episkopos* in Titus 1:7 and in several of the parables; *hyperatos* describes Paul's first call to service in Acts 26:16. For a full description of all of the 'servant' groups of words, see David W. Bennett, *Metaphors of Ministry*, Paternoster, 1993, particularly pp. 119–29.
20. The word 'last of all' picks up the words of Jesus in Mark 9:35 (see below).
21. 2 Corinthians 4:5.
22. 2 Corinthians 6:3–10.
23. Philippians 2:4–8. Philippians 2:6–10 is generally recognised to be one of the oldest statements of the churches' faith in Christ and belief about Christ within the New Testament. Paul is quoting here a hymn or creed, either of his own making or by others within the Church. For detailed commentary and extensive bibliography, see Peter O'Brien, *The Epistle to the Philippians*, Eerdmans, 1991 pp. 186ff.
24. Mark 9:33–35. The parallel in Matthew 18:1–5 has Jesus appealing to the disciples to become as children in order to enter the kingdom of heaven. Luke 9:46–48 develops this theme also, yet preserves the saying about the least becoming the greatest.
25. Mark 10:41–45. The parallel in Matthew 20:24–28 is very similar.
26. Matthew 23:6–12.
27. As indicated above, Luke seems to deliberately avoid the noun *diakonos* here, perhaps because it has become a technical term by his generation.
28. *Diakonos* is used only three times in John's gospel. One reference is in John 12:26 which sums up *diakonia* as following Jesus: 'Whoever serves me must follow me, and where I am, there will my servant [*diakonos*] be also.' The other two references describe the servants who draw the water in the story of the wedding at Cana (John 2:5, 9). The changing of the water into wine is rich in its allusions to the

Eucharist. It may be that John is here reflecting an early liturgical role for the deacons of his own day as servants at the Holy Communion and at Holy Baptism.

29. John 13:3–5.
30. John 13:12–17.
31. The four 'songs' are generally reckoned to be Isaiah 42:1–4; Isaiah 49:1–7; Isaiah 50:4–9; and Isaiah 52:13–53:12.
32. Exodus 12:11–15.
33. Numbers 12:3.
34. Isaiah 42:2–3.
35. Luke 1:37, 52.

CHAPTER 5

1. Those interested in the diaconal ministry should contact, in addition to their Diocesan Director of Ordinands, the Diaconal Association of the Church of England (DACE), which exists to 'help the Church of England to develop its distinctive diaconal calling and ministry, and to promote the diaconate as a full and equal order, and to support those – both lay and ordained – in such ministry.' The contact address is The Secretary, DACE, 95, Ballens Road, Lordswood, Chatham, Kent, ME5 8PA.
2. What follows is a retelling of an account told in more detail in a number of sources: James M. Barnett, *The Diaconate – A full and equal order*, The Seabury Press, 1979; Jill Pinnock, '*A History of the Diaconate*', in *The Deacon's Ministry*, edited by Christina Hall, Gracewing, 1992; *Deacons in the Ministry of the Church*, General Synod Papers, 1988, 802. The subject has been studied largely from the perspective either of liturgical history or as part of the Church's journey of exploring the ordination of women to the priesthood.
3. Pliny, *Letter x.96.8.*
4. Ignatius, *Trallians 3*, quoted in Barnett, p. 48.
5. '*The Epistle of Clement to James*', 12 in Vol. 8: *Pseudo Clementine Homilies in Ante Nicene Fathers*, 8:220. The Epistle probably dates from the beginning of the fourth century. Quoted in Barnett, p. 59 and footnote, p. 84.
6. Barnett, p. 72.
7. Justin, *Apology* 65, 1.286.
8. *Didascalia Apostolorum*: The Syriac Version tr. R. Hugh Connolly (Oxford, Clarendon Press, 1929), p.147; quoted by Pinnock op. cit., p. 15. The Didascalia dates from the first half of the third century. Pinnock goes on to explore the Didascalia's representation of the women deacons as a representation of the Holy Spirit in their femininity as male deacons are a representation of Christ.
9. Barnett, p. 97.
10. Barnett, p. 105.
11. *Deacons in the Ministry of the Church*, p. 15.
12. Romans 12:1–12; Mark 10:35–45.
13. ASB, p. 344. The gender-specific language is almost always now amended in ordination services.
14. ASB 1980, p. 348. The Post Communion collect for the service (p. 350) also uses the language of *diakonia*.

15. 'The recommendation is made that the Church of England make provision for, and encourage, men and women to serve in an ordained distinctive diaconate. This conclusion is drawn from a consideration of Scripture, tradition and contemporary experience which would seem to complement and affirm one another. Furthermore, the future ministry of the Church will be greatly enriched by the restoration of a diaconate after the model and pattern of Christ's diaconate. He came "not to be served but to serve and to give his life as a ransom for many" (Mark 10:45), to provide an example and support for the diaconal ministry of all – laity, presbyters and bishops. All who follow him are called to be "servants for Jesus' sake" (2 Cor: 4.5).' *Deacons in the Ministry of the Church*, p. 119. The four major divisions of diaconal ministry in the report are seen as servant to the community, enabler of the Church, servant within the Church, and liturgical ministry (pp.109–18).

16 *Baptism, Eucharist and Ministry*, World Council of Churches, Geneva, 1982.

17 Pope John XXIII, *Journal of a Soul*, Geoffrey Chapman, 1965.

18 Matthew 25:35, 36, 40. In verse 44 when those at the King's left hand reply to his accusation, they say: 'Lord, when was it that we saw you hungry or thirsty or a stranger or naked or in prison and did not take care of you.' The word translated 'take care' is *diakoneo*, to serve.

19 From the Scottish Ordinal, 1984, quoted in *The Anglican Tradition, A Handbook of Sources*, edited by G. R. Evans and J. Robert Wright, SPCK, 1988, p. 553.

CHAPTER 6

1. National Association for the Care and Rehabilitation of Offenders, active at that time in working with young unemployed people in the locality.

2. The recent ABM document *Beginning Public Ministry* contains as an appendix a long checklist of ministerial skills and experiences which should have been gained in the first four years of public ministry. Little scope and space is given within this list to the service of the wider community. Again the emphasis is church-based and church-centred. *Beginning Public Ministry*, ABM Ministry Paper 17, 1998, pp. 19–26.

3. Gordon MacDonald, *Ordering Your Private World*, Highland, 1987, pp. 81ff.

4. Luke 24:13–35. For an exposition of this story as it relates to sharing faith, see *Introduction to Emmaus: the Way of Faith* by Stephen Cottrell, Steve Croft, John Finney, Felicity Lawson and Robert Warren, Church House Publishing and Bible Society, 1976; for the story as it applies to pastoral encounters, see the very different but very helpful reflection in *Eccentric Ministry* by Christopher Moody, Darton, Longman & Todd, 1992, pp. 89–108.

5. Peter M. Senge, *The Fifth Discipline: The art and practise of the learning organisation*, New York; Doubleday/Currency Books, 1990.

6. See Thomas R. Hawkins, *The Learning Congregation*, Westminster, John Knox Press, 1997. The Church of England's Boards of Mission and Ministry held consultations on the subject in 1996 and 1997.

7. See the comments by Robert Warren on learning from failure in *On the Anvil*, Highland, 1990, pp. 35.

8. *The Rule of Benedict*, Chapter 3.

9. It follows from this that one of the essential skills in *diakonia* and therefore in Christian leadership is the skill of listening. Listening is a discipline which can be

learned. A great deal has been done within the Church of England and elsewhere to help churches develop listening skills by the Acorn Healing Trust.

10. Luke 17:7–10.
11. 1 Timothy 6:8.
12. Psalm 123:2.
13. Psalm 131:1–2.
14. So Acts 9:3–6 (Saul's conversion); Acts 9:10ff (the Lord's word to Ananias); Acts 10:9ff (Peter's vision and commandment to go to Cornelius); Acts 11:27ff (the prophetic word through Agabus that there would be a severe famine); Acts 13:2 (the instruction to the church in Antioch to set aside Barnabas and Saul); Acts 16:9–10 (Paul's vision of the man of Macedonia). This list is by no means exhaustive.
15. Colossians 1:18 and elsewhere.
16. Romans 1:32, 1 Corinthians 16:7–9.
17. For more on this, see David Pytches, *The Holy Spirit* and Wayne Gruden, *The Gift of Prophecy*, Kingsway, 1988.
18. John 10:4.
19. To explore further, see Gerard Hughes, *God of Surprises*, Darton Longman & Todd, 1985, 1996.
20. For more on this, see the recent study by Vanessa Herrick and Ivan Mann, *Jesus Wept: Reflections on Vulnerability in Leadership*, Darton Longman & Todd, 1998.
21. See Andrew Burnham, 'The Liturgical Ministry of a Deacon', in *The Deacon's Ministry*, ed. Christine Hall, Gracewing, 1992, pp. 67–89.

CHAPTER 7

1. For references here and other details, see the articles by G. Bornkamm and *Theological Dictionary of the New Testament*, vol. VI, pp. 651–83 and J. Rhode in the *Exegetical Dictionary of the New Testament*, Vol. 3, pp. 148f. See also the extensive and detailed study *The Elders: Seniority within earliest Christianity* by R. Alastair Campbell, T. & T. Clark, 1994. Campbell's conclusions about the ministry of presbyters in the Old and New Testaments differ at a number of points from my own.
2. The Hebrew word used throughout these references is *zaqan* – always translated by the Greek word *presbyteros* in the LXX, the Greek translation of the Hebrew Scriptures.
3. Exodus 3:16, 18; 12:21.
4. Numbers 11:16ff.
5. See, for example, Joshua 8:33; 24:1; Judges 11:5; 21:16; Ruth 4.
6. 1 Samuel 8:4.
7. 2 Samuel 3:17.
8. See, for example, 2 Kings 6:32; 10:1; Isaiah 3:14; Jeremiah 19:1; Ezekiel 8:1.
9. Ezra 5:5; 6:7; 10:8.
10. See Campbell, *Elders*, p. 54.
11. In Luke 7:3 the Centurion sends the presbyters of the local synagogue to intercede with Jesus, asking for the healing of his slave.
12. Matthew 21:23; 26:3, 47; 27:1, 3; 28:2.
13. Acts 4:5, 8, 28; 6:12; 23:14; 24:1; 25:15.

14. Matthew 15:12; Mark 7:3, 5.

15. See Acts 6:1–6: there is no mention of presbyters at the setting aside of the Seven.

16. Acts 15:2, 4, 6, 22.

17. Acts 15:23.

18. Acts 16:4.

19. Acts 21:17.

20. Campbell argues that the title 'elder' was not originally a formal office but a general honorific describing heads of households in the ancient world.

21. See J. D. G. Dunn, *The Acts of the Apostles* (Epworth, 1997) p. xi.

22. Acts 13:52. Campbell favours the view that the apostles are here blessing or ordaining the elders who had already emerged naturally within the household churches rather than themselves appointing elders to a formal position.

23. Acts 14:21–23.

24. Acts 20:35 and the tenor of the whole speech.

25. See I Corinthians 4:16; Philippians 1:9; I Thessalonians 1:6.

26. Acts 20:18.

27. Acts 20:24. Note the link made again between *diakonia* and laying down one's life for God and for others.

28. Acts 20:35.

29. Matthew 2:6; 25:32; Mark 14:27; Luke 15:3–7; John 10:1–18.

30. Acts 20:21.

31. Richard Baxter, *The Reformed Pastor*, first published in 1656 and available now from the Banner of Truth Trust.

32. Acts 20:26–27.

33. From the Bishop's Charge in The Ordering of Priests of 1642. The element of accountability has largely disappeared in later revision of the service.

34. Acts 20:34.

35. Acts 20:35.

36. Acts 20:36, 37.

37. 1 Peter, like all the general epistles, is hard to date, given the lack of both internal and external evidence which is conclusive. More conservative commentators argue that the Epistle fits the writings and situations of Peter in Rome or else the Roman church shortly after his death (see J. Ramsey Michaels, *Word Biblical Commentary*, 1988). Others would see the Epistle as pseudonymous and therefore later, dating from the end of the first century.

38. 1 Peter 5:1–6.

39. Mark 10:41ff and parallels.

40. James 5:14,15. Again, James is very difficult to date. Peter Davids sees merit in the traditional view that the letter originates with James the Just, brother of Jesus and leader of the Jerusalem Church and therefore its final redaction is to be set *c.* AD 75–85 (*New International Greek Commentary*, Eerdmans, 1982); Martin Dibelius sees the letter as certainly pseudonymous and probably later, within the parameters of AD 80–130 (Fortress Press, 1975).

41. Titus 1:5–6.

42. Titus 1:7–9.

43. J. N. D. Kelly follows this interpretation in *The Pastoral Epistles*, A. & C. Black, 1963, pp. 230f.

44. I Timothy 3:1–13.
45. I Timothy 4:14.
46. I Timothy 4:14.
47. I Timothy 5:22.
48. I Timothy 5:17–20.
49. John 10:10–16.

CHAPTER 8

1. Act 6:4.
2. Matthew 28:19.
3. Ephesians 4:13.
4. Hebrews 2:17.
5. Hebrews 4:14–15. See also the whole of Hebrews 2–9.
6. 1 Peter 2:5.
7. Revelation 5.9. The song is sung by the heavenly elders (*presbuteroi*). See also Revelation 1:5–6.
8. Romans 12:1. To extend the metaphor, it is of course priests in the old covenant who offer sacrifices.
9. Romans 15:16.
10. John Webster, Ministry and Priesthood in *The Study of Anglicanism*, Revised Edition, SPCK, 1998.
11. From the Ordering of Priests, quoted from the service of 1662.
12. As evidenced, for example, in the heated debate in General Synod on the 1986 report by the Board of Mission and Unity on their report 'The Priesthood of the Ordained Ministry'; General Synod Report of Proceedings, Volume 17, No. 3 pp. 743ff.
13. WCC, *Baptism, Eucharist and Ministry*, 1982, p. 30. Not surprisingly in view of the debate through the years, the later WCC report on the responses to the document comments: 'The description of the functions of bishops, presbyters and deacons was unsatisfactory according to many responses ... There are indeed so many cultural and time-bound differences of tasks and functions that a uniform description is hardly possible.'
14. The Alternative Services Book, 1980, A Commentary by the Liturgical Commission, Church Information Office, 1980, pp. 140 ff
15. ASB 1980, amended according to the principles in 'Making Women Visible'.

CHAPTER 9

1. For example, the recent and helpful book by David Pytches, *Leadership for New Life* (referred to above) is set out as a comprehensive manual for incumbents and covers many areas of parish life in great detail – yet the theological language of ordination, priest or presbyter is hardly used. The basic category used in the chapter headings and text has become that of 'leader' – reflecting, as we have seen, the call from both clergy and parishes for more help in this area.
2. The way in which the pendulum swings in this or other contexts has as much to do with what is assumed as what is emphasised. For example, a generation of ministers who assume and take for granted from their own process of formation that, central to ministry, is prayer and service of the Word, begin to emphasise

leadership skills and qualities as something which is lacking (as with David Pytches and, in different ways, Bill Hybels). The next generation hear what is being said about leadership skills and place a high priority on these. However, they have not been taught, and do not automatically assume, that prayer and service of the Word are central to ministry. Their guiding model therefore becomes entirely that of the 'leader'.

3. Isaiah 61:1 (NEB); Old Testament reading in the ASB ordination of priests.

4. Malachi 2:7 (RSV); Alternative Old Testament reading in the ASB ordination of priests and making explicit in the service the link with Old Testament language of priesthood.

5. 2 Corinthians 5:19 (NEB); New Testament reading in the ASB ordination of priests.

6. From the Declaration at the Ordination of Priests, ASB pp. 356f.

7. The fifth of eight questions asked of the candidates by the bishop in the same service (ASB, p. 358).

8. The bishop's words to the newly ordained priests at the presentation of the Bible in the service. This bifocal priestly ministry of Word and sacrament is expanded to embrace the care for God's people in the proper preface in the service: 'And now we give you thanks because within the royal priesthood of your Church you ordain ministers to proclaim the word of God, to care for your people, and to celebrate the sacraments of the new covenant.' The service returns to the classic dual focus in the Postcommunion collect: 'Father, you have appointed your Son to be our high priest for ever. Fulfil now your purpose in choosing these men and women to be ministers and stewards of your word and sacraments' (ASB, pp. 363–64).

9. John Stott, *I Believe in Preaching*, Hodder and Stoughton, 1982, pp. 180–211.

10. Gordon MacDonald, *Ordering Your Private World*, Chapter 5. The whole chapter has helpful advice on study generally.

11. Psalm 1; Jeremiah 17:7–8; see also Psalm 19 and 119 – a lengthy meditation designed to be learned by heart and to encourage diligent study of the law.

12. Stephen Covey, *The Seven Habits of Highly Effective People*, Simon and Schuster, 1989, pp. 287ff.

13. Isaiah 55:10–11.

14. John 1:1ff.

15. 1 Timothy 3:15–17.

16. Hebrews 4:12–14.

17. One of the principal themes of the Book of Acts as it seeks to draw lessons from the missionary practice of the early Church is to continually emphasise the three elements of the proclaiming of the Gospel of Jesus Christ (primarily his death and resurrection); the inspiration of the Holy Spirit empowering the life of the Church; and the proper ordering of ministry within the life of the Church.

18. See the collected essays in Christopher Green and David Jackman (ed), *When God's Voice is Heard*, IVP, 1995.

19. See Amos 1:3–2.5; Isaiah 15–21; Jeremiah 46–50.

20. Jeremiah 1:5.

21. Acts 2:14–36; Acts 3:11–26; Acts 10:34–43; Acts 13:13–51; Acts 17:22–34.

22. For examples, see Colossians 3:1–17; Philippians 3:17–21; Ephesians 5:21–22; Romans 14:13–23.

23. P. T. Forsyth, *Positive Preaching and the Modern Mind*, Independent Press, 1907; Donald Coggan, *The Sacrament of the Word*, Fount, 1987; John Stott, *I Believe in Preaching*.

24. David Day, *A Preaching Workbook*, Lynx, 1997.

25. The pioneering research here was that of John Finney in *Finding Faith Today* (Bible Society, 1992) and *Stories of Faith* (Bible Society, 1995). See also John Clarke, *Evangelism that Really Works* (SPCK, 1995); my own *Growing New Christians* (CPAS/HarperCollins, 1993); and Stephen Cottrell, *Catholic Evangelism* (Darton Longman & Todd, 1998).

26. 1 Corinthians 3:10.

CHAPTER 10

1. Article XXV of the 39 Articles reads: 'There are two Sacraments ordained of Christ our Lord in the gospel, that is to say, baptism, and the Supper of the Lord. Those five commonly called sacraments, that is to say, Confirmation, Penance, Orders, Matrimony and extreme Unction are not to be counted for Sacraments of the gospel, being such as have grown partly of the corrupt following of the apostles, partly are states of life allowed in the Scriptures; but yet have not like nature of Sacraments with baptism and the Lord's Supper, for that they have not any visible sign or ceremony ordained of God.'

2. John 20:23 (RSV) from the gospel reading at the Ordination of Priests (ASB, p. 354).

3. From the Declaration at the Ordination of Priests, ASB, pp. 356f.

4. For the most recent Church of England reflections on the issue, see the report *On The Way: Towards an Integrated Approach to Christian Initiation*, CH.', 1995.

5. Quoted from the extract from the findings of the International Anglican Liturgical Consultation, Toronto, 1991, *On the Way*, p. 121.

6. For guidelines on working with under-fives, see Ann Croft, *Caring for Children through Crèches and Toddler Groups*, CPAS, 1994.

7. The Emmaus material contain some outline rites. The Liturgical Commission is shortly to publish 'Rites on the Way' in draft form.

8. One possible model is given in the Emmaus nurture material, Session 6.

9. For more on this individual ministry of reconciliation and the practice followed, see *Growing New Christians*, pp. 190–201 and *Making New Disciples*, pp. 165–181.

10. Again, it is not necessarily only a ministry of the ordained yet it is an area of priestly ministry which the ordained ideally need to understand and be equipped for as part of the work of the 'cure of souls' to which they are commissioned.

11. From the Declaration, ASB, Ordination of Priests, p. 356.

12. From the Bishop's blessing of the newly ordained. ASB, Ordination of Priests, p. 363.

13. The language of presidency was used in ARCIC discussions and passed into common parlance in the Church of England with the publication of the ASB. The concept is made the defining concept of priesthood by Robin Greenwood: *Transforming Priesthood*, SPCK, 1994, Chapter 6.

14. This, of course, is a whole subject in itself. To explore it further, see Richard Giles's excellent book *Repitching the Tent*, Canterbury Press, 1996.

15. James 2:1–7.

16. I am very conscious that each of the chapter headings in this and the previous

chapter deserves a book in its own right – and many books have been written on each of the areas of ministry. I hope the reader will forgive the brevity of the treatment of each vital area of ministry in serving the primary interest of this particular book: seeing the way in which the whole of ordained ministry fits together.

17. Genesis 18:16–end.

18. Exodus 32:30ff and elsewhere.

19. Exodus 28:6–14.

20. Jeremiah 7:16ff.

21. 'My little children, for whom I am again in the pain of childbirth until Christ is formed in you' Galatians 4:19.

22. Colossians 4:12.

23. Gary Smalley and John Trent, *The Blessing*, quoted in Robert Warren, *Being Human, Being Church*, p. 75, with perceptive comments on subsequent pages.

CHAPTER 11

1. Homer, *Iliad*, 22:254ff. This and other elements in what follows are drawn from the very full article by Beyer in *Theological Dictionary of the New Testament*, Vol. 2, ed. G. Kittel, pp. 606ff.

2. So in Plato, women should be overseers of young married couples (Laws, VI, 748a); market overseers watch over the market to ensure trading is fair (VIII, 849a).

3. 2 Chronicles 34:12, 17; Nehemiah 11:9, 14:22; Numbers 4:16.

4. Philippians 1:1.

5. Acts 20:28.

6. 1 Peter 5:2 – a small number of manuscripts omit the word *episkopountes*, presumably thought by some to be a later insertion.

7. Titus 1:7–9.

8. 1 Timothy 3:1–7.

9. The Greek terms used are *prostenai* – to lead – and *epimelesetai* – to take care of or look after. The image picks up on the metaphor of parenting used elsewhere in Paul's writings to describe Christian nurture and leadership: 2 Corinthians 12:14; 1 Thessalonians 2:7; 1 Corinthians 3:1–3; Philippians 2:22; 1 Corinthians 4:15. The image of gentleness and discipline in the context of a relationship lies behind the memorable phrase from the charge to bishops in the Ordinal: 'He is to be merciful, but with firmness, and to minister discipline, but with mercy.' For more on the image in general, see David W. Bennett, *Biblical Images for Leaders and Followers*, Paternoster, 1993, pp. 80–84.

10. Mark 1:38.

11. Mark 2:14.

12. Luke 8:1–3.

13. Luke 9:1–6, Luke 10:1–20.

14. Matthew 28:16–20; Luke 24:44–52; John 20:19–23; John 21:15–19; Acts 1:6–11.

15. Matthew 11:28–30. Although in one sense this is an invitation to faith offered to all, and is used in this way liturgically through the incorporation of the sayings into the 'Comfortable Words' of the Book of Common Prayer, it is also a very tender expression of Jesus as *episcopos*. The way we live our lives often seems to deny the truth in the words.

16. Acts 2:42.
17. For example, Peter's preaching to Cornelius in Acts 10 and the beginnings of the Gentile Mission in Acts 13:2.
18. The Council of Jerusalem recorded in Acts 15.
19. Acts 20:28.
20. See, for example, Romans 16:1–16; 2 Timothy 4:9–18.
21. For a history and summary of the development of the ministry of bishops (that is, of episcopacy as opposed to *episcope*), see *Episcopal Ministry, The Report of the Archbishops' Group on the Episcopate*, CHP, 1990; and 'Episcopacy' by Richard Norris in *The Study of Anglicanism*, edited by Stephen Sykes, John Booty and Jonathan Knight, SPCK, revised edition, 1998, pp. 333ff, covering the period from the Reformation to the present day.
22. *Baptism, Eucharist and Ministry*, pp. 26.
23. The Declaration from The Ordination or Consecration of a Bishop, ASB, 1980, pp. 388f.
24. The second sentence of the charge relates more to episcopacy than to *episcope*: 'As chief pastor he shares with his fellow bishops a special responsibility to maintain and further the unity of the Church, to uphold its discipline and to guard its faith.' The words 'He is to ordain and send new ministers' would need to be amended to something like '(S)he is to seek out and commission new ministers, guiding those who serve with her/him and enabling them to fulfil their ministry.'

CHAPTER 12

1. For convenience in this and the following chapters I have used 'vicar' or 'incumbent' as a shorthand for anyone charged with oversight of a local congregation, whether their title is rector, minister, parish priest, etc.
2. Useful questions for a new incumbent to ask members of the Church Council and other representatives of the congregation are: 'Tell me the story of this church through your eyes. What has made this church special or distinctive through the years? What do you think are the most important things we need to hold onto? What directions do we need to develop over the next period of our life together?' It is possible to gather some of this information through written questionnaires but there is no substitute for simply sitting and listening.
3. Bill and Lynn Hybels recount in great detail the ways in which the vision Bill Hybels was given for the local church at his theological seminary, based on a picture of the Church in Acts, has formed and shaped their own vision for the life of Willow Creek Community Church: Bill and Lynn Hybels, *Rediscovering Church*, Zondervan, 1996.
4. Romans 12:1 and the ASB prayer of dedication, p. 145.
5. Both rhythm and road are implicit in Robert Warren's list of characteristics of missionary congregations (*Building Missionary Congregations*, CHP, 1995, p. 52) yet there remains a tension in understanding the missionary congregation about what is at the centre of its life ('Are missionary congregations sustainable?', pp. 31–2).
6. Equally discouraging is the situation in which the church members articulate what is wrong with the incumbent without a clear vision of how things might be different.
7. For additional reflections on vision and planning, see Peter Brierley, *Vision Building*.

8. For information on how to go about this process of Mission Audit, see the *Faith in the City Report*, pp. 367ff.

9. 'Whenever anything important has to be done in the monastery, the Abbot must assemble the whole community and explain what is under consideration ... It is often to a younger brother that the Lord reveals the best course.' Rule of Benedict, Chapter 3.

10. Among the most helpful books on change in congregations are: Thomas Hawkins, *The Learning Congregation*, Westminster John Knox Press, 1997; John Finney, *Understanding Leadership*, Daybreak, 1989, Chapter 6, pp. 133–52; Robert Warren, *On the Anvil*, Highland, 1990, Chapters 7 and 8, pp. 103–31.

11. Again, see the chapters on conflict in *Understanding Leadership* and *On the Anvil*. Both change and conflict within congregations deserve a longer and fuller treatment than is possible here.

CHAPTER 13

1. Exodus 18:1–27 and Deuteronomy 1:9–18.

2. 1 Kings 19:1–21.

3. The Emmaus Growth material provides several courses, particularly in Growth Books 3 and 4, which will be of great help to churches wanting to do more in this area.

4. Eddie Gibbs has a fascinating analysis of the separation of these worlds in Chapter 5 of *Winning Them Back: The Protestant Mindset and Urban Reality*, Monarch, 1993, pp. 123–59.

5. Carl George, *Prepare Your Church for the Future*, Revell, 1993 especially Chapter 9. See also Paul Simmonds (ed.), *A Future for Housegroups*, Grove, 1996 (Grove Pastoral Series 66) for worked examples by John Leach and myself.

6. The plantpot reference is to John Finney, *Understanding Leadership*, p. 30, in which the more usual pyramid is inverted to make the leaders the bottom layer of soil. It's a better picture in terms of direction and focus (upwards and outwards) but implies an increasingly one-dimensional ministry for the ordained.

7. See Romans 12; 1 Corinthians 12–14 and Ephesians 4 as a beginning.

8. One of the most helpful places to begin this process is as people come to faith and at the beginning of their Christian lives. The Emmaus nurture course for this reason contains a session on ministry which attempts to teach the basic principles outlined in this section and contains a helpful exercise to begin to help the group discern one another's gifts. Often after leading this session of the course it has been possible to suggest to people that they begin to find out a bit more and possibly join in this or that area of the church's life (Emmaus Stage 2: Nurture, Leaders Guide, pp. 58–60 and Members' Handouts pp. 46–48). Willow Creek also produce a more developed multimedia kit for helping people discern and begin to use their gifts: *Network*, Bruce Begbee, Don Cousins and Bill Hybels, Zondervan.

9. For convenient written summaries of the guidelines see James Behrens, *Practical Church Management*, Gracewing, 1998, Chapter 8, pp. 142–60; David Pytches, *Leadership for New Life*, Appendix 2. For the interpretation of the Children Act and local social services guidelines as they apply to crèches and toddler groups, see Ann Croft, *Caring for Children in Crèches and Toddler Groups*, CPAS, 1994.

10. One of the best of these, widely used as a basis for similar documents, is the

Diocese of Norwich handbook, *Tend my Flock, Good Practice in Pastoral Care*, available from the Diocesan Office, 109, Dereham Road, Easton, Norwich, Norfolk, NR9 5ES.

11. Some of the material in the following chapter may be of use here. An excellent course to use with those engaged in leadership in different ways within the local church is Colin Buckland's 'Liberating the Leadership', a Ministry Survival Course, from the Oak Hill Learning Centre, Oak Hill College, Chase Side, Southgate, London, N14 4PS.

12. *The One-Minute Manager*, Kenneth Blanchard and Spencer Johnson, HarperCollins, 1994. The book is in the form of a short story. The three keys to effective management are the One-Minute Goal Setting, the One-Minute Praising and the One-Minute Reprimand. It's not the whole story but the three skills are an essential part of *episcope*.

13. A manageable span of care for lay visiting schemes is much nearer 1:5 – allowing for time off and missed appointments that works out at one visit per week and contact every couple of months. A similar ratio for working in small groups would be 1:10 where the emphasis is on the leader enabling the group to care for one another.

14. My own theory of why so many clergy love to delegate unmanageable tasks is because the pastoral care workload we carry ourselves feels so unmanageable. An essential part of being a pastor, we think, is feeling impossibly overstretched, and so we create exactly those conditions for others.

15. John Finney has an excellent section on delegation and delegation interviews in *Understanding Leadership*, pp. 84–85. His list of questions to ask in forming the shape of the task and as a guideline to a 'delegation interview' is reproduced here for those who cannot obtain the book – but the whole section is well worth reading: 'What commitment of time does the job require? What resources are available? Who is also engaged in the same sphere of work? How much authority is being allowed – can money be spent, people approached to help, publicity distributed, without reference to anybody else? Where can the person seek help if difficulties arise? Is any training available to help the work to be done better? What opportunities will there be for review of the work? With whom? When? Is there any term to the work? Is there anything the person is already doing which needs to be dropped to make way for this new enterprise? Above all the vision for the job should be spelt out.' John Finney, *Understanding Leadership*, Darton Longman & Todd, 1989, p. 85.

16. This principle is also borrowed from Carl George's Metachurch Model, which is strong throughout on practical ways of supporting lay ministers in church ministries.

17. Described in detail in *Prepare Your Church for the Future*, pp. 135–44.

18. Lest anyone think otherwise this reference is not tongue in cheek!

19. It has been wisely said that a church rich in musicians will always attract many more; a church without musicians will struggle to do so. Seed corn may be needed.

CHAPTER 14

1. Acts 20:28.

2. Irvine's work on clergy identity was highlighted above. His second major under-lying cause of clergy stress is isolation, at the root of which is too much personal energy focused into a great many superficial relationships, too little into deeper friendships: Andrew Irvine, *Between Two Worlds – Understanding and Managing Clergy Stress*, Chapters 7, 8, 9.

3. Stephen Covey helpfully explores what he describes as the P/PC balance where P stands for production and PC for production capacity. Where the production capacity is ignored, ultimately nothing is produced: the goose which lays the golden egg has been killed by neglect. Stephen Covey, *The Seven Habits of Highly Effective People*, pp. 52ff.

4. It seems to me that dioceses need to invest much more heavily in those who are able to give pro-active support to the parochial clergy, switching resources away from 'sector ministers' . . . but that would be the subject of a different chapter.

5. One of the inhibiting features here are the changes in personnel at senior level in a diocese. In nine years as Vicar of Ovenden I related to two diocesan bishops; two suffragans; three Archdeacons of Halifax and three rural deans.

6. For a description of what is involved and a survey of the issues involved, see the collection of essays edited by Kevin Eastell, *Appointed for Growth: A handbook of ministry development and appraisal*, Mowbray, 1994.

7. This aspect of group clergy life is underlined by Irvine.

8. Larger groups will need to break down into smaller units of around four people within the meeting if this is to be effective.

9. Andrew Irvine, *Between Two Worlds*, pp. 160–179.

10. Philippians 4:8.

11. For more on this theme, see the excellent chapter on 'Discerning' in *Living at the Edge, Sacrament and Solidarity in Leadership* by Penny Jamieson, Mowbray, 1997.

APPENDIX 2

1. Arlin Rothauge, *Sizing up a Congregation for New Member Ministry*, New York, The Episcopal Church Center. An initial Anglicised version of the research was pre-sented in my own *Growing New Christians*, CPAS/Marshall Pickering, 1993, pp. 68–81, using Rothauge's categories of Family, Pastoral, Programme, and Corporation Church. Since then I have presented and reflected upon different versions of the model with many different groups of clergy, ordinands and lay leaders and it has been refined considerably in the work presented here. The original observations on the Family and Pastoral Churches have been largely retained and his findings have found echoes in many peoples' experience within the United Kingdom. The other 'models' of church have been developed as a more accurate and helpful picture for the evolving dynamic of churches in the 1990s. An analysis based on the work of the Alban Institute has also been published recently in Malcolm Grundy's book *Understanding Congregations*, Mowbray, 1998, Chapter 2.

2. For the purposes of this analysis of dynamic numbers should be taken to refer to adults and to average Sunday attendance. 'Membership' figures may be much higher.

3. The most stretching and uncomfortable analysis of addictive patterns of behaviour is that of Carl George, *How to Break Growth Barriers*, Revell, 1993, Chapters 6, 7 and 8.
4. Rothauge has two further categories of Programme and Corporation Churches to describe congregations of 150+ and 450+. These are described in an Anglicised form in *Growing New Christians*, pp. 74ff. There are some churches corresponding to the 'Programme Church' in the UK but hardly any 'Corporation Churches'. I have not found the models as useful in seminars as tools for understanding what is happening; nor would I particularly want to commend them as models to seek to build intentionally. The dynamic of size implied in them tends to be alienating to members of the congregations involved.
5. The 'Nurturing Communities' model is in part a development of Carl George's 'Metachurch' model described in *Prepare Your Church for the Future*.
6. The 'Transforming Communities' model is a development of the ideas of the Cell Church and Base Communities movement referred to in Chapter 1. For an introduction to Cell Church, see Howard Astin, *Body and Cell*, Monarch, 1998.

SELECT BIBLIOGRAPHY

Astin, Howard, *Body and Cell*, Monarch, 1998

Ball, Peter, *The Adult Way to Faith*, Mowbray, 1992

Barnett, J. M, *The Diaconate – a Full and Equal Order*, Seabury, New York, 1989

Baxter, Richard, *The Reformed Pastor*, Banner of Truth (1656)

Beckham, William, *The Second Reformation*, Touch Publications, 1995

Behrens, James, *Practical Church Management*, Gracewing, 1998

Bennett, David, *Biblical Images for Leaders and Followers*, Paternoster, 1993

Bennett, David, *Metaphors for Ministry*, Paternoster, 1993

Blanchard, Kenneth and Johnson, Spencer, *The One Minute Manager*, HarperCollins, 1994

Bosch, David, *Transforming Mission*, Orbis, 1995

Brierley, Peter, *Vision Building*, Hodder and Stoughton, 1989

Buckland, Colin, *Liberating the Leadership: A Ministry Survival Course*, Oak Hill College, 1997

Campbell, R. Alistair, *The Elders: Seniority Within Earliest Christianity*, T & T Clark, 1994

Clarke, John, *Evangelism that Really Works*, SPCK, 1995

Coate, Mary Ann, *Clergy Stress*, SPCK, 1989

Cormac, David, *Team Spirit*, Marc Europe, 1987

Cormac, David, *Seconds Away*, Marc Europe, 1986

Cottrell, Stephen; Croft, Steven; Finney, John; Lawson, Felicity and Warren, Robert, *Emmaus: The Way of Faith* (eight volumes), Church House Publishing/Bible Society, 1996 and 1998

Cottrell, Stephen, *Catholic Evangelism*, DLT, 1998

Covey, Stephen and Merrill, A. Roger, *First Things First*, Simon and Schuster, 1994

Covey, Stephen, *The Seven Habits of Highly Effective People*, Simon and Schuster, 1990

Croft, Ann, *Caring for Children in Crèches and Toddler Groups*, CPAS, 1996

Croft, Steven, *Growing New Christians*, CPAS/Marshall Pickering, 1993

Croft, Steven, *Making New Disciples*, Marshall Pickering, 1994

Davey, John, *Stress in the Ministry*, Gracewing, 1995

Davey, John, *Burn Out: Stress in the Ministry*, Gracewing, 1995

Day, David, *A Preaching Workbook*, Lynx, 1997

Eastell, Kevin, *Appointed for Growth: A Handbook Of Ministry Development And Appraisal*, Mowbray, 1994

Etchells, Ruth, *Set My People Free*, HarperCollins, 1995

Evans, G. R. and Wright, J. Robert, *The Anglican Tradition: A Handbook of Sources*, SPCK, 1988

Finney, John, *Church on the Move*, Daybreak/DLT, 1992

Finney, John, *Finding Faith Today*, Bible Society, 1992

Finney, John, *Understanding Leadership*, Daybreak, 1989

Francis, James M. and Francis, Leslie J. (eds.), *Tentmaking: Perspectives on Self-Supporting Ministry*, Gracewing, 1998

Francis, Leslie and Jones, Susan H., *Psychological Perspectives on Christian Ministry*, Gracewing/Fowler Wright, 1996

Francis, Leslie J. and Richter, Philip, *Gone But Not Forgotten*, DLT, 1998

General Synod, *Under Authority, Report on Clergy Discipline*, Church House Publishing, 1996

General Synod, *All Are Called*, Church House Publishing, 1985

General Synod, *Breaking New Ground*, Church Planting in the Church of England, Church House Publishing, 1994

General Synod, *Deacons in the Ministry of the Church*, Church House Publishing, 1988

General Synod, *Episcopal Ministry: The Report of the Archbishops' Group on the Episcopate*, Church House Publishing, 1990

General Synod, *On the Way – Towards An Integrated Approach To Christian Initiation*, Church House Publishing, 1995

General Synod, *Working As One Body: The Report of the Archbishops' Commission On The Organisation of the Church Of England*, Church House Publishing, 1995

General Synod, *Youth Apart*, Church House Publishing, 1996

George, Carl, *How to Break Growth Barriers*, Revell, 1993

George, Carl, *Prepare your Church for the Future*, Revell, 1991

George, Carl, *The Coming Church Revolution*, Revell, 1994

Gibbs, Eddie, *Followed or Pushed?*, Marc Europe, 1987

Gibbs, Eddie, *I Believe in Church Growth*, Hodder and Stoughton, 1981

Gibbs, Eddie, *Winning them Back*, Monarch, 1993

Giles, Richard, *Re-Pitching the Tent*, Canterbury Press, 1997

Gill, Robin and Burke, Derek, *Strategic Church Leadership*, SPCK, 1996

Goodliff, Paul, *Care in a Confused Climate*, DLT, 1998

Green, Christopher and Jackman, David (eds.), *When God's Voice Is Heard*, IVP, 1995

Greenwood, Robin, *Transforming Priesthood*, SPCK, 1994

Grieve, Jane, *Fundraising for Churches*, SPCK, 1999

Grundy, Malcolm, *Understanding Congregations*, Mowbray, 1998

Hall, Christine (ed.), *The Deacon's Ministry*, Gracewing, 1992

Harvey-Jones, John, *Making it Happen*, Collins, 1988

Hawkins, Thomas, *The Learning Congregation*, Westminster John Knox, 1997

Hebblethwaite, Margaret, *Base Communities*, Geoffrey Chapman, 1993

Herrick, Vanessa and Mann, Ivan, *Jesus Wept: Reflections on Vulnerability in Leadership*, DLT, 1998

Higginson, Richard, *Transforming Leadership*, SPCK, 1996

Hughes, Bryn, *Leadership Tool Kit*, Monarch, 1998

Hybels, Lynne and Bill, *Rediscovering Church*, HarperCollins, 1996

Irvine, Andrew, *Between Two Worlds: Understanding and Managing Clergy Stress*, Mowbray, 1997

Jamieson, Penny, *Sacrament and Solidarity in Leadership*, Mowbray, 1997

Kennedy, Carol, *Guide to the Management Gurus*, Century Business Books,1998

MacDonald, Gordon, *Restoring Your Spiritual Passion*, Highland, 1986

MacDonald, Gordon, *Ordering Your Private World*, Highland, 1984

Moody, Christopher, *Eccentric Ministry*, DLT, 1992

Nash, Wanda, *Christ, Stress and Glory*, DLT, 1997

Neighbour, Ralph, *Where Do We Go From Here?*, Touch Publications, 1991

Nelson, Alan, *Leading your Ministry*, Abingdon Press, 1996

Nelson, John (ed.), *Leading, Managing, Ministering*, Canterbury Press, 1999

Nelson, John (ed.), *Management and Ministry*, Canterbury Press, 1996

Pattison, Stephen, *The Faith of the Managers*, Cassell, 1997

Peters, Tom and Austin, Nancy, *A Passion for Excellence*, Fontana, 1986

Pytches, David, *Leadership for New Life*, Hodder and Stoughton, 1998

Schwartz, Christian, *Natural Church Development*, British Church Growth Association, 1997

Senge, Peter M., *The Fifth Discipline: The Art And Practise Of The Learning Organisation*, Doubleday/Currency Books, 1990

Spriggs, David, *Christian Leadership*, Bible Society, 1993

Stott, John, *I Believe in Preaching*, Hodder and Stoughton, 1982

Sykes, Stephen; Booty, John; Knight, Jonathan, *The Study of Anglicanism*, SPCK, revised edition, 1998

Tidball, Derek, *Skilful Shepherds: Explorations in Pastoral Theology*, Apollos, 1997

Tiller, John, *The Gospel Community and its Leadership*, Marshall Pickering, 1987

de Waal, Esther, *A Life Giving Way*, SPCK, 1995

Ward, Pete, *Growing up Evangelical*, SPCK, 1996

Warren, Robert, *Being Human, Being Church*, Marshall Pickering, 1995

Warren, Robert, *On the Anvil*, Highland, 1990

Warren, Robert, *Building Missionary Congregations*, Church House Publishing, 1995

Wimber, John, *Power Evangelism*, Hodder and Stoughton, 1994

World Council of Churches, *Baptism, Eucharist and Ministry*, Geneva, 1982